Working in the Countertransference: Necessary Entanglements

Working in the Countertransference: Necessary Entanglements

Howard A. Wishnie, M.D.

A JASON ARONSON BOOK

ROWMAN & LITTLEFIELD PUBLISHERS, INC.
Lanham • Boulder • New York • Toronto • Oxford

A JASON ARONSON BOOK

ROWMAN & LITTLEFIELD PUBLISHERS, INC.

Published in the United States of America
by Rowman & Littlefield Publishers, Inc.
A wholly owned subsidary of The Rowman & Littlefield Publishing Group, Inc.
4501 Forbes Boulevard, Suite 200, Lanham, Maryland 20706
www.rowmanlittlefield.com

PO Box 317
Oxford
OX2 9RU, UK

Copyright © 2005 by Rowman & Littlefield Publishers, Inc.
Originally published in 2002 by Jason Aronson, Inc.

This book was set in 12½ pt. Perpetua by Alabama Book Composition of Deatsville,
Alabama.

British Library Cataloguing in Publication Information Available
A previous edition of this book was catalogued as follows by the Library of Congress:

Wishnie, Howard A.
        Working in the countertransference / by Howard A. Wishnie.
            p. cm.
        Includes bibliographical references and index.
        1. Countertransference (Psychology) 2. Psychotherapist and Patient. I. Title.
        [DNLM: 1. Countertransference (Psychology) 2. Physician-Patient Relations.
        WM 62 W814 2002]
        RC489.C68 W574 2002
        616.89'14—dc21   2002018572

ISBN 0-7657-0369-6

Printed in the United States of America
⊖™ The paper used in this publication meets the minimum requirements of American
National Standard for Information Sciences—Permanence of Paper for Printed Library
Materials, ANSI/NISO Z39.48-1992.

*To Cathy with love and appreciation
for who she is
and all that she has done to fulfill our lives*

Contents

Preface

In writing this book, I sought to address clinicians: psychologists, psychiatrists, social workers, and lay therapists, people who are just getting started in their careers as psychotherapists, as well as experienced clinicians who have begun to consider the necessary entanglements of countertransference. While I have reviewed some historical and theoretical materials, my main interest is to provide clinical examples illustrating the many kinds of interpersonal responses that occur in clinical practice. A more thorough examination of the theoretical issues I raise and a more in-depth analysis of the related questions can be found in the writings of the referenced authors.

Many of these examples draw on my own errors, mistakes, and misunderstandings. These miss-steps occurred as I struggled to be genuinely present in the interpersonal process, while attending to the legitimate needs and boundaries of the work. The errors described here represent only a fraction of those I made. In this text, my objective is to elicit your interest in the vital process of continuous reexamination of one's role as a clinician, and in the challenges presented by the impact of one's own personality upon the psychotherapeutic endeavor.

Because I'm writing as a clinician, my examples are rather plainly stated. Many were taken directly from the office experience with alterations made only to disguise the identity of those involved. The work of psychotherapy requires continuous reflection on one's own role and involvement, along with frequent consultation with colleagues, both in person and through their writings.

Many people have helped me over the years: teachers, colleagues, authors. But the greatest assistance has come from the people with whom I have worked in psychotherapy and psychoanalysis. I am thankful to all of them and to the institutions that existed when I began my training. I fear that today's students are caught in a whirlwind of competing pressures and spend insufficient time learning about, listening to, and talking with patients. The demand for short-term quick fixes and the fantasy that such fixes are possible has contributed to a situation wherein too little emphasis is put upon the kind of meaningful interpersonal work that leads to change and growth in a person's character.

When this pressure for quick change is combined with recent advances in neuroradiology, neurochemistry, neurobiology, and neuropsychiatry, there is a seductive pull towards the belief that rapid symptomatic improvement represents the best we have to offer. Yet, the history of medical and psychological treatment shows us that medicines or treatments prescribed apart from an interpersonal relationship between physician[1] and patient are frequently abandoned. While newer modalities may enhance the potential for improvement, it is only when they are thoughtfully used (or not used) and integrated into ongoing intensive psychotherapy that genuine change occurs within the individual.

When I began my medical career, I loved the excitement of the emergency room. Working in a large city hospital with huge numbers of patients and in the midst of scenes like those portrayed on the television show *ER*, I felt confident and effective in spite of the surrounding chaos.

After several months of work in this setting, I was struck by the number of people returning with the same, self-inflicted problems: the man who got into struggles with his wife and "messed up" his insulin; the adolescents with repeated drug overdoses; the screaming teenager whom

---

1. Physician here refers to a therapist who may come from one of a number of disciplines.

I sutured on multiple Saturday nights; the 15-year-old, pregnant for a third time, who felt empty and abandoned unless pregnant; the cardiac patient hospitalized each time his daughter began to move out and begin her own life.

Watching these endlessly repeated scenarios, I began to feel that I was only patching and re-patching recurrent problems, while missing the deeper root issues. As I reported this observation to more senior physicians, some candidly stated that most of the medical issues they saw in their offices were psychogenic in origin—or at least contained some significant underlying emotional factors that exacerbated the medical issue. Some dealt with this complex problem by giving advice and admonitions. Others threw up their hands and said, "That's how people are! What can I do? I'm just a doctor."

One Monday morning after finishing a 56-hour weekend shift, I was in the screening clinic (also known as the "screaming clinic"). This was "easy" work. Three or four of us, all medical interns, would screen the first 200 people to come through the door that morning. Most were there for medication renewal. Anyone needing examination in the specialty clinics would be weeded out and referred upstairs.

The guidelines were clear: get the chart and keep your medical bag with stethoscope and sphygmomanometer out of sight. Do not take anyone back to be examined. If you do, *everyone* will want to be examined and we'll never get done. This was a huge New York City public hospital, with an equally large, immigrant, polyglot population anxious to be treated in the imposing medical center.

On this particular morning, I saw a woman with her daughter. The woman was there for medication renewal: pain-killers and sleeping medications for terminal cancer. The daughter had quit her job in order to stay home and care for her dying mother. Both were miserable together. While the mother was slow-moving and gaunt, I could see no progression of her illness. Quickly reviewing her record, I saw mention of her underlying illness but no documentation. The chart was bigger than a New York City phone book. Maybe some part of the record was missing? Something didn't feel right, so I took her into the examining area and did a quick physical. I could find no sign of an underlying medical problem other than depression.

I spoke with mother and daughter and suggested that along with getting the older woman to the appropriate medical clinic for further evaluation of the alleged terminal cancer, we should consider the strong possibility that depression was contributing to her distress. Would they agree to go to the psychiatric clinic? Both seemed upset and initially rejected my recommendation. So I proposed a deal. I would renew the medicines for two weeks and send the mother to the medical clinic without the usual several-week delay—if they would in turn agree to a psychiatric consultation. They agreed, but I heard nothing further from them.

Four months later, the daughter sought me out. She was back at work. Her mother had no cancer and in fact had been depressed. Reluctantly, she had agreed to see a therapist in the psychiatric clinic. As it turned out, records and information from the first hospital had been misplaced, then mixed with those of another patient's, and reassembled. "Cancer" had been considered as a possibility much earlier in her evaluation, but was then excluded. (This had been the source of the erroneous diagnosis in her chart.) The daughter reported that her mother was now improved and was beginning to consider returning to work.

I was shocked at the dramatic change in both mother and daughter. This was not the outcome I had anticipated in making the referral. How many other, similar problems had I failed to identify in my haste to get through the huge volume of patients? How many unnecessary prescriptions had I written that provided only symptomatic relief, even as they reinforced or contributed to distortions in how these patients understood themselves?

I decided that I needed to find a way to achieve a more enduring impact, a way of reaching the underlying issues that contributed so heavily to a person's causing or contributing to his or her own problems. In the end, I decided to pursue a career in psychiatry instead of internal medicine, which had been my original choice.

In 1967, first-generation psychoactive medications were being widely used. They included antidepressants and antipsychotics. Around the same time, lithium was being introduced for bipolar disorders. Thus, a whole new range of medications had been introduced that were more specifically useful than the previously available ECT, sedative-hypnotics, wet-packs, and seclusion. While the medications were effective, they could also trigger more disquieting side effects than those associated with older medicines. However, these new substances represented a major shift in psychiatry towards a biological understanding and treatment of an individual's difficulties. Up to that time, psychiatry had been divided between organic and psychological approaches. Within each of these divisions, there were many subdivisions and schools of thought. For many years the various psychological approaches had dominated the thinking in the field. The development of specific and effective psychoactive agents resulted in a major shift in the field that is still evolving. Many psychiatrists welcomed the development of effective medications. They could now rejoin the mainstream of medicine as "real doctors," prescribing medicines and treating symptoms. More dynamic and analytically oriented psychiatrists and psychologists worried about being displaced and having their valued perspectives put aside and ignored.

The center where I trained emphasized the need to understand the dynamic, interpersonal, psychological process unique to each individual. Medications were used in combination with this understanding in order to help the patient focus upon an intra-personal understanding of himself. At the time I trained, medications were employed routinely, but were still considered suspect. There was a concern that they could be used to avoid the resolution of underlying psychological issues. At the same time, it was clear that in many cases a struggling individual could not begin to meaningfully engage in treatment until there was some reduction in the level of distress or confusion.

Instead of immersing ourselves in the literature of psychiatry, we were encouraged to spend our hours in multiple psychotherapy sessions each week with our patients. These treatment sessions were then reviewed in conferences, groups, and under individual supervision. What was said, heard, understood, and potentially implied during these sessions was to be carefully considered. Our course of study focused heavily on spending time with the patient, on being supervised, and on trying to understand the patient's perspective, along with our own involvement.

While there were many demonstration-interviews with senior clinicians, one such event took on particular importance for me. Elvin

Semrad,[2] the senior clinician at our center, met each week with small groups of resident physicians. Our training group would crowd into his small office as one of us presented the history of a patient with whom we were working. Dr. Semrad would then interview the patient. In a quiet, gentle manner, he would ask a question or two, or perhaps limit himself to a comment.

The patient, previously reticent or monosyllabic with the resident therapist, often responded with an outpouring of heartfelt material that had not been expressed earlier. After a further gentle but clear exploration of the issue at hand, Dr. Semrad would ask the patient, "Do you think that your doctor can bear to hear this? Can you help him to understand this?"

As resident doctors who were struggling to learn (while also hoping to appear knowledgeable to ourselves and our colleagues!), we squirmed at these questions about our capacities. Yet, these questions went to the heart of the work of effective psychotherapy. *Could we bear to hear what was genuinely important to the patient, or would our own defenses and superficial needs obstruct our capacity to be present and engage with the patient in the most helpful way?*

The issue of a "therapist's capacity" to understand the perspective of the other, both emotionally and intellectually, informs this manuscript, and also looms as a crucial aspect of our practice.

Another powerful aspect of my early psychiatric training involved the way in which mistakes were treated. The message was: "You *will* make mistakes. We need to discuss, examine, and understand them in order to learn." This principle was in fact practiced for the most part by my colleagues and teachers. As one finds in any other circumstance in life, there were also issues of pride, competition, and self-esteem. Yet there did seem to be more acceptance and genuine interest in understanding errors than in concealing them. In my prior experience of medicine and surgery, people had tried to approach this level of honest examination, but there had always been too much pressure to conceal and displace

---

2. Descriptions of this can be found in S. Rako and H. Mazer, eds., *Semrad: The Heart of a Therapist* (New York: Aronson, 1980).

responsibility. The medico-legal and societal pressures of today were also present in the 1960s. They seem to have intensified greatly in recent years, however, while creating even more barriers to the frank disclosure and examination we need in order to learn from our mistakes.

In the spirit of my early and later training, I have tried to use some of my clinical errors to illustrate issues in this book. While preparing the text, I have had to endure the humbling memory of many countertransference enactments, as well as live through others yet ongoing; all of which presents me with formidable challenges, as I struggled to find the responses that would most help my patients and also allow me to honestly write this manuscript.

There are many people whose help I have deeply appreciated. There is not enough space to mention everyone who has helped me to learn. I don't purposely exclude anyone and hope that those who are not mentioned will forgive the omission.

First and foremost, I wish to thank the people who have worked with me as patients; together we have learned and grown through the process of therapy.

For twenty-five years I have met weekly with Bob Berezin to examine the process of our work. Bob has taught me the value and necessity of understanding and directly engaging characterologic realities on a continuous basis, both within myself and within my patients. The invitations to sidestep and gloss over troubling issues are ever present, and he has helped me to understand this key fact, while also helping me to see the effects on patients of both encountering and avoiding.

Harry Penn has been a continual source of thoughtful reflection. Many times he waits until the end of a conversation in order to draw in the many dynamic elements that I have previously not considered. In this way, he gathers together all that we have said. Then he asks a question that opens a window previously unnoticed by me, or directs me to an article or consideration that further clarifies what I need to learn.

Joseph Schwartz regularly brings a combination of immense clinical and teaching experience to his comments, en route to synthesizing a difficult case. With self-reflective humor that both accepts and highlights our personal limitations, he has kept me on track.

M. Jeanne Smith has given all of these efforts a personal and specific meaning in our work together over many years. Theory has become living reality, and I have been able to rely on it in order to appreciate the multidimensional aspects of meeting people where they are. Her quiet sense of professionalism, dignity, and respect for boundaries has given me a sense that one can be very personally involved and yet keep the necessary distance in the work that gives the patient the freedom to find his or her own answers.

Stuart Hauser, Louis Kirshner, Nick Kouretas, and more recently Alec Morgan have been part of monthly clinical meetings that regularly introduce aspects of clinical and theoretical understanding that humble me and send me back to learn more. All are profound clinical and theoretical psychiatrists. These meetings give me the repeated opportunity both to hear the same problems approached from different vantage points and to allow me to synthesize better understandings of a multifaceted issue.

Steven Sands for many years has helped me with gentle and considerate understandings of the dilemmas introduced by narcissistic injuries. Scholarly and thoughtful, he also owns a sense of wry humor and an appreciation of the human condition that have been a continuous source of help.

Bruce Hauptman helped me to integrate developmental psychology, neuropsychiatry, and psychodynamics as we collaborated in family work. He values both the emotional-psychological basis of human experience and the emerging clarity of neurobiology.

Nicholas Avery, a teacher during residency and a supervisor during analytic training, has guided me with direct observation and considerate reflections on the details of my endeavors. His years of clinical experience and appreciation of the distress of narcissistic injuries and their origins remind me that I must continually attune myself to the patient's perspective. He patiently reviewed this manuscript and encouraged me to pursue it to completion.

As a supervisor during analytic training, George Fishman was a source of enthusiastic support. His capacity to look beyond and beneath the moment toward deeper insights helped me to pursue the explorations and understandings vital to furthering a patient's treatment.

During the early years of my work, Irene Briggin was a teacher, friend, and consultant who provided thoughtful reflection and insight. George Vaillant supported my pursuits in this area, at a time when countertransference was considered a problem "not to be discussed." Jim Harburger was a companion in the struggle to understand and constructively engage issues of character and countertransference.

A special thanks to Laurie Sokolsky, who in researching her doctoral thesis led me to resurrect and reconstruct my experiences into this book. Her final research helped me outline the historical review in Chapter One and she coined the term "Disclosurist" to refer to those interpersonal therapists who believe that self-disclosure is an important element of the treatment process. When the manuscript was completed, she carefully read and edited it.

I am also grateful to the Massachusetts Institute for Psychoanalysis for providing a program in which older clinicians could bring together their diverse experience and complete training in psychoanalysis. The broadly defined understanding of the psychoanalytic process embraced by this institution, one that includes many schools of thought, has significantly contributed to my own thinking. The opportunity to immerse myself in learning with like-minded colleagues, years after completing my residency, has been an enormously useful experience. It has challenged me and introduced me to many thoughtful and dedicated psychotherapists.

At a time when the value of this work is being increasingly challenged and marginalized, it has been an immense support to find such a group of committed clinicians who continue to practice and learn together about the intra– and interpsychic processes.

Twenty-two years ago, my son Mark composed the original diagrams for these chapters and related lectures, while his brother Mike labored at the keyboard to put together the various notes and lectures. I hope that finishing this work will provide them with some useful if belated recompense.

Finally, I want to thank Tom Nugent, who has worked with me in editing notes and ideas written over many years into a more cohesive document. Hopefully our joint efforts will provide you with an introduction to the necessary, fascinating, and complex world of the countertransference. Dr. Eve Golden was an immense help to me in smoothing out my presentation so that ideas that were clear to me, might become clear to you, the reader.

In the book *The Dancing Wu Lai Masters*, each chapter is labeled "Chapter One." That perspective would seem appropriate for this work as well! I always feel that I am at the beginning.

1

Living in the Countertransference

As our understanding of the processes of psychotherapy has evolved, its practitioners (psychotherapists and psychoanalysts) have come to realize that *countertransference* is an *inescapable and important part of the therapeutic process*.

In the following material, I intend to demonstrate how the interactive dynamics of psychotherapy expose and frequently exacerbate distressing issues and imbalances within a clinician's own character. When this occurs, there will almost always be an arousal of the therapist's transferences and defenses against them.

Such countertransferences can be briefly defined, drawing on the writings of Gill, Hoffman, McLaughlin, Racker, Sandler, Stolorow, and others, as the therapist's personal transferences aroused during work with a patient. These responses within the therapist pose a formidable challenge for the clinician. In the context of the psychotherapeutic work, he or she must carefully examine and break down—"metabolize"—often distressing responses into their constituent elements. It then becomes possible to make use of those aspects of the digested information that have bearing upon the treatment.

The resonances[1] contained in the countertransference, potentially distracting and threatening though they may be, are a valuable source of understanding that can deepen the therapeutic process. Thus countertransference, when thoughtfully understood and integrated into the process of therapy, can be of great service to patient and therapist. In this book I will present, in concepts and clinical examples, some of the numerous manifestations of countertransference interaction and how they can influence the treatment process. I will also elaborate basic evolving guidelines designed to help therapists make the countertransference a useful element in the treatment. Each of these guidelines is connected to case examples that illustrate the therapeutic principles on which it is based. As I noted in the introduction, I will draw upon mistakes—my own and others'—to clarify the issues and to give the reader a sense of how the guidelines are still evolving for me.

COUNTERTRANSFERENCE: THE BACKGROUND

The term *countertransference* has been in use since the early days of psychoanalysis to denote unresolved conflicts or deficits that are awakened in the psychotherapist during the treatment process.

The "ideal" therapist of the early psychoanalytic model was conceived of as a benignly neutral, yet empathic individual who had been freed by personal analysis from troublesome neurotic conflicts. This analyzed therapist/analyst was an objective professional, both removed from and deeply involved in the ongoing therapeutic work. It was believed that this greatly desired balanced emotional distance would allow the patient to experience a necessary frustration in the treatment setting, and that this would force unconscious infantile wishes into consciousness,

---

1. *Resonance* here refers to often inchoate and hard to define, but strongly experienced, feelings. First reactions to these feelings may be impulses to avoid—by denial, dissociation, reaction formation, or frank withdrawal—or impulses to control, by authoritarian defenses. In addition, we may first feel responses as sensations, and only then internally react with responses to the feeling. We may describe the reaction to an initial feeling as the feeling itself, as in "I felt angry" when it might more accurately be that "I felt hurt and became immediately angry."

allowing the therapist to clarify, examine, and help the patient to resolve them. The patient's transference distortions were seen as a route into this unconscious world of archaic and infantile forces, and it was believed that the intrusion of personal responses from the clinician might interfere with and contaminate the unfolding process. Implied in this view is a degree of unilateral authority and capacity on the part of the analyst that has only recently given way to a more realistic perspective.

For much of the history of psychoanalytically oriented psychotherapy, therefore, the reactivation of unresolved conflicts in the clinician was regarded as a significant treatment complication. It was usually considered an unseemly development, to be eradicated in a responsible practitioner by further personal analysis.

Although the creation of an environment in which the therapist's personal issues would be excluded seems a desirable objective (as the patient must always be the focus of treatment), the assumption that such crystal-clear objectivity is possible now appears to have been a manifestation of the same intellectual grandiosity that distorted certain other early psychoanalytic doctrines.

I was fortunate enough to be a psychiatric resident in a program dedicated to learning from errors. Even so, I witnessed and experienced the distorting effects of the objectivity myth. "Objectivity" as a desirable goal had become firmly imbedded in psychoanalytic doctrine in the U. S. during the 1930s and 1940s. The idea of the benignly neutral clinician had been a central organizing concept in the training of practitioners of analytic psychotherapy in the U. S., and, even though it was changing, it was still a dominant feature of psychodynamic training at the end of my residency in 1970.

Before completing that training, we aspiring psychotherapists were implicitly expected to explore and resolve our conflicts sufficiently so that they would not affect a patient's treatment. While it was understood that one would need to continue in one's own analysis well beyond training in order to accomplish this goal, the goal itself was clear. At the same time, it was expected that we would make mistakes, and that we would have to learn to examine them. To us as residents, coming from the greater certainty of the medical model, the simultaneity of these two ideas seemed paradoxical. As the years went on, however, it became easier to understand the inevitability of errors and their uses, even while certain doctrinaire clinicians/theoreticians maintained an attitude of certainty.

At first glance, the goal of objectivity seemed to be well advised and even achievable provided that the therapist-in-training worked hard at his or her analysis. During my training, I witnessed my friends' and colleagues' struggles, as well as my own, as we strove to conceal the evidence of our own conflicts from ourselves and others, and especially from our supervisors and analysts.

For many of us, our most useful personal analytic experiences occurred well after training, when we were no longer trying to conceal our personal responses. Perhaps we had gained enough experience in our lives and work to be assured that it was safe to explore our own characters. In our first analytic experiences during residency, we had wrestled with so much shame and fear of being found to be "unanalyzable" that we avoided important issues in our own lives. This avoidance was one of the distorting and delaying effects of the "myth."

But there are other contradictions at the heart of this doctrine, and they have been apparent for a long time, as a closer look at its development reveals.

By 1937, Freud was advising that practitioners should return to their own analyses every five years, to counter the stress of immersion in psychoanalytic work. This precept clearly suggested that objective neutrality could not be achieved by analysts, as their own internal issues could never be permanently excised. (Today we also have a clear awareness that our characters are always in a state of evolution. Life experiences and aging, new understandings, change our perspectives and bring up new versions of old issues, which must be relived and reexamined. This is another reason that realistic practitioners today periodically return for further analysis throughout long careers.)

Even so, Freud's recommendation makes clear his belief that practitioners' internal issues can never be permanently removed, that we will always be powerfully affected by the emotional intensity of our work with patients, and that we will never achieve the perfect objective neutrality embodied in the early psychoanalytic ideal.

This understanding, that we must expect to be continuously affected by the intensity of our involvement in our work, unlike the earlier one, has stood the test of time. It highlights an ambiguity that has haunted psychotherapy almost from the beginning: it is an enterprise that seems to require its practitioners both to acknowledge and to deny their subjective responses. However objective we strive to be, our work always takes place in a two-person domain, a free-flowing context in which the subjectivity of both patient and therapist are fully engaged.

The reluctance of early psychotherapists to address this innate ambivalence was understandable. Freud and his followers feared that psychoanalysis would not be regarded as a pure and objective science if the taint of subjectivity were admitted. "Real" science in the nineteenth and early twentieth centuries rested on a bedrock of so-called objective neutrality, which it conceived to be the source of its validity. Psychoanalysis emerged at a time when the "scientific method" of reproducible experimentation was changing the way we lived and worked, and encouraging the hope that science would be the path to a new, more perfect world. However, science had to be free of distorting subjectivity; no amorphous mysticism and magic could be permitted in this new Age of Reason. A "talking cure" for psychological issues raised suspicions enough of a nonscientific process. If the subjectivity of the scientist were acknowledged, the psychoanalytic enterprise would be even more suspect than it already was.

* * *

As a physician, I had been trained in this tradition of scientific objectivity. At the end of my psychiatric training, however, I could not pretend to myself that I had eliminated subjective responses in my work. I continued to notice all kinds of inner reactions to my patients. Whatever time I spent sorting through these responses, I could not find a way to make them disappear. For a long time I considered this a personal failing, and a limitation within myself.

With the passage of time and the acquisition of experience—plus continued supervision, consultation, and therapy with practitioners less wedded to the objectivity ideal than I was—I gradually came to regard these inner responses as opportunities that could sometimes open a window into the patient's experience. I began to see a range of experiences as forming an enactment of some drama, from subtle to dramatic. At times, usually more distressing ones, my inner turbulence told me that I was caught up in some re-creation of an experience that seemed to me primarily orchestrated by the patient, with me as an unwitting (and sometimes unwilling) participant. Sometimes I could only see my own role later, after the dust had settled; I had known that I was caught up in something, even if I hadn't known what! While the purpose of the scenario seemed to be communication, I learned that I couldn't discern the message until I could begin to sense some of my own role in the drama. Frequently my confusion and affective retreat into some defensive mode re-created something important in the patient's experience and my own. As I discovered the transference elicited in me by my own life, I began to have hints as to what it might be for the patient. I also was now free to consider a wide range of options in my patient's experience.

Uneasy about my reactions to these situations, I worked hard to avoid them. I hoped that increased skill would help me fend off such messy and distressing entanglements. Part of me still believed that more senior and talented clinicians did not suffer such distress. This was another distorting effect of the myth of "benign neutrality" and the "fully analyzed therapist," and of my own wish to believe that there were all-knowing practitioners who could teach me to be as they were. Who would want to imagine that the future would forever hold more of the same distress and uncertainty?

REVIEW OF THE CONCEPT

Seeking to understand these troublesome transference entanglements better, I reviewed the literature and looked hard at descriptions of the process by other clinicians. At first Freud had believed that a therapist would be able to discover the unconscious processes of the patient, gradually understand how they fit together to influence the patient's inner life, and eventually find the opportune moment to convey these discoveries to the patient. He thought that the power of his paternal observations, coupled with their compelling truth, would effect change within the patient. Too often, however, he found that patients could not grapple with such insights in a productive manner.

When he realized that it was not always possible to locate the targeted unconscious content, or to communicate effectively what he believed that he had found, he devised the strategy of working through what he called "resistances," to help the patient recall and confirm unconscious material. His belief at that time was that such conscious integration allowed the best resolution of the patient's suffering.

In spite of these efforts, however, it became clear to Freud that most patients still could not remember all repressed material, and that they therefore had to *re-live* the hidden content as a contemporary experience in treatment. In 1920, he termed this reliving of repressed materials the *transference neurosis.*

It was increasingly clear to Freud that the therapist would necessarily be drawn into the struggle via the transference neurosis. As the patient grappled with the original, but now internalized and buried unconscious material, the psychoanalyst too had to grope through the distress, now disguised in the form of the transference. The key to this complicated dynamic lay in the fact that the patient was now emotionally experiencing the therapist as some aspect of the original problematic person or circumstance in the patient's own life. Both analyst and patient had to try to understand the experience of the transference: the analyst being unknowingly perceived as someone from an earlier time. To the patient, such sensed feelings about the analyst's demeanor, attitude, etc., were experienced as a true reflection of the analyst, and not seen as a distortion. The analyst needed to listen carefully to get a sense of what the patient might be experiencing, to develop a theory of its origin within the patient, and to find a way to interpret it meaningfully. Today, we would also say that the analyst must examine his or her own transferences and their role in the patient's perception, as a means of more readily understanding an experience that involves both of them and to which both contribute.

Freud's recommendation that analysts reenter analysis every five years because of the impact of the work upon the analyst shows how, from the earliest work in this field, there was a recognition of the interactive and experiential nature of the psychoanalytic endeavor. This knowledge coexisted with the attitude that the analyst existed above the fray in a removed neutral position. Indeed, Freud seemed to be suggesting as much, when he advised that his colleagues take a cautious and structured approach to psychoanalysis, even as he allowed himself considerable freedom in responding to and involving himself in the patient's process.

Freud made it clear that interacting with the patient's transference neurosis is often extremely challenging, precisely because the unconscious content must also resonate with the therapist's own unconscious. When that happens, the clinician often experiences the disorienting and distressing turbulence of the countertransference. It is no wonder that many practitioners prefer to believe that effective treatment involves only the *patient's* transference—thus permitting the clinician to remain a neutral, empathic, observer.

One factor that seems to have limited Freud's understanding of the full nature and intensity of this countertransference, and its impact upon the clinician and treatment process, was his exclusion of pre-oedipal material from the analytic process. This led him to force powerful and urgent issues into an ill-fitting Oedipal frame, or to regard earlier material as unanalyzable. Again, this error in his perspective can best be understood in the context of the temporal and professional pressures that impinged upon his endeavors.

Although the trend in mainstream psychoanalysis had clearly been toward the idealization of the analyst as an allegedly neutral observer, from the beginning a few influential individuals and groups contended that the therapist's subjective responses to the patient were also an important part of the therapeutic process.

Ferenczi (1926), for example, introduced a series of "relational" concepts and argued for their central importance in the dynamics of psychotherapy. His was an uphill struggle, in part because of his own lack of judgment and boundary violations. Until the 1970s, the psychoanalytic movement in the U.S. (as opposed to Europe and Latin America) always insisted on preserving the rigid, objectivity-based framework that it had originally constructed around such key concepts as transference, the unconscious, transference neurosis, and the Oedipus complex. As a result, such relational concepts as those proposed by Ferenczi were unwelcome and considered contaminates in the process.

Even a brief reading of some of these early disputes is enough to show how greatly practitioners feared that boundary violations and wild, unstructured analyses could have destroyed the early psychoanalytic movement, and how they worried that open support for such techniques would have eroded confidence in the authenticity of the work. And indeed, there is much to be said for this cautious approach to therapy, especially in light of recent disclosures of inappropriate behavior on the part of both early and more recent practitioners.

Although many psychoanalysts were reluctant to admit, that the countertransference had a significant impact on therapy, some clinicians and theoreticians did recognize that it could be used to help patients during sessions. Deutsch (1926), for example, pointed out that the countertransference involved much more than mere transference from patient to analyst, and suggested that further study of this complex phenomenon might provide useful insights about the tangled dynamics of psychotherapy:

> Under certain conditions which are not altogether clear, but which are probably connected with transference (in the analytic sense), the transmission of ideas to a given person elicits in that individual a reactive process, which is then transformed into a perceptual thought content. . . . One may therefore suspect that the condition for this transfer of "emotionally colored recollections" consists in a certain unconscious readiness to receive them. Only if this condition is fulfilled can the recipient function as a "receiving station." These emotionally cathected ideas must mobilize in the unconscious of the second person analogous ideas of similar content, which then manifest themselves in the conscious as "internal experiences." [p. 135]

Here, Deutsch not only suggests that the therapist is personally responding, but that such responsiveness and involvement are necessary for the work to proceed!

The British Object Relations School

Melanie Klein and the British school of object relational clinicians (Balint, Fairbairn, Guntrip, and Winnicott) were open to the therapist's involvement in the process, and articulated the significance of transferential distress in the therapist and its potential impact on patient outcomes.

Winnicott (1947) described the functioning of hate in the countertransference. He emphasized the need for the therapist to recognize and wrestle with intense countertransference responses, if he or she were to be able to concentrate most effectively on the needs of the patient. In 1960, again discussing the countertransference, he sought to define a professional attitude that would permit the therapist/analyst to remain vulnerable and open to his or her responses to the patient. He cautioned that countertransference must be well examined before being included in interpretations.

Other important contributors, such as Heimann (1951), Little (1951), and Guntrip (1971) added insight into the dynamics of treatment as a two-person field, in which the therapist's capacity to be aware of his or her own responses was crucial for an accurate perception of the patient's experience of the therapy.

The Interpersonalists

In the U.S., Harry Stack Sullivan (1953) was assembling the elements of what would soon become the interpersonal school of psychoanalysis. Sullivan, like Klein and the other object-relational clinicians, felt that it was precisely in the interpersonal and intersubjective aspects of the therapeutic relationship that psychotherapy took place. He regarded psychotherapy as a reciprocally interactive process between the individual and his communal environment (developmental and current), which includes the therapist. Sullivan saw the therapist as needing to be in control of the therapeutic situation and of his own participation. He was to titrate the patient's level of anxiety, and learn about the patient's distortions and illusions from the responses to his participation. His controlled participation was not seen as countertransferential, except for occasional diversions of the therapist, which he was then to correct. While the therapist/analyst participated, he had a function: to gather data that would allow him to help the patient sort out his distortions and his illusory beliefs from reality. Although he did not call it transference,

Sullivan saw all perceptions of others as shaped and influenced by experiences with previous others. Given his logic of the shaping function of interpersonal influences, it is difficult to escape the conclusion that the treatment process is a two-person domain of mutual influence, with the shadows of numerous others contributing to each participant's experience of the other (even though he viewed the therapist as carefully gathering data and in control of the treatment). Sullivan influenced a number of American practitioners, including such major figures as Fromm, Thompson, Fromm-Reichmann, and Searles. Havens (1973, 1976), building on Sullivan's work and his own clinical experience, continued to define the role of the therapist as the participant–observer.

Self Psychology

By the 1960s, the writings of Kohut (1959, 1968, 1971, 1977) and the rapid emergence of Self psychology were focusing even more attention on the therapist's responses. One of the crucial issues emphasized by the Self psychologists was the need for the therapist to engage empathically with patients around the narcissistic deficits and injuries reexperienced in the treatment situation. Kohut and the Self psychologists increasingly focused their interest upon the exploration of how and when issues are brought to the patient's attention by the therapist. What is the state of the therapeutic alliance at such times, and what is the form of the transference? How attuned is the therapist to the patient? What is the nature of the empathic bond? Kohut saw clearly that many difficulties in treatment were the result of empathic failures (lapses in empathy on the part of the therapist) that re-created for the patient early traumatic injuries, and he urged that such lapses on the part of the therapist be included and examined as an important element in treatment.

Infant Research

At the same time, observational research was leading to better understanding of the mother–child interaction (Escalona 1968), and new insights into separation and attachment issues. Bowlby (1956, 1958), and Mahler and her colleagues (1965), inspired dramatic revisions of earlier assumptions about the pre-oedipal period. While their research did not confirm the presence of many of the previously hypothesized developmental phases, these authors made clear that very early phases of personality development were actively present in the analytic interaction, and could be understood analytically using different explanatory frameworks: attachment, bonding, separation, attunement, etc. This confirmed the attention to early development and pre-oedipal issues that had been fundamental to the theoretical work of Melanie Klein and the British object relations school long before they were accepted on this side of the Atlantic.

Repercussions of Kohutian Theory

Kohut eventually envisioned a separate evolutionary path for narcissism. He believed that the early parent–child (frequently mother–child) interaction would sooner or later be recapitulated in the treatment process. When that occurred, the patient would first use the therapist as a self–object, and then increasingly as an object with whom to repair deficits established during his own narcissistic self-development. The potential impact of this transference upon the therapist, along with the possibility of countertransference reactions in the form of empathic lapses, underlined the significance of interpersonal attunement in this approach to interactional therapy. Kohut's insistence, that lack of attention to the countertransference risked repeating the patient's earlier injuries, was an important contribution that further affirmed the interactional nature of our work.

Eventually, as an outgrowth of Kohutian theory, the capacity for the therapist/analyst to live as a self–object or mirror, or self–object and mirror in the treatment came to be seen as a significant demand of the analytic work. Such structural pressure on the analyst's psyche requires that the therapist be acutely aware both of self and of patient, as well as keenly responsive to and anchored firmly in the patient's perspective.

In the 1970s, broader definitions of countertransference found their way into the literature. It was no longer taboo to acknowledge that psychoanalysts were subject to the same reactions that affected everyone else during intense dialogues, including such ordinary reactions as fatigue, annoyance, and boredom. This recognition occurred too late to be of use to me in my residency, but it provided a context for my own later working through of the neutral object myth.

The Study of Countertransference as a Phenomenon

As this changing psychoanalytic perspective began to admit the reality of countertransference reactions, they began to be studied as an important phenomenon in their own right. Perhaps as a step in the movement away from previous denial, they were at first considered by some practitioners as an "ordinary" normative state. Such generalizations, however, failed to acknowledge an important distinction: in every treatment situation, countertransference reactions are specific to the psyches of the two individuals involved in the therapeutic dialogue. That oversight was significant. Countertransference reactions, however unremarkable in terms of their seemingly ordinary quality, cannot be dismissed as merely "ordinary." In fact, *they are* always *the specific interactional responses of two unique personalities framed by identifiable structures and discernible boundaries.*

These reactions, which are never ordinary or routine, deserve careful attention from the therapist, who needs to ask, Why now? What is being touched? What might this represent or be in response to? These seemingly ordinary exchanges are actually invested with the power to trigger, and then exacerbate, early developmental issues, traumas, conflicts, and deficits in both psychotherapeutic participants. Charged as they are with this triggering energy, the defensive operations of both participants, along with their "usual" reactions, must be carefully examined and thoroughly understood.

Racker (1968) wrote:

The truth is that it [the analytic situation] is an interaction between two personalities, in both of which the ego is under pressure from the id, the superego, and the external world; each personality has its internal and external dependencies, anxieties, and pathological defenses; each is also a child with his internal parents; and each of those whole personalities—

that of the analysand and that of the analyst—responds to every event in
the analytic situation. [p. 132]

By the 1980s, the stage was set for a synthesis of many of these
views. A group of theoreticians emerged to combine some of the earliest
insights about psychoanalysis with later findings from object relations
theory, Kleinian theory, Self psychology, and the seminal observational
research in mother–infant dynamics (Stern, Beebe, Tronic). This group
focused heavily on the subjectivity of therapist and patient both, and
tended to regard the work of treatment as taking place in a subjective
space shaped by the two of them. Their work provided supporting
evidence for the shift in our basic perceptions about psychotherapy and
the availability of pre-oedipal material. For one thing, the therapist was
no longer considered to be a benignly neutral, distant figure. The playing
field was leveled with the move from the authoritarian, neutral, uninvolved analyst to the description of the process given by Racker, and the
process of therapy was now regarded as an intersubjective field in which
two unique personalities mutually influenced each other as they responded to the unfolding dialogue taking place during each session. Of
necessity, this dialogue would rekindle the earliest developmental transferences for both.

One of the clearest descriptions of the evolved understanding of
transference (and by inference, countertransference) has been presented
by Stolorow and Lachman in their 1984–1985 paper, *Transference: The
Future of an Illusion*. After an initial review of the conceptual frames and
evolution of the concept of transference, they present their understanding of the nature of transference as a flexible, dynamic, developmental
process.

> In our view, the concept of transference may be understood to refer to all
> ways in which the patient's experience of the analytic relationship is
> shaped by his own psychological structures—by the distinctive, archa-
> ically rooted configurations of self and object that unconsciously organize
> his subjective universe (Stolorow, Atwood, and Ross 1978). Thus trans-
> ference, at the most general level of abstraction, is an instance of *organizing
> activity* . . . The transference is actually a microcosm of the patient's total

psychological life, and the analysis of the transference provides a focal point around which the patterns dominating his existence as a whole can be clarified, understood, and thereby transformed.

From this perspective, transference is neither a regression to nor a displacement from the past, but rather an expression of the *continuing influence* of organizing principles and imagery that crystallized out of the patient's early formative experiences . . . . The concept of transference as an organizing activity does not imply that the patient's perceptions of the analytic relationship distort some more objectively true reality. Instead, it illuminates the specific shaping of these perceptions by the structures of meaning into which the analyst and his actions become assimilated.

The concept of transference as an organizing activity offers an important clinical advantage over the other formulations in that it explicitly invites attention to both the patient's psychological structures and the input from the analyst that they assimilate (Wachtel 1980). As Gill (1982) repeatedly observes, it is essential to the analysis of transference reactions to examine in detail the events occurring within the analytic situation that evoke them . . . . *Transference as an organizing activity focuses more narrowly on the specific patterning of experience within the analytic relationship, to which both patient and analyst contribute.* [p. 26–27; emphasis added]

Psychotherapy had clearly taken an egalitarian turn. *Yet the practitioner still bore and bears the crucial responsibility for containing and maintaining the boundaries and frame of the work.* This is a challenging assignment, obviously, since such "participant observation," as Sullivan and Havens called it, requires the therapist to observe *both* parties, while involved in a distinct and bounded way. At the same time, the clinician must always keep the focus on the patient's issues, while monitoring and sorting out his or her own responses to this material as it comes up in the hour.

It is no surprise, therefore, that the better we understand the crucial importance of countertransference, the more we appreciate with greater humility the prodigious challenges that confront therapist and patient alike. Psychotherapy is a daunting task, and Freud's early instruction— that practitioners return to their own analysis every five years—appears to be even more relevant now than when he first offered it. Yet this increased awareness of the therapist's involvement in and impact upon the process also offers the possibility of helping patients understand themselves in ways that are deeper and richer than ever before.

THE DISCLOSURISTS[2]

What role, then, should the countertransference play in therapy, and how can a clinician best incorporate this inevitable phenomenon into treatment?

The debate over this question has become wide-ranging and intense. Practitioners on one end of the spectrum regard the countertransference as an issue involving only the therapist, who must deal with it alone. On the other end, psychotherapy (including the countertransference) is seen as a process that requires both parties to communicate openly and candidly about their reactions to whatever comes up in the course of an hour.

What, then, of the issue of disclosure? What feelings, contents, insights should the therapist disclose to the patient? What material should be held back, and why? How can a clinician determine the proper timing of a significant disclosure, and how should this material be presented? These questions lie at the heart of the ongoing debate over the meaning and possible therapeutic value of the countertransference.

An elegant response to some of them can be found in a paper by Levenson, (1996, p. 237):

> In my efforts to delineate an interpersonal perspective on self-revelation and disclosure, I must reiterate that "being interpersonal" and getting interpersonal are not, by any means, synonymous! *The essence of the interpersonal position lies in the analyst's self-awareness, that is, in an exquisite attention to the nature of his or her participation. As Gill put it, "The emphasis falls on being aware of what one is doing, rather than on what to do."* (Gill 1983, p. 211; emphasis added)

---

2. *Disclosurist* is a term coined by Sokolsky (1993), to refer to the range of clinicians and theorists who believe that some form of personal disclosure is a requisite part of the work.

Searles

Searles, a clinician who grappled with many of these questions, developed a number of useful understandings and ideas about clinical engagement, arising from his intensive work with schizophrenic patients. One of these (1959) was that the therapist's attempts to repress his or her own emotional responses to the patient inevitably mirror the oedipal repression experienced by a parent, who feels compelled to struggle towards a beloved child, even while making strenuous efforts to retreat from intimacy in the encounter.

Searles saw that the arousal of this distressing conflict in the therapist, and his or her attempt to suppress, repress, and retreat from it, introduced a factor that could easily undermine treatment. He was convinced that the clinician needed to confront these responses openly, and that acknowledging them would both clarify the experience and validate the patient (Searles 1961, and Searles 1959, pp. 284, 299 in L. Sokolsky, 1993). He believed that the therapist who refuses to admit the presence of these feelings will be required to keep them unconscious, and thus to avoid any related issues that might risk arousing them or bringing them into consciousness during treatment. Such an avoidance of fundamental issues would influence and limit the clinician's capacity to be empathically with and responsive to the patient. This could hardly be expected to produce a good outcome. Searles (1961) addressed this complex problem by focusing on the need for recognition and disclosure of the therapist's positive affective and fantasy involvement in the treatment.

While Searles's understanding of the positive and negative transferences aroused in the therapist were respected by many, the profession as a whole tended to view them as limited in usefulness, relevant to the "special" needs of schizophrenic patients, or materials to be employed only by such experienced and talented practitioners as Searles. Disclosure, as Searles described it, was seen for many years as an exception to the general rule prohibiting therapists from introducing countertransference issues into treatment.

Searles' insights found support in the earlier work of Winnicott (1947), and in the later work of Epstein and Feiner (1979) and Little

(1991), all of whom concentrated on the importance of working openly with hatred and the other hostile responses evoked in the therapist during treatment. Their findings, like those of Russell (1976), emerged primarily from the treatment of patients with nonpsychotic character disorders.

In 1974, Maltsberger and Buie noted the countertransference difficulties presented by suicidal patients, and the risks of avoiding this dimension of the treatment.

Epstein

Epstein (1979) suggested a process by which clinicians can acknowledge within themselves the hatred aroused in work with patients. They should:

1. remain inwardly open, and admit all feelings and fantasies provoked during therapy;
2. identify all destructive counter-reactions to these feelings as they unfold;
3. distinguish between their own inner issues (empathetic, hostile, erotic, etc.) and those feelings triggered by their engagement with the patient—admittedly a difficult process, consuming much time and energy. This process represents a formidable and ongoing challenge to the therapist;
4. reduce the affective intensity of these inner responses by first recognizing and then carefully assessing them;
5. finally, after completing this process, which helps to reduce the hatred to irritation and frustration, they must consider the most useful means of introducing this response for joint assessment and understanding, and then examine its impact on the treatment.

Epstein, like Searles before him, notes that a therapist who fails to address such issues risks inadvertently acting on the hostility evoked in treatment.

Kernberg

Kernberg (1984) was struck by the countertransference elicited by patients with character disorders. He recognized the significance of its impact on treatment, especially in its hostile and aggressive aspects. He describes aspects of the dilemma for patient and therapist:

> The concern for the patient, especially at times of violent acting out of the negative transference, also renders the analyst more vulnerable. His attempt to keep in touch with the patient's "good self" while being berated for his comments and silences and to maintain not only respect for the patient, but awareness of the loving and loveable aspects of his personality, requires that he be emotionally open to the patient. This, of course, exposes the analyst even further to the onslaught of the patient's aggression. The defensive withdrawal from attack, the sharpened affirmation of social boundaries that protect us from sadistic assaults under ordinary social circumstances, is deliberately reduced in the analytic situation, a circumstance that may tempt the patient to extreme unreasonableness and demandingness.
>
> By the same token, the threat of unbearable guilt forces the patient to resort increasingly to primitive projective mechanisms to justify his aggression; and primitive projection, particularly projective identification, is a powerful interpersonal weapon that "unloads" aggression onto the analyst. The patient may provoke the analyst into counteraggression and then, triumphantly, utilize this development as a rationalization of his own aggression. [p. 269]

Kernberg relied on direct forms of clarification, such as calling the patient's attention to his or her hostility and its effect upon the interaction as it occurred during the treatment hour.

One of Kernberg's significant contributions was his recognition that the therapist must maintain a keen awareness of the patient's split-off, positive aspects of self. A patient who has abandoned his positive sense of self through splitting-off will invite the therapist to do likewise. This awareness on the part of the therapist serves as an emotional safeguard during treatment (1984, p. 205). When the therapist loses sight of this aspect of the patient—in situations, for example, where a patient enacting a negative introject pressures the therapist to reject him—the patient may reexperience the original trauma of parental abandonment that had been formative of the character deficit.

Kernberg effectively described a psychological dynamic in which the patient seeks confirmation of a negatively introjected view of himself by reenacting in the treatment sessions the circumstances that initially established his "unworthiness" or "badness." Only when the therapist retains awareness of the patient's split-off positive sense of self in the face of this pressure, can the treatment succeed. In many instances, this need to retain a sense of what the patient is disowning while under the pressure of the repetitive dynamic is a most trying task that elicits many negative countertransference reactions from the therapist.

In order to intervene successfully, said Kernberg, the clinician must remain steadfastly aware of those disowned affective regions of the patient's personality that still yearn to be loved and cherished, but that were devalued and disallowed during development. These exiled facets of the personality must be retrieved through the interactional work of the therapy, and integrated by the patient. For this reason, the therapist's determination to remain centered in the process, even while identifying and articulating the hostility of the patient, often provides an acid test of the practitioner's commitment to the patient.

Kernberg, unlike Winnicott, chooses to identify the patient's hostility with less of a personal response. His approach confirms the clinician's awareness of the hostile intent, even as it demonstrates the practitioner's refusal to flee from it, or to react destructively. Although Kernberg might not label it as such, it seems to result in a genuine corrective emotional experience.

Kernberg's direct clarification of patient hostility in the treatment provides another built-in safeguard, preventing the clinician from taking a masochistic stance that might engender destructive counterhostility.[3] To avoid this trap, the therapist needs a clear sense of his own boundaries and also a keen awareness of the nature and extent of his or her own

---

3. In later examples, I show myself falling into this trap.

sadism and proclivity for masochistic avoidance of this aspect of him or herself.

Both Epstein and Kernberg struggled to develop guidelines for the use of direct intervention and disclosure in situations where resonantly aggressive issues impact powerfully on the treatment dyad.

Bollas

Bollas (1983, 1987) emphasized an understanding previously noted by Kernberg and others: that the countertransference may be a means by which some key aspect of a patient's early-life experience is communicated. Obviously, the patient can benefit from this communication only if the therapist remains open and vulnerable to the responses generated within him- or herself by the countertransference, and can then find a useful way to reintroduce them into the treatment.

Bollas (1983) describes this phenomenon clearly, and, like Epstein, delineates his own vision of the work it requires of the analyst. Because the patient engaging in the enacting of the transference drama is so often unaware of the process and the message being communicated, Bollas recommends the following:

1. The therapist registers the drama and its impact by experiencing it affectively and containing it.
2. The therapist then breaks down his or her emotional response to the situation into component parts (this is "metabolizing"), a process that requires the clinician to confront his or her own feelings and fantasies, and to identify the triggers that set off reactions within the treatment and within the practitioner, for example, perceiving what is being personally touched within the therapist, etc.)
3. The therapist recognizes that his response is a replay of something in the patient's experience. Most likely he or she has become an identifiable object in the patient's past and is playing a specific role. The therapist's understanding of what has been aroused within him– or herself may give a clue to the role in the patient's life.

4. The therapist connects this insight to his or her affective state.
5. Finally, the therapist describes aspects of his or her experience to the patient, and begins to suggest possible meanings *for the patient*. These potential meanings, presented for mutual consideration, must be described by the therapist as "possibilities," and not as ironclad conclusions.

Bollas is cautious about this process, and recommends that such self-disclosures be infrequent, judicious, and limited to statements that describe a specific aspect of the patient's impact on the therapist.

Hoffman (1983, p. 417), a proponent of view that use of the countertransference is helpful to patients in intensive treatment, is nonetheless careful to warn clinicians, "Such regular self-disclosure is likely to pull the therapist's total personality into the exchange in the same manner that it would be involved in other intimate social relationships."

Throughout this paper Hoffman suggests that too frequent self-disclosure may undermine the transference process, and thus foreclose deeper and broader understandings. He also points out that the practitioner must be careful not to "overestimate" the helpfulness to the patient of premature disclosure or inclusion of transference responses. Otherwise a kind of therapeutic *chutzpah* or arrogance may be enacted by the analyst:

> Admissions of countertransference responses also tend to imply an overestimation of the therapist's conscious experience at the expense of what is resisted and is preconscious or unconscious. Similarly it implies an extraordinary ability on the part of the analyst to capture the essence of the experience of the patient in a few words, whereas the patient may grope for hours in his free association before he reaches a verbalization that fully captures something in his experience of the analyst. (1983, pp. 417–18)

Hoffman's assessment continues: "Although countertransference confessions are usually ill-advised, there are times when a degree of personal, self-revealing expressiveness is not only inescapable but desirable [Ehrenberg 1982, Bollas 1983]. In fact, there are times when the only choices available to the analyst are a variety of expressive responses" (p. 418).

Like Little (1951), Hoffman believes that sometimes the therapist is forced to respond to the patient. On such occasions, a reference to the countertransference may be the least harmful approach. But once again, he takes pains to warn the therapist that it is always a mistake to assume that disclosure will be useful. Instead, he says, the practitioner must carefully assess the responses to it by thoroughly scrutinizing the patient's associations.

As the 1980s progressed, this question of how to make the best use of disclosure in the service of the patient became ever more prominent as more and more therapists began to regard countertransference responses as a useful tool in psychotherapy. Ehrenberg (1984), for example, summarized the problem like this: "Too much of one's . . . participation can destroy the integrity of the analytic relationship, as does too much caution. What is obviously needed is a delicate, judicious balance which establishes optimal distance."

Another proponent of judicious countertransference disclosure in therapy was Gorkin (1987), who contended that this practice often confirms reality for patients. Gorkin found that such disclosures were especially helpful for patients, borderline, narcissistic, or psychotic, who were struggling with pre-oedipal issues and whose reality sense was greatly shaded and colored by fantasy. Gorkin's conclusions were consistent with much of the earlier work of Winnicott, Searles, and Kernberg.

A major voice in the debate over countertransference disclosures belongs to Renik, who begins his discussion of the issue (1995) by declaring that analytic work goes best when the analyst can reasonably maintain anonymity. Noting that such anonymity can never be fully realized, however, Renik goes on to say that many therapists would probably agree that "judicious self-revelation under certain circumstances can be the least evil" (p. 467).

In addition, the fact that perfect anonymity is "impossible" (p. 468), clearly suggests that some disclosure is inevitable. Renik notes that every intervention, and equally every nonintervention signals something about the practitioner.

Most therapists have had experiences that suggest that Renik is correct in his argument that every silence, pause, change in posture, inflection, hesitancy, etc., reveals[4] something to the patient about the clinician's character. Such telltale clues may be seized upon by patients, and when they are, they necessarily become part of the work. Whatever the patient perceives, senses, and interprets in treatment, whether accurate or not, sooner or later becomes part of the intersubjective work of reliving and examining the transferences. Renik points out: "Careful examination shows that any way an analyst decides to deal with his or her emotional responses is consequential. . . . To suggest that an analyst can minimize communication of his or her idiosyncratic psychology . . . is to advocate the pursuit of an illusion" (p. 468).

He goes on to challenge Bollas's conception of the analyst as a receptive container of the patient's mental projections. The effective analyst as envisioned by Bollas examines such projections through his own affective and cognitive responses, in order to locate and accurately identify the patient's experience within himself. Once metabolized in this manner, these new understandings are reintroduced into the treatment.

Renik finds this concept unsatisfactory, since it perpetuates the illusion of a perfectly neutral clinician whose own analysis has completely removed his or her psychology from the treatment process. Only such an analyst could conduct this internal processing of the patient's projected experience without fear that his own psyche would distort the emergent understanding. This imputed state of psychological neutrality would allow him to internally examine and understand the patient within his own container, apart from the patient and their interaction. Renik is herein defining an area of danger: namely the consideration that one may be tempted to invest excessively in one's own understanding. Bollas does in fact see this danger and suggests a caution similar to Hoffman's (1983).

Renik (1995), while persuasively arguing that the erasure of one's own intrapsychic life is impossible, and that treatment is actually an intersubjective experience shared by two equivalent individuals, suggests that the analyst take pains to "clarify his analytic purpose and activity in the treatment setting," a step that he believes will "clear the field of those

---

4. Revealing and disclosing are different processes.

idealizing and confusing projections that are the inevitable product of the analyst's striving for perfect nonrevelatory anonymity" (p. 482). He sees the nonself-disclosure as a means of keeping the mysterious analyst at the center stage: "It makes the analyst into a mystery, and paves the way for regarding the analyst as an omnipotent sphinx whose ways cannot be known and whose authority, therefore, cannot be questioned" (p. 483).

Here Renik's valid premise of intersubjectivity is stated without consideration of the multiple levels of understanding in any communication: cognitive, conscious, paraverbal, nonverbal, and unconscious. His suggestion that the analyst take pains to clarify his reality and purpose seems to me to represent the common mistake of ascribing too much power to cognitive, conscious disclosure of analytic purpose and activity, as if that alone will reduce distortion and projection. This is a position that implicitly denies the same unconscious transference that therapy struggles to bring into awareness. As Hoffman notes, "What the patient's transference accounts for is not a distortion of reality but more a selective attention to and sensitivity to certain facets of the analyst's highly ambiguous response to the patient in the analysis" (1983, p. 409).

Given that both participants in this endeavor bring the capacity for selective sensitivity and attention to the situation, it is naive to believe that the assertion of our purpose and activity represents anything more than our consciousness, even as our unconscious infiltrates our clarification. In fact, intersubjectivity is based upon the premise that both parties engage with their whole psychological repertoire, which they then struggle to make sense of. While we hope that our experience, training, and personal analyses give us a broader capacity for understanding, in any given moment we have to keep a degree of uncertainty about our beliefs, perceptions, and understandings.

The reality is that such distortions of our purpose cannot be wiped away by assertions and clarifications. Renik's suggestion implies that we possess sufficient knowledge of our own unconscious to know what is accurate about our purpose at any given moment, and that merely stating it will remove the cloud of inevitable ambiguity. Renik's theoretical prescription, therefore, may create new distortions for both parties, even as it seeks to avoid distorting mystifications of the therapist.

Furthermore, although such clarifications may provide information that is helpful, they may also be defenses, avoidances, or distortions of our own. They may be necessary at certain points in a treatment, but to learn how such information is interpreted and used by both parties is in fact the work of psychotherapy. How does it impact upon both, and what do the two parties learn from the process?

Clarifications and affirmations of mutually perceived reality do have a place in our work. Most frequently they are useful when one has lived through and examined a transference-laden experience, and there is a need to clarify its meaning. Affirming elements of the experience while seeking further meaning may also promote deeper examination; confirming a patient's observation about us during the examination of a countertransference phenomenon, with a focus upon more associative examination, may deepen the work.

On the other hand, we must remember that some efforts to avoid mystification may paradoxically provoke it. When we believe that an explanation of our analytic purposes or activities has definitively cleared the therapeutic arena of distortions about our *persona*, we are probably deluding ourselves.

Renik views the quest for anonymity as an attempt to shroud the analyst in mystery. He further asserts that this mystification soon becomes the false center of the treatment, both enforcing the therapist's arbitrary power, and shielding him or her from the patient's critical scrutiny. His observations do legitimately suggest that somewhere between the illusion of anonymity and the intersubjective reality there is a therapeutic balance that will provide appropriate space for observation and knowledge of the therapist by the patient. In this elusive and sought-after place of balance, more authentic (we are always approaching authenticity) therapeutic work can emerge. Accordingly, he suggests that the clinician needs to clarify his or her own views. This step will encourage frank scrutiny of all issues by both parties in the process. Renik is convinced that this kind of open dialogue will ground the therapy in a reality where both parties confront real issues and solve real problems, rather than merely addressing hypothetical questions in a setting where correct answers are the property of the therapist alone.

As with most issues in life, "the devil is in the details." With the exceptions I've noted above, much of Renik's vision of the therapeutic process seems to me compelling and accurate. His perspective on the fundamental intersubjective nature of the process is especially helpful. His assessment lacks guidelines, however, and his approach is undermined by what seem to be glib dismissals of the risk of acting-in by the analyst. He also tends to oversimplify the enormous complexity of intersubjective work, a flaw that appears to encourage potentially impulsive, self-serving, and unstructured interventions by the therapist.

Several years ago, I heard a prominent intersubjective theoretician present clinical material at a conference. He related the history of a woman who was nearing the completion of her treatment.

Describing the closing phases of their work together, he said, he had asked her some questions about the level of intimacy and satisfaction in her marriage. His exploratory questions were phrased in a way that felt to me like an invitation for her to consider having an affair. (It wasn't clear with whom.) He then went on to relate how she subsequently found and became involved with an old boyfriend from her early college years, left her marriage, and finished her analysis.

I wondered to myself, Was this a way of maintaining a fantasy of no endings, no grieving, and no loss? A dream of never-ending relationships and object substitution? A vicarious affair for one or both parties in the treatment? Or was I being too critical? Did her midlife course adjustment represent an appropriate change in her circumstances? The timing and presentation didn't sit well with me, although the analyst proudly declared the patient to be "pleased with the treatment!"

It seemed possible to me that the patient's affair and subsequent marital breakup had provided both a vicarious experience and a possible countertransference enactment for the therapist. If that scenario had in fact occurred, was it a way for the analyst to play out his own issues of loss or separation? Was it serving other needs in the analyst's life? I knew that such acting-in can occur in any treatment as both parties face the ending of an intense and personal relationship; in this instance I was concerned that an intersubjective perspective had become the vehicle for enactment.

It is clear to me that such hazards exist in an unguided intersubjective approach. And yet, it's also true that the intersubjective nature of our work must be recognized. Awareness of this dual necessity sharpens the need to maintain the boundaries and attend to the multiple parameters of treatment.

PROJECTIVE IDENTIFICATION AND DISCLOSURE

Having outlined the emergence of countertransference as an acknowledged part of the treatment relationship, and having noted some concerns about its recognition and function, I want to turn now to another prominent element in the treatment process: namely, the defensive mode called projective identification.

This early form of projection, first defined by Melanie Klein (1946), is an important element in the dynamics of countertransference. Klein saw it as a way of disowning by means of projection an unacceptable, frequently aggressive aspect of oneself, which is then experienced as residing in another. Rather than avoiding the other person, as one might observe in ordinary projection, the subject instead seeks to control the object perceived as owning the dangerous trait. The subject therefore remains involved in an often contentious relationship with the person who seems to own the unacceptable aspect of the subject's self (Segal 1964, Kernberg 1984).

Ogden (1979, p. 358) describes projective identification as a three-stage process:

1. An individual who feels compelled to rid him— or herself of some discomforting self-aspect fantasizes the expulsion of it into another, and the expelled part then taking over the other from within;
2. The projecting person pressures the recipient through interpersonal interaction to claim the projected element and "think, feel, and behave in a manner congruent with the projection;"
3. After the recipient has accepted and internally processed the projection, the subject relates to him or her as though the projection defines the other.

Kernberg has also described this process; he sees it as a primitive form of communication (1984, p. 139), in which the projector hopes to control the projected aspect of the self by controlling its recipient:

> In the transference, projective identification is typically manifested as intense distrust and fear of the therapist. The therapist is experienced as attacking the patient, while the patient himself feels empathy with that projected intense aggression and tries to control the therapist in a sadistic overpowering way. . . . It is as if the patient's life depended upon keeping the therapist under control. The patient's aggressive behavior, at the same time, tends to provoke counteraggressive feelings and attitudes from the therapist. It is as if the patient were pushing the aggressive part of himself onto the therapist and the countertransference represented the emergence of this part of the patient from within the therapist. (Money–Kyrle 1956, Racker 1957) [1984, p. 114]

Continuing his description, Kernberg (1984, p.114) describes a rapid oscillation as the patient alternates between self and object representations in transference:

> Characteristic of borderline patients is a rapid oscillation between moments of projection of self representation while the patient remains identified with the corresponding object representation, and other moments in which it is the object representation that is projected while the patient identifies with the corresponding self representation. For example, a primitive, sadistic mother image may be projected onto the therapist while the patient experiences himself as the frightened, attacked, panic-stricken little child; moments later, the patient may experience himself as the stern, prohibitive, moralistic (and extremely sadistic), primitive mother image while the therapist is seen as the guilty, defensive, frightened, but rebellious child. These complementary role reenactments in the transference may also induce corresponding countertransference reactions in the therapist, an example of "complementary identification" (Racker 1957).
>
> Rapidly alternating projection of self and object images representing early pathological internalized object relations produces a confusion of

what is "inside" and "outside" in the patient's experience of his interactions with the therapist. [p. 115]

Unfortunately, such insights say nothing about the emotional experience of the therapist in this situation. Difficulties in treatment often begin when the therapist resists the projection or submits to it (consciously or otherwise), rather than identifying it and grappling with it in the transference.

Understandably, in such a turbulent scenario there will be many times when we cannot recognize the projective material, and find ourselves complying or resisting unknowingly. The ensuing struggles are painfully familiar to most of us.

Paul Russell (1976) described the therapist's affective experience in these situations, when projected fragments of self and object are oscillating rapidly in the transference, as "the Crunch." In a lecture at a Tufts University psychiatry conference and in a subsequent paper, Buie (1981) warned that these "resonance experiences"—these rapid oscillations— were one of the most frustrating and wearing experiences that can impede therapy.

There's no doubt that the discomfort experienced by both therapist and patient in this state of blurred boundaries accounts for much of the distress in intense treatments. *I believe that the urge to make disclosures to the patient is frequently triggered by the hope of relieving this sharp discomfort.*

How does projective identification occur? Tansey and Burke have attempted to outline the steps in this process, in which projection allows the therapist to recognize affective states in the patient by experiencing them. Their analysis shows how the therapist processes this information, then taps his or her empathic or cognitive skills to make sense of it (as in Bollas). After that, the challenge is for the therapist to find a way to reintroduce the experience into treatment.

At this point, Renik's observation that the therapist is bound to communicate something back to the patient, whether consciously or unconsciously, takes on great importance, since the former's words, silence, avoidance, gestures, etc., are all laden with communicative messages. The clinician needs to verbalize and communicate effectively his or her sense of the possible meaning of the projection. This response must be clear and genuine, while also grounded in a sense of the patient's perspectives and needs in the treatment. If it is not, the response can result in misperception or misinterpretation. Struggles within the therapist in these circumstances may also become the basis for the kinds of continuing internal obstacles to treatment progress described by Searles.

For all of these reasons, it is important that the therapist maintain an empathic connection with diverse elements of the patient, and also maintain the therapeutic framework, while verbally clarifying the situation. This is no small or simple undertaking; it is fraught with risk and the unknown. Yet this understanding supports Racker's and Kernberg's explication of primitive communication mechanisms.

One of the major understandings I have gained from the clinical material that follows is that most patients in these circumstances require more than mere acknowledgment that the therapist has received the idea conveyed by the projection. As the later examples show, the patient needs to understand that the clinician actually *felt* something in response to the projection, and has been emotionally affected by it.

As noted above, it is not easy to define how and when one can include this material most helpfully; the decision requires of the therapist both self-awareness and empathic attunement with the patient.

Having recognized and clarified to myself that I am having such an emotional response, once I introduce it into the treatment setting I have found it useful to point out that I regard my response as a sign that the patient is communicating an experience by helping me to *feel* it as the patient feels it. During such exchanges, I am careful to speak in a tentative manner of "possible" links to any known experience or genetic formulation that the patient and I can safely examine together. Tansey and Burke (1989, pp. 133–150) recommend the same careful internal assessment before a therapist decides to disclose inner experiences. They also attempt to formulate some guidelines for the clinician who has decided that judicious disclosure is appropriate.

SUMMARY

After decades of psychoanalytic discourse, study, and treatment, it seems clear that in every treatment a particular relationship evolves between patient and therapist in which the events, affects, and experiences generated by early object relationships are recapitulated for both members of the dyad. As the process unfolds, both verbal and nonverbal communication modalities influence both participants.

During the early history of psychoanalytic psychotherapy, this recapitulation-via-therapy was believed to involve only the patient, whose transferences could be analyzed by a benignly neutral and objective therapist. Ideally, the therapist would clarify early conflicts, distortions, and injuries in the patient, allowing their resolution and removing obstacles to further growth.

This early view of the psychotherapeutic process has been dramatically modified in recent decades. Increasingly therapy is seen as an interactional process involving the subjectivity of both participants. Today most therapists regard empathy, countertransference, projective identification, affective intersubjective communication, and keen receptivity as vital elements in the process. The price of this expanded understanding of psychotherapy is a greatly increased awareness of the responsibility upon the practitioner to analyze his or own character and examine its impact upon the treatment.

Analysts today recognize that emotional responses to patients are inevitable, and that they will be influenced by the clinician's own early life experiences, character structure, defenses, and current emotional circumstances. As noted above, this new and expanded psychoanalytic reality vastly increases the responsibility of the therapist to remain exquisitely attuned to the ever-shifting topography of his or her own psyche, while continuing to monitor transference events.

In this book, I am defining countertransference to mean "the therapist's personal transference, as aroused in the process of working with a particular individual," and I treat it as a mutual transference event, in which each party brings his or her past history to the session (McLaughlin 1981, 1991).

This definition emphasizes the crucial importance for the therapist of analyzing his or her own transference, in order to avoid acting on it. The therapist needs to recognize affects and enactments as they occur. After that, it's necessary to examine his or her own internal issues, in order to understand where, why, and how they intersect with those of the patient.

The therapist must ask the key question, What is being touched in me by this particular encounter, and how is it relevant to this particular treatment?, while simultaneously grappling with the patient's own transference. What is the meaning of this experience for the patient, and is there some reason that the patient might need to reach me in this manner at this time? Is the patient's enactment triggering some reaction in me that is linked to other situations in my life? If that is the case, then why is the reaction taking place now—and why with this patient?

Faced with the multi-layered challenge of countertransference, today's practitioner must depend more than ever upon rigorous self-scrutiny, ongoing analytic treatment, consultation, supervision, and whatever other means enable him or her to stay attuned to the vicissitudes of his or her own psyche during the treatment hour. The therapist's careful self-analysis may very well illuminate the patient's own struggle, even as it sharpens the clinician's empathic understanding of the subject's transference.

Once we recognize the fact that the therapist cannot realistically hope to conduct treatments without having his or her own transferences reawakened, the need for effective countertransference guidelines becomes self-evident. This requirement becomes even more urgent in a field of endeavor that is changing rapidly, and in which more and more therapists consider the advisability of making personal disclosures to their patients. Again quoting Levinson (1996, p. 247): "Self-disclosure often seems to be a reparative effort by the analyst after some acting in on his or her part."

When tempted to disclose something about myself in treatment, I review what I understand about the dynamic of this particular interaction and my own psychological status. Frequently I find that I am feeling helpless, irrelevant, and excluded, or that I want to flee, or assuage a pain that seems unbearable. I call to mind my own treatments and former analysts. I am grateful that somehow they bore the distress of my anguish and despair without acting, knowing as I do that even when I was curious about them, I didn't *really* want to know about them. I wanted the space that they afforded me to struggle with my own demons while they held the frame.

In my first analysis, I developed a fantasy about my the analyst's identity in order to protect accompanying fantasies of joining and completion. And yet I actually resented the intrusion of revealed or disclosed material. In later work, I finally gained a sense of the conflicts within me, and the need therefore for a transferentially created *persona* with whom I could interact. I wanted a transference object, and felt that the inclusion of the *reality* of my therapist's life would interfere with my making sense of my own.

The title of this book, *Working in the Countertransference*, is an effort to underline the importance of recognizing on a continuing daily basis that the therapist's own transferences are an essential part of the psychotherapeutic dynamic—and that they are *not* something to reveal without due consideration. How well we work in this dimension of psychotherapy will have a major impact, for better or worse, on the treatment of our patients.

2

Styles of Communication

This chapter explores the ways in which patients and therapists exchange information and communicate via nonverbal means. The chapter concludes with considerations of the ways in which the infant-mother relationship influences adult communication, and the implications for treatment. A case study provides illustration.

If we the professional therapists find the process of treatment and the countertransference aspects to be complicated and demanding, what then drives the patient to engage in this stressful and turbulent process? In most instances, one finds that a significant component is the patient's hunger for authentic communication with another human being, a genuine emotional connection in which the patient finds his or her true self recognized. Such a communication can only be achieved if the other person in the dialogue, here the therapist, responds in a way that recognizes and validates the complexity and intensity of the patient's unique perspective.

How can a therapist respond to a patient's messages in an appropriately forthright manner, while carefully monitoring and sorting through those inner resonances that are being triggered by the clinician's own transferences?

Kernberg (1984) provides a good starting point for such an inquiry, by describing the power of nonverbal communication in the treatment of borderline personality disorders.

> Borderline personality organization always involves . . . the expression, mostly by nonverbal means, of unconscious intrapsychic conflicts in the form of chronic, repetitive behavior patterns. Therefore the nonverbal aspects of the interaction with the therapist supply fundamental information, replacing to a considerable extent what the verbal communication conveys in the standard psychoanalytic situation. [p. 138]

Kernberg observes that nonverbal expression by the patient plays a key part in the communication that takes place during the hour. For that reason, the clinician will be required to participate in the therapy with his or her entire being, including those emotional resonances inevitably provoked by nonverbal messaging.

Indeed, Kernberg himself takes pains to point out that even in the so-called standard psychoanalytic situation, nonverbal cues often form a communications circuit of their own. And this second circuit, Kernberg suggests, may sometimes be more effective than mere words in transmitting meanings back and forth between the partners in the treatment dyad: "One might say that in this transformation of intrapsychic conflict into interpersonal action, the patient is resorting to a form of communication and relationships that, genetically speaking, predates the predominance of verbal communication (p. 139)."

Kernberg's analysis of nonverbal communication demonstrates that such elements as vocal tone, intonation, facial expression and gesture—along with various types of actions (or the absence thereof)—combine to create deep, rich meanings in the treatment setting.

These wordless clues powerfully evoke feelings and reactions in both patient and therapist. As in any communication, the affects generated and the responses to them are then interpreted and associated to by both parties. Such "silent messages" evoke a chain of complex reactions charged with emotion based on personal experience and individual needs.

As therapists, we are obligated to carefully scrutinize all of these communications and also the responses they evoke within us. Thus we must remain perpetually vigilant, while repeatedly asking ourselves such questions as:

—What am I feeling now and why? Where is it coming from within me and within this situation?

—Is there some message in this? What might it be?

—What is the impact of the messages I believe I am picking up from the patient?

—What do these clues lead me to feel, remember, fantasize, or generate in my own responses?

—How do my responses potentially relate to the patient, apart from my own separate life and experience?

—Is there some way in which my internal responses can help me understand something new about the patient and his or her experience?

—Can I use my response to better understand something in our current interaction?

—How does my response relate, specifically, to the content of this hour and preceding hours?

PARAVERBAL COMMUNICATION

The term "paraverbal communication" describes the process in which significant and powerful information is transmitted from one person to another, not through words but through sounds, gestures, attitudes, and shifts in demeanor, all of which can serve to elicit feelings in the treatment setting.

How does such paraverbal communication take place? One way to understand the process is to look at what happens between adults and infants before spoken language becomes fully present. As researchers (Escalona, Stern, Beebe and Lachman, Tronick, Demos, Mahler, and others) have pointed out, a great deal of significant emotional information is exchanged between the child and his or her important caretakers during the earliest moments of life and for long periods of time afterward, without the use of organized language. Thus noises, silences, gestures, movements, facial and bodily expressions, along with touching, hugging, squeezing, etc., constitute our earliest and most basic modes of communicating with one another. These aspects of communication are never lost and always remain part of our repertoire, particularly when communicating significant emotional material.

With increasing maturity, most people come to rely more and more on words as the primary means of communication, with emotional intonation and expression giving color and depth to the content. But other senses and expressive modalities retain much of their force, and it takes but a moment's thought to realize that all of us rely upon a combination of nonverbal mechanisms to convey many of our significant perceptions and experiences. Such intimate forms of communication require a high degree of trust that the other person is fully engaged with us. There must also be a solid assurance that our communication partners are keenly attuned to us and determined to comprehend our full meaning. Thus, in adult communication, we are constantly assessing the other person's facial and eye expressions, gestures and sounds, to make sure that they are still with us. We shift our emphasis or restate a point, slightly alter or amplify an issue, all for the purpose of maintaining the most optimal sense of engagement and understanding.

But what happens when one of the parties to a communication is struggling with characterological disorders that distort their understanding of what is being stated; or someone is depressed and distracted; or psychotically preoccupied and cannot engage? For these individuals, achieving effective verbal communication is often difficult. All too often, experience has taught them that other people will not truly be attuned to their thoughts and feelings. Like all of us, their entry into a discussion is shaded by expectations based upon past experience.

One of the challenges faced by the clinician working with individuals with significant emotional difficulties relates to a crucial aspect of human communications: the universal need to feel that other people can see and appreciate issues and experiences from our point of view.

Intent upon obtaining this sensed understanding and validation from others, most of us will do everything we can to get the other person to feel as we do. If we have had the experience that important others carefully attend to our words and understand our state of being in that way, then we will first use words. If not, then what better way to get others to "walk in our shoes," than to attempt to create for them experiences in which they feel something similar to what we have felt?

Defined by some practitioners as "mini-re-creations," and by others as "resonances" or "enactments," these scenarios are a necessary part of treatment. Russell used a highly evocative expression, "the Crunch," to capture the essence of what one feels while living through this kind of communication. Russell also suggests that "the Crunch" is a common experience that presents a formidable challenge to most therapists: "These crises have a way of generating so much affect and consuming so much energy, that one of the major problems in the treatment situation is the disorientation of the therapist. The feeling is that if only the storm would clear, the treatment could begin [or resume]. Take this point, when the confusion is the greatest, when the therapist's anxiety and helplessness and sweat are at levels not before possible, and call this the 'Crunch' (p. 2)."

As Russell makes clear, this disturbingly familiar state of confusion, distress, fatigue, and self-doubt on the part of the therapist is usually evoked by the patient, who is unconsciously asking us to re-live some painful problem or experience in order to understand it better. Sandler (1976, 1990) has described the patient's effort to transmit these feelings to the therapist via nonverbal, unconscious cues. He views it as a means of imposing a particular role upon the analyst that will create a reenactment of a particular internal object relationship. Like the patient at an earlier time or an object in relation with the patient at that time, we find ourselves feeling and associating in ways that are initially unclear. We may feel bothered, bored, avoidant, overwhelmed, wishing to end the hour, hurt, angry and wishing to destroy the one responsible for such hurt, or potentially enraptured or enthralled with our fantasy relationship.

Disorienting and painful at times, the therapist's reexperiencing of something akin to the patient's earlier discomfort is actually essential to treatment. The challenge for the clinician is precisely this: how to contain these conflicted feelings while not acting upon them. The clinician must:

1. First, recognize that the distress or upset being experienced is part of the mini drama which he has unwittingly, but necessarily, fallen into.

2. Second, observe the effects of, and the responses to, this emotional reenactment within himself.
3. Third, work at deciphering and metabolizing the experience, before bringing these transformed materials back into treatment and attempting to reintegrate it.

As the following examples seek to illustrate, this interactional paradigm of patient–therapist communication is an essential aspect of working with most forms of psychopathology. While more easily seen with people struggling with character disorders, it is by no means limited to these individuals. A brief look at the dynamics at work in these more dramatic instances will help us to discern the complex mental operations at work in "orchestration."

For many patients struggling with more severe character disorders, this mode of communication begins in the very first moments of encountering the therapist. Whether the clinician is meeting a haughty, distant narcissist character or a depressed, disorganized, and yet fiercely demanding borderline personality, the process usually includes interactions that are familiar and predictable.

Almost invariably, the patient will attempt to reduce the perceived psychic danger of the encounter with a stranger[1] by quickly constructing a rigid mental image, or *persona*, of the other, here the therapist. In part a fiction, this pre-fabricated persona will be based upon hastily perceived aspects of the therapist's character, matched up with elements selected from the patient's preexisting internal object world.

The patient's motivation at this stage is quite understandable. He or she is struggling to defend against the potential danger of meeting a stranger in unfamiliar circumstances. By quickly constructing the persona of the therapist and then relating to it, rather than gradually getting to know the therapist as the person he or she is, the patient is in effect saying, "I have assured myself that I don't have to be afraid of you. You are like

---

1. We need to keep in mind that our unknowness is to the patient a danger. Thus they must quickly define us in terms of a few known character types to reduce their anxiety.

so-and-so from my past, and I learned how to deal safely with you long ago."

During these early sessions, the therapist will almost inevitably be drawn into the patient's projective world of dominance and submission, control, and exploitation. Work with more neurotically constructed individuals (as opposed to those with more severe character pathology) has shown that similar, if less emotionally intense enactments will emerge later in treatment.

Nonetheless, some neurotic patients with more internalized conflicts and fewer projective defenses will engage in the same kinds of reenactment scenarios during the early phases of treatment—especially if they are struggling with severe emotional stress at the time that treatment begins.

UNDERSTANDING ORCHESTRATION

What is the process by which the patient learns to ease the anxiety of relating to others by relying upon inwardly scripted projections, rather than remaining open and vulnerable to a more gradually constructed sense of the other?

In recent years, research on the dynamics of early development has opened fascinating windows on the process of paraverbal communication as a key step on the road to selfhood. Increasingly, the research shows that such wordless communication has a vitally affective and evocative impact on the developing infant and his or her primary objects.

During the first year or so of life, as rudimentary vocalizations begin to emerge, the infant relies primarily on paraverbal messages to engage both the environment and caretakers. While the child is learning how to vocalize needs, desires, and responses, most of them must be communicated through these behavioral clues.

The intensity and urgency of the child's affective state varies with the sensed or anticipated capacity of the respondent to provide required care and empathy. Thus behavioral learning based upon experience becomes an early learning modality. In most cases, the infant whose cry regularly elicits a speedy and comforting response will become quiet after hearing the parent's approaching footsteps, voice, or other familiar sounds that signal approaching comfort. Similarly, the child will be sensing the vocal tone, facial expression, easy or rushed qualities, physical tension or relaxation in the touch and holding. All of these comprise vital elements of the communication.

Obviously, the interaction with the responding adult is a key variable in the "feedback learning loop" that results from paraverbal communication.

But what happens in situations where the mother is frequently unable to correctly interpret the child's cries, or misreads the nonverbal communication? What if the mother turns out to be preoccupied, distressed, depressed, or otherwise unattuned? In that unfortunate happenstance, the child's affective sense of security will be weakened, triggering increased discomfort.

If one takes the following hypothetical example, a child, a toddler around age two years is playing with some toys in a room adjacent to his mother. Each is busy with their activity but aware of the other nearby. The child slips, and in the moment before landing, he feels the disequilibrium and loses the fragile early integrated sense of self. In a split second, he feels a hot searing pain as his knee hits the edge of his toy truck and he screams and begins to cry and hold his knee. The pain has further fragmented his organized sense of himself and his environment. He needs his mother to put him back together.

We now postulate two hypothetical mothers, A and B. Mother A hears the cry and puts down her work and stands up calling "I'm coming." She has sensed the quality of the cry and discerns that while her child has hurt himself, he's probably bruised and frightened but not seriously injured. As she reaches the door, she quickly assesses the scene and realizes that it is a fall and a scrape. Approaching the child, she is already reassuring by the expression of simple declaratives: "You fell." "It hurts." "I'll help." "We'll fix it." "It will be fine." "The hurt will go away." While saying this calmly, without tension, she has scooped the child into her arms and gently rocked him and holds him closely. Her muscle tone and body are comforting and relaxed as she holds him. Her voice is soothing. She strokes him while continuing to express the simple declaratives that define the situation and begin the reintegration of the child's ego sense of definition. The child's crying diminishes and she asks to see the injured knee. The child begins to howl at the prospect of uncovering the injury. Mother does not persist, but continues to soothe and does not force the issue. She allows the child to continue to cover the wound. Again she mentions that she'd like to look but assures that she won't touch it. This becomes a brief negotiation in which the child's need for assurance about not touching will be respected. The child gradually uncovers the wound and begins crying at the site of the blood and scrape. Again, mother affirms that there is blood; that it will feel better; that it will heal. She carries the child to the sink and holding him places him on the counter. She asks if they can see it again and maybe wipe the blood away. He cries and says it will hurt. She says that if it hurts she'll stop. He agrees (more negotiation). Gently she dabs it with a wet paper towel. He cries and she stops, as she said she would. Deciding that it can go without further cleaning, she says, "All done. How about a bandaid?" He perks up and says, "A Pooh one?" She gets the box and he picks the one he wants. As they put it on together, the crying stops as if there is anesthetic in the bandaid. She gives him a cookie and he goes off to play. The negotiation, respect, comforting gestures, tones, and experiences have resealed the ego boundaries, and the event has left both parties feeling intact, respected, and mutually involved.

In the same circumstance, Mother B hears her child cry and gets up suddenly with a tense, "Oh God! What's wrong? Are you all right? I'm coming." She hurries to her child. At the doorway, she sees the child and realizes that it's a fall and a cut. She approaches the child tensely. "It's OK." "I told you to be careful." Her voice has an edge of concern and blame. Her gestures are slightly sharp and not soothing or easy. She picks the child up to comfort him and his cries continue. Her arms and body are tense as she tries to comfort him. She says, "You cut your knee. It will be fine. Let me see it." The child howls, and she feels terrible. Trying to assert control, because she feels the situation is out of control, she again says, "I need to see it so that I can fix it." This time, she is more insistent. Reluctantly, he uncovers it and cries more loudly at the sight of the blood. She also gasps slightly and carries him to the sink. She tells him that they will have to wash it. His cries become louder. Not feeling successful in comforting him, and feeling distressed herself, she explains that they must clean it to get rid of the "germs." He covers his knee vigorously and she insists on his taking his hands away. "How can I make it better if you won't let me clean it?" Whimpering, he again submits. She washes it and tells him that big boys don't cry and it will get better. He tries to be a big boy, but can't help crying. He wants her to comfort him and submits in the hope of gaining her softer voice. The "bandaid" does not work the magic as in the first instance. He goes off to the other room, returning frequently to reconnect with his mother who also feels badly about the interchange. He can be heard kicking his truck and saying "bad truck" several times during the day. Rather than having a reintegrating experience, he has felt shame, a lack of comfort, and externalizes the pain to the "bad truck," deflecting his pain away from the hurt and shamed little boy who cries and isn't yet a big boy.

Both mothers love their children, and any of us can be either Mother A or B at any given moment. The more integrated and personally comfortable we are, the more we are in the experience of Mother A. The more we are anxious, depressed, distracted, self-critical, and preoccupied, the more we are Mother B. For the child who gets enough of Mother A, there are sufficient integrating experiences with a trusted other and an evolving self to weather the periodic relational disappointments. When there are too many Mother B experiences, one's character develops with a mistrust of self and others and character deficits emerge.

Frustrated and filled with undifferentiated anxiety, fury, and panic as a consequence of the caretaker's misattuned response, the struggling infant and child will try various means to engage the adult, and will repeat those methods that prove effective, even when they include negative aspects. In this way, the feedback-based learning system is established early in life. As Escalona's and Stern's observations of infant-mother interactions have powerfully demonstrated, miscues and missed communications play an important part in the development of the child's affective responses during the first weeks of life.

Other investigators, including Beebe and Tronick, have also shown how distorted communication between infants and their caregivers often has a negative impact on affective responses in the developing child. (Their work also suggests that patients in therapy can be negatively affected by the therapist's failure to read and then respond to their nonverbal messages.) In a like manner, attuned communication facilitates the flourishing of the child's development and evolution.

What happens to a young child whose paraverbal signaling is regularly ignored, misunderstood, or poorly responded to by the mother or other significant caregiver? In most cases, the developing youngster will make increased efforts to gain the response that has not been forthcoming.

Such signaling usually involves attention-seeking behaviors, since these are most likely to win a response. And while these behaviors often contain active and aggressive components, they can also be passive and restrained, without involving significant actions of any kind. In situations of regular and continuing misattunement and lack of response, there can be a profound resignation and shutting down leading to attachment disorders and failures to thrive.

This process becomes maladaptive if it leads to fixations in which developing children continually use negative behaviors to earn validation of self and to engage significant others. The problem is that the development, through negative introjection and repetition of experience, of a malformed sense of self becomes the basis for repeated destructive transferences. All too often, the result is an individual with serious character pathology and a penchant for endlessly reexperiencing childhood trauma (getting important others to react with aversion and rejection). Unfortunately, these adults possess little or no confidence that they will be noticed, understood, or appropriately responded to. *They will find a way to evoke the familiar response, however, even if it proves to be destructive!*[2] This unfortunate syndrome plays itself out across all socioeconomic levels, and regardless of the affected individual's intelligence or worldly achievements.

---

2. If there are, simply defined, only three response states: positive, negative, and nonresponse, and the first is eliminated, most of us would choose a negative response that recognizes our existence over a nonresponse that denies our existence.

BRENDA–A STRUGGLE WITH "COERCIVE PSEUDO-FAMILIARITY"

Several years ago, I received a call from an industrial psychologist who asked me to see a middle-aged woman whom my colleague had been forced to fire from her job. The psychologist liked her, but finally decided that her behaviors were too disruptive in their work group. Brenda, highly trained, with a background in mathematics, physics, and economics, was apparently unaware of the impact of her behavior upon others, despite my colleague's attempts to discuss it with her. This would be her third job loss within the past three years. All three firings had been related to her character problems.

I agreed to see her for an evaluation. When she arrived for her first appointment, her inappropriately casual attire bordered on outright sloppiness. She approached the chair intended for her, then made an ostentatious display of bending over and "brushing off the seat." The effect of this maneuver, an incongruous concern for cleanliness, was to bring her ample posterior very close to my face!

After this apparently unconscious action had been completed, the new patient took her seat. What was she showing me—that she was an ass? Was she saying that this was important to notice, and not what she said? Was there was more "behind" this presentation, or was this an obstruction of other issues? I didn't know. A moment later, she was chattering away in a casual and familiar manner, as if we had known each other for many years. I was surprised, engaged, charmed, humored, and getting uncomfortable with the assumed familiarity.

She talked at length about her job situation, and dismissed her fellow workers as intellectually inferior clods who could not possibly understand a person of her complexity and intelligence. She described herself as generous in accepting their limitations and insisted that she worked very hard not to judge them. I wondered if I might also be "managed" in this way.

I listened carefully to all of this, then commented about the recent loss of her job and the possible disappointment or consequences it caused for her. Without hesitating, she informed me that she had been "completely misunderstood" by her supervisors, and that she had simply been

scapegoated as the result of political chicanery on the part of her bosses—
"But, I understand, that's how some narrow-minded people are."

Because I sensed that this patient already felt judged and shamed,
and that she would respond defensively to any further comments, I did
not interrupt her again, except to wonder out loud if she might be feeling
some disappointment over the loss of her employment. Unsurprisingly,
she waved this concern away with airy disdain, saying that I should not
trouble myself about that.

After the session, I noted that I felt intruded upon by the patient's
unctuous and false-seeming familiarity, which struck me as enveloping
and suffocating. It seemed aimed at controlling my participation in the
session from beginning to end. Such feelings set off familiar alarm bells
from my own early life.

Later, I examined my responses with the help of a colleague who
frequently joins me in reviewing sessions and exploring our work. He
chuckled as he reflected on previous situations in which others had been
discomfited by this patient's ersatz bonhomie and her bullying, if jocular
tactics. "It sounds like this is an old issue for you," said my friend, "trying
to stay the course with someone who turns out to be controlling and
enveloping all the while, concealing it in the best of intentions and
concern. So, how's your Mom these days?"

I laughed as we both recognized a piece of my experience. We knew
each other well, and each other's character pitfalls! I was grateful for the
opportunity to discuss this encounter with a colleague, because I understood that this patient had triggered some painfully familiar resonances
within my own psyche. Talking with another practitioner allowed me to
articulate some of my own painful feelings and reactions to being manipulated and coerced. Here the strategy of inauthentic and demanded con-
viviality felt like an impenetrable wall. Why did I feel the urge to
penetrate this? A counter-intrusion perhaps? I don't like being cornered
or forced into something false. Such situations could arouse my guilt-
driven penchant for trying to "stay the course" rather than examining
deeper concerns about my own aggression. Imagine my surprise and
consternation at the start of the next session, when I entered my office to
find the patient already there and busily engaged in rearranging all of the

books and papers on my desk! (My door had been slightly ajar as I talked with a friend in an adjacent office.)

Amazed, I asked the patient quietly, with some incredulity, what she was doing. She replied that she'd arrived to find the door ajar, and had simply walked into my office. After taking a quick look around, she'd decided to do me a favor. Was I aware, she wanted to know, of the chaotic disorganization of the papers and journals that littered my needlessly cluttered desk?

I paused for a few moments as she continued to explain, and then I interrupted what had become a booming monologue. I asked her, with an evident sense of smiling wonderment, what were **we** to make of this rather remarkable behavior: her decision to enter my office in my absence and then serve as a self-appointed rearranger and organizer or helper?

Anxiously, she started to interrupt me in order to justify her actions. I raised one hand in a gesture intended to both calm and silence her. In a soft but firm voice I insisted, "It's all right, please let me finish." I then spoke to her slowly and quietly (remarks paraphrased slightly):

> Have you brought in for our understanding the very issues that were causing you problems elsewhere? You've barely met me, yet you jumped in to "help" me. The reality is that you don't know me yet. Were you so fearful that our relationship would not succeed? So you rushed ahead in this surprising and dramatic manner? Did you feel that we would not be able to take those numerous, small, sequential steps that are the necessary prelude to genuine relatedness?

> Perhaps you felt compelled to leap past those intermediary steps, before the opportunity for a meaningful relationship evaporated on you? Did you assume that I would not want to get to know you of my own volition? Did you further decide to remove my choice by acting so precipitously—by coming into my office and "helpfully" moving things around—forcing me to be grateful or something else? Could it be that your fear of being rejected led you to tell yourself, "Since I know you will reject me, I'm going to act preemptively. I will force him to either submit to my control, or break off our relationship early, before you've even gotten to know me, the person you are rejecting. That way, I won't have to feel that my true self is being rejected, just my behavior?"

As I asked these assumptive questions quietly but persistently, the patient tried several more times to interrupt. But when I continued to pose these queries, not as attacks, but as meaningful speculations, she gradually began to listen. Soon, she sank down into her chair and began to weep. Then she told me that my response had shown her something new: the fact that she, herself, had orchestrated the sequence of events that might have led to my breaking off the relationship. Previously she was always convinced that no one understood her good intentions.

In this early moment of treatment, the dynamics underlying a piece of her familiar behavior had become clear to both of us. Her aggressive intrusion was a coded message in which she was presenting me with two options: either I could allow her to take over and control me (by coercing me with pseudo–intimacy), or I could reject her right at the start of our relationship. If I chose the latter option, I would at least be sparing her the pain of a later, even more terrible rejection.

This patient was also asking me to experience some of the shame and humiliation she had so often felt in her own life, while enduring a forced submission to a superficially caring and friendly person feigning unctuous joviality, even as they cynically exploited and manipulated her.

When I refused to reject this patient because of her behavior, and instead asked her calmly but firmly if she understood her need to make others turn away from her as quickly as possible, she was able to begin exploring her fears and earlier traumas in earnest. Eventually, her lifelong characterologic victim's stance began to give way to a clearer understanding of her own role in orchestrating these scenarios of rejection. More importantly, she began to see the underlying vulnerability and assumptions about herself, and the negative introjects forming a falsely identified self which had concealed her genuine, instinctual self.

Had I not taken the time to review the first hour of her treatment with my colleague, I don't believe that I would have been able to respond as helpfully. My own anger and reaction to intrusion and violation would have clouded my judgement. My defenses against my own feared aggression would have led me to endure her behavior masochistically until I had invited her to perform a sufficient number of intrusive acts to justify an angry rejection. Instead, in this instance, I was able to use my aggression in a more helpful way.

3

Force and Coercion

This chapter examines the dynamics of the orchestrated "mini-dramas", predominantly, but not exclusively shaped and driven by the characterologic needs of the patient. How does enactment affect the therapist's approach, and what will help the clinician to stay in the enactment until its hidden meanings are revealed through mutual understanding of the transferential dynamic?

Having defined the mini-drama (or enactment) as the process in which the therapist reacts consciously and unconsciously to messages (paraverbal or other) from the patient, we are now prepared to explore some of the ways that patients unconsciously orchestrate, and we participate in (and sometimes also orchestrate), these experiences.

As many clinician-authors (including Sandler, Russell, and Bollas) have noted, these behavioral orchestrations are usually employed as a means of "forcing" the therapist to understand the patient's experiences in a deep and compelling way. I use the term force deliberately, since there is undoubtedly an element of coercion in the dynamics of the process, as noted in the first example.

Why does this disturbing, coercive element so often emerge to threaten the equilibrium of the treatment dyad? In many instances, patients feel compelled to drag us into their characterological dramas because they fear that we will not be truly capable of understanding or willing to understand their painful inner state unless we actually feel it with them. And there is some truth in this assumption. Could we truly understand them and their experience without some taste of what their life is like? And yet, who would willingly agree to feel such distress?

In other words, these anxious patients fear that we will prove to be no different than the significant others who abandoned them to their lonely suffering earlier in their lives.

All too often, the patient's coerciveness during sessions will trigger resistance from the therapist, setting the stage for a therapeutic struggle that can become brutal and exhausting over time. This complication can be observed quite vividly in the enmeshed, part-object relationships that occur so frequently with borderline patients.

Describing the process, Melanie Klein (1946) posits an early developmental state, the paranoid–schizoid position, in which the infant experiences destructive and malevolent drives as externally located, while happily claiming positive and pleasurable senses as features of his or her internal landscape. In this dynamic, the infant attempts to protect the "good" inner self from the destructive "outsider," which is merely a projected aspect of the same self.

After establishing this framework, Klein goes on to develop the concepts of splitting and projective identification. Splitting is a way of emotionally separating off an aspect of oneself and one's character as not one's own. The trait or behavior is not mine or doesn't exist. It is then projected, seen as residing in another, with whom one stays in a relationship, in order to control the disowned aspect of the self.

For example, in working with a couple who were in a chronically strained relationship of long duration, the following occurred:

The two were reviewing what seemed to be a minor difference in their understanding and memory of an event. As she was saying something quietly, he looked over and said with venomous intensity:

Husband: You're disgusting!
Wife, shocked: What's that about? Why did you say that?
Husband: Say what?

Wife: You said that I was disgusting.

Husband: No I didn't say that, you did!

Therapist, quietly to her: Actually, you did say that.

Husband, more agitated, voice rising: Well, if I did, I didn't mean it!

Therapist: You meant something, perhaps we can understand it.

Husband, in a fury: You hate me, you're picking on me. I don't say
things like that. You're both disgusting. You're liars. No one
likes me!

He went on a few moments longer before storming out.

What had happened? As events were later reconstructed, he had
immediately repressed his words. When faced with the wife's statement
that the words originated in him, he immediately split off his hostility and
projected it: "I didn't say that, you did." For him, to be the source of
hostility rather than a victim responding to it would mean that he was
irrevocably "bad."

In his childhood, he had been subject to extremely vitriolic anger
from his father for minor errors. His mother had ignored him and not
protected him. Thus, any issue that reflected adversely upon him was
vehemently defended against for fear that it confirmed his innate badness
and unworthiness (negative introject misidentified as the genuine self).
When the therapist confirmed the statement, it was as if both parents had
overtly joined to condemn him. There was nothing to be understood. In
a panic-driven rage, he fled the scene.

He was not lying when he said that he did not say, "You're disgusting." He did not recall saying it. He had truly repressed it. Several days
later, he and his wife talked about the incident. She quietly reiterated her
words and his. At first he yelled and cursed and threatened her. She
quietly repeated what she had said. After many repetitions of this, he
looked up and said sadly, "Oh my God, you're right. I can't believe that I
said that!" He calmed down and they then had a quiet evening.

The next morning he was furious, saying, "You are so cruel. You
made me agree that I said terrible things last night." Again, he had
reexperienced that she was the aggressor and he the victim. The projection warded off the intolerable sense that he had done something that he

found unacceptable and therefore meant he was a worthless, awful person. While it protected him internally, it made relationships impossible to sustain.

Melanie Klein's meta-psychological model for infants accurately describes the behavior and interactions that occur with characterologically disturbed patients such as the woman noted above. She lived in a paranoid–schizoid state, in which she could not contain a recognition of her mixed and conflicting wishes and emotions. Thus, a developmental movement into a depressive position that allows one to bear ambivalence about oneself and others, and to grieve lost fantasies of perfection, was precluded, and with it, stable relationships. It is at this level of emotional functioning that many patients present themselves at their initial entry in psychotherapy.

Although most of us find intensive psychotherapy to be extremely challenging and evocative of painful and frightening feelings, it should be pointed out that patients with characterological issues live at this high level of fear and rage during much of their daily lives.

Mercilessly tormented, the typical borderline patient struggles with desperate feelings of imminent abandonment, isolation, and disintegration. Inwardly, these burdened individuals hold themselves responsible for their inner turmoil and, in the same moment, they must project (disown) this responsibility by attributing it to others, whom they perceive as critical, rejecting, and abandoning of them. These inner agonies are only exacerbated by the internal splitting and the part-object attacks from within themselves that so often leave patients feeling overwhelmed by bleak emptiness. This emptiness represents their rejection of the genuine core self that was not valued and cherished in their earliest object-relationship. Instead they have identified with the negative introject, while defending against it.

Even as they sweat through these violent assaults from within, many patients engage in outrageously self-centered acts based on a perception of themselves as powerless victims entitled to anything they wish. Hoping to reverse or undo their losses, they also hope to punish the one whom they perceive as injuring them. The fact that their actions are frequently most destructive to themselves indicates the deeper sense of belief that they are indeed to blame for their state.

Complex and maddening, this tortured dynamic is difficult to untangle. In situation after situation, these patients will tend to see others as malevolent, dangerous forces and will rage against them with a fury born of righteous indignation at such alleged mistreatment. This accounts for the apparent lack of boundaries or limits in their assaults upon others. They are defending their right to exist and are in a constant panic about survival.

Seeing themselves as victims externalizes the reason for the loss and emptiness. It is not their fault, and yet, somehow, they fear it is. In the next moment the same individual may find himself overtaken by panic and self-devaluation, as the projected malevolence that was seen in others suddenly appears to have taken up residence within him. This painful oscillation between inner and outer orientations often saddles both patient and therapist with a chronic uncertainty. Yet this maddening and terrifying state is the ordinary internal life of the patient, which the therapist needs to sense in order to fully appreciate.

Quite often, the therapist in this circumstance begins to experience his or her reaction to the continual object inconstancy as personally threatening. The therapist anxiously wonders, "How will today's session with this patient unfold? What will I face? How can I prepare effectively, when I never know what to expect?"

Interestingly, the therapist who finds him— or herself asking these sorts of rhetorical questions now seems to be mirroring the patient! Suddenly the clinician feels required to pour all of his or her psychic energy into surviving the hour. He has very little emotional reserve left for empathizing with and understanding the patient, because he has come to experience the state of lonely perpetual panic that the patient lives in!

One of the most common fears experienced by these patients relates directly to the issue of communication. Describing that anxiety, a patient might explain: "You will not genuinely understand my experience until you feel it inside you. In order to get you to know me, and in order to feel known, I must compel you to undergo an inner experience closely akin to the experience that so powerfully affects me."

In my view, this painfully urgent need to be known and not abandoned is the motivating force behind the coercive element in the dynamics of treatment. In a nutshell: The patient cannot trust that you have understood his or her dilemma until it becomes evident that you have actually felt it.

In the same way, many patients will not be able to believe that you really wish to be present with them, unless they can see for themselves that their behavior has "forced" you to suffer through the same emotional turbulence that haunts them day in and day out. The patient is usually not consciously aware that he or she is demanding this of you. To the patient, these moments are "just what happens with people."

Over the years, many of the people with whom I have worked have described these essential steps in the mini-drama of the transference enactment: "I didn't know it while we were in it, but I had to get you to feel it. Words just aren't enough. I couldn't believe you really knew it until I knew you felt it."

For most patients, this perspective becomes clear and conscious only after the patient-orchestrated transference mini-drama has been worked through and appropriately clarified.

If coercion of the therapist is a major factor in the treatment of borderline patients, what about those individuals who are able to maintain a more intact sense of self, while remaining ego-observant and avoiding the dangers of excessive splitting and projection? For these more stable patients, the clarifications and interpretations of the therapist usually serve as a welcome additional perspective on problems and issues. Such individuals may be characterized as being more adequately differentiated, while also possessing a more stable internal self and object constancy. Yet, even these relatively stable and healthy individuals will quickly resort to the same types of psychological defenses and mini-dramas of reenactment when faced with painful treatment issues that evoke powerful inner conflicts. None of us is free from this potential regressive pull. The characterologic difference may be in the amount of our life spent in these modes.

The more troubled patients who struggle with developmental problems linked to deficit and trauma usually view the therapist through a lens significantly distorted by mistrust and early disappointment. Indeed, there is frequently a powerful sado–masochistic dynamic at work in these people, who have come to regard every relationship as a "power dyad" in which one member looms as dominant, while the other remains submissive but also resentful of this subservient position.

Fraught with anxiety, such power-based relationships are inherently unstable because they depend on control and manipulation of one party by the other. This leads to resentment and mistrust: the dominant person fearing loss of control, and the dominated person seeking to reverse position.

Most patients who are struggling and relating in this way will assume that the therapist also views every relationship as based on control and dominance. For these individuals with significant character disorders, the idea of interactions built around trust, respect, and mutual regard is unrealistic, even if longed for in fantasy. These assumptions play an important part in shaping the patient's transferences,[1] an irritant.

Little (1981, p. 130) provides some useful insights into treatment difficulties that often occur with patients of this kind:

> There are two ways in which the desired way of working is frustrated. The first is that what to the analyst are "interpretations" are often meaningless to the patient.[2] He may sometimes accept them (superficially) on the basis of, "Well, if you say so, I must believe you," but this, of course, is not conviction [it is a mere pseudo-submission]—and next time he will behave exactly as if he had never heard the interpretation.
>
> The second [obstacle] is that he will frequently present the analyst with a situation that does not allow time enough for an examination or sifting to happen, before some remark or action [the result of force/

---

1. The broad range of personality types who may share in this projective style includes not only individuals with borderline and narcissistic characters, but people with masochistic, sadistic, passive–aggressive, and passive-dependent characters as well as individuals with obsessive compulsive personality disorder, eating disorders, etc. In other words, this includes people who still split the world into the early Kleinian, paranoid–schizoid manner and have not reached the developmental depressive position.

2. Because words, which do not feel personally connected to our felt experience, are meaningless. The patient in these moments wants to feel something with the therapist and hears the words as annoying static.

coercion, as described earlier] must be made to forestall him in some way if a dangerous piece of acting out is not to happen.

One of the difficulties for the therapist in this situation emerges when the patient signals the need to know that he or she has impacted the clinician at the level of personal feeling.

Because many patients cannot trust mere words as vehicles of affective meaning, they unconsciously seek other kinds of evidence that will prove that they are real in the treatment and seen as discrete individuals, not just one in a series of two-dimensional patients in the therapist's life. Little offers a compelling example:

A patient enters her office in a familiar frenzy, while announcing that she feels compelled to smash something. Convinced that the distraught patient is about to destroy a favorite pot, Little (1951) quickly reacts, "I'll just about kill you if you smash that pot!" The patient falls silent for a few moments. Little takes advantage of the pause to review her statement by asking the patient what meaning she has taken from it. First, however, she presents a possiblity to the patient: "I think you thought that I really would kill you, or perhaps that I had done so." The patient replies, "Yes, I felt like that. It was frightful, but it was also very good. I knew you really felt something, and I so often thought that you didn't feel anything at all!"

Little's experience with this individual provides a dramatic example of how patients may sometimes go to great lengths to evoke reactions in the therapist.

Although the outcome of the "flower pot incident" appears to have been positive, I try to avoid such unpredictable, shoot-from-the-hip episodes in treatment, even as I do my best to remain open to spontaneous responses triggered by patient enactments.

With hindsight, I would wonder about her experience of "the familiar frenzy." What was Little's sense of it that day? What was her mood and internal experience as the patient entered the session? When did she first sense the familiar frenzy was reoccurring? What were her reactions as she had the premonitory awareness of the building frenzy? Might there have been a way to engage the issue of the familiar frenzy and the fear, anger, aggression in Little before this moment?

When faced with threatening enactments such as the one described above, I do my best to gain time for reflection and consultation. I also make every effort to remain aware of even the mildest hostility being directed at me, while endeavoring to openly engage and clarify it before it builds to a crescendo. Obviously, this is not always possible. My concern is that I will break empathic connection and react only from my own anxiety, fear, or anger.

I've often noticed that patients who enact hostile feelings and negative transferences are in fact seeking the same validation of their unique existence from the therapist. They want us to give meaning and aliveness to the interaction with them. Unconsciously, we are equated with those early objects who seemed coldly indifferent and untouched by all efforts at authentic communication. This cool distance was seen as confirming the patient's badness—or worse, it was evidence that the patient did not matter—or most terrifyingly, the patient did not exist. It also seeks to confirm that they do exist as the familiar, reliable, negative introject they mistook for themselves long ago.

As one patient who had a penchant for seeking this kind of negative reinforcement, confirmation through action, explained to me, "Dr. Wishnie, when the only choice is being a black sheep or no sheep, the black sheep wins every time!"

When asked if there were "no other options available," this struggling patient answered emphatically, "None that I've ever seen!"

Because they have little hope of being loved, cared for, or even recognized as separate selves, these patients often become caricatures of their parents' negative self-projections. They took in and became the negative introject as a way to affirm their existence in the parent's world, as if to say, If this is the only way you will see and react to me, then that is what I will be! It is as if they're announcing to the world, "I desperately need to be responded to, so I'll have to be content with the only possible response, a negative one" (Sandler 1990).

In many cases, these patients then become convinced that only negative responses can be trusted. Positive responses from others are swiftly devalued as mere deceptions and manipulations aimed at keeping them off-guard until the more genuine underlying negativity emerges.

Understandably, these people who felt invisible as children have come to expect that their adult words and actions are equally invisible and meaningless. They have great difficulty believing that they have any real impact upon others, unless there is some dramatic proof.

Because they do not believe that what they say or do has any genuine impact on others, they tend to treat the therapist in an unreal fashion, like a shell whose words are meaningless, false, and empty (a projection of their sense of themselves). This is most clear in situations involving narcissistically injured patients. Our responses to these individuals are crucially important. We are being carefully assessed and judged to see if we will confirm the projections. The reactions to our real and inferred responses allow us to learn more about the dynamics of the patient's internal world that are continuously being projected into the environment and relived.

The impact upon the therapist of living in this kind of projective world is profoundly discomforting. However, it is important to remember that the threatening dynamic does not occur because of the implantation of a foreign body or affect within us. Instead, it is the distress we feel because something in this relationship has reactivated some aspect of our own character, some troubling conflict, associations to an old pain or fear, old defenses, etc. It is not, as some authors imply, that the patient has projected into us some aspect of themselves which we then react to.

In other cases, this dynamic may result from our defensively discounting or minimizing aspects of ourselves, due to our fear that such aspects might assume too great a centrality in our mental functioning.

Patients in this situation are often exquisitely sensitive to the cues we send them. They recognize, albeit unconsciously at times, that there are troubled issues at work within us. Is it any wonder that they often seek them out, as a means of validating themselves by compelling us to experience these painful inner analogues of their own turbulent emotions?

Acknowledging this reality emphasizes the importance of admitting to ourselves that we carry discomforting deficits and conflicts within us. Concurrently, we recognize that fearful and mistrustful patients will often feel the unconscious need to touch upon these painfully unresolved areas. They do so by sending messages, verbal and behavioral, aimed at provoking such pain.

If the therapist attempts to deny the inner turbulence caused by such countertransference arousal, the result will often be the kind of struggle between clinician and patient that can only impede the progress of the treatment. Several of the examples in the next chapters include instances of therapist resistance, and the dilemmas that ensue.

4

Maintaining Empathy

This chapter describes some of the dynamics at work during therapy sessions, as patients unconsciously present and attempt to repair deficits caused by trauma in their earliest relationships. The chapter includes a discussion of part-object relationships in borderline patients, as well as a schematic representation of a model for treatment aimed at recovering the core self.

The struggle to empathize with an overtly hostile, distant, or self-involved patient will often prove arduous, primarily because of the way in which the patient's inner conflicts inevitably engage and expose conflicted aspects of our own characters.

When this occurs, the therapist laboring to maintain inner equilibrium by trying to ignore or minimize the impact of these materials may easily fail to maintain the empathic sense required to protect the all-important emotional connection with the patient.

An example of this occurred when I briefly treated "Blake," a former career military officer, now a successful businessman who had sought therapy at the demand of his spouse.

Let me include some of my initial reactions to this man. Before he entered the office, I heard a car pull into my driveway and park. I noted this arrival for two reasons. First, the car's engine was remarkably loud. Was my visitor a veteran of the NASCAR circuit? And second, the huge vehicle not only dwarfed my driveway, it obstructed my office window and completely blocked my modest family sedan parked in front of it! Startled and also amused, I chuckled to myself, "Hmmm . . . what's *this* all about? Boundaries? Entitlement? Power?"

A moment later the man appeared. He turned out to be a tall, powerfully built gentleman with an impressive tan. He wore an expensively tailored suit and a military-style "brush cut." Wary and resentful, he stalked into my office for our first appointment, then paused to scrutinize the room. His demeanor and his movements were brusque and abrupt. Power clearly seemed to be an issue for him. Was it an issue for me, as well? How did I feel about his sudden appearance in this small, rather nondescript home, as I prepared to greet a man who obviously lived in circumstances more affluent than my own?

I also found myself wondering how *he* must be feeling, as he surveyed the environment in which he would be asked to talk about his own emotional issues. Was he undergoing a narcissistic injury at the moment, because he felt the need to bring his troubles to a man who lived and worked in these pedestrian surroundings?

Only one thing seemed certain, at that moment: My visitor didn't like the layout! Sneering with obvious disdain, he growled at me, "For the prices you guys charge, at least you could get decent furniture. This is crap!"

Nodding with a smile, I agreed that the furniture had seen better days. But then I responded to him by saying that I felt sure he hadn't scheduled an appointment with me in order to critique the furniture. He laughed and seemed to appreciate my refocusing on his reasons for coming, rather than responding personally to the attack on my furniture.

After a few more uneasy exchanges, he began talking about himself. Smirking, he stated bitterly, "I don't give a damn about anyone or anything in my life. No one matters." So why was he here? Simple: He had to come; he felt required to consult with me in order to placate his wife. Otherwise, she might divorce him, and he hadn't yet sequestered enough assets to protect himself. "Besides, why should she get anything? And who knows, maybe I'll learn something!" (Was that last comment perhaps an indirect expression of a wish? Maybe!)

Oh, he knew how to say the right things, knew how to "play the game," but it was all "an act." The naked truth was that his family and so-called friends meant nothing to him, nothing whatsoever. If they "died tomorrow, I'd be well rid of them!" They were "hypocrites," every one, total frauds who spent their days "merely going through the motions" in order to get by, while he at least was honest about not pretending to care.

Sure, he'd learned to "mouth the platitudes and homilies" required of him, but that didn't mean he believed any of the garbage he was forced to spout. Why should he kid himself about the emptiness he saw all around him, from one day to the next?

I sat silently listening in my chair while he described the lack of meaning and human connectedness in his life. At first, I felt a sense of shock at the relentless fury and intensity with which he expressed utter contempt for anyone who believed there were people capable of genuine attachment or authentic care. He stated, "The truth is that people are only interested in using each other, and in getting power. My wife thinks that my coming here will get her something. Bullshit!"

Listening, I focused on this angry man's demeanor: his intense furious gaze, his facial and bodily expressions of fury, disgust, and futility, the hand and shoulder gestures. Beneath his angry disdain, I thought I sensed a profound despair. (Or was I only looking for a vulnerable emotion in which I could participate with him, since his presence was otherwise so devastatingly barren?)

What had occurred in this man's life to teach him the futility of hoping to be cared for, along with the terror of abandonment? I silently wondered: Had a fear of being abandoned led him to preempt this inevitable catastrophe? Had he learned to shut people out of his life before they could devastate him with their own rejection? As we sat together, wasn't he driving me away and thus attempting to confirm his belief that no one would ever treat him with authentic respect and regard?

It was a difficult session because of the intensity of his relentless fury at anything humanly valuable in life. Buffeted by his angry speeches, I paid close attention to his physical gestures. I noted his shrugging of his shoulders, the dismissive swipes of his hands, his grimaces of disgust about emotional concerns, and his sarcastic and disdainful tone of voice.

I described his gestures and said that they seemed to express a great deal of feeling. I asked him if he thought his strident tone and furious body language might reveal more than a simple need to control others by endlessly devaluing them. Could these scornful gestures and expressions perhaps be a way of protecting himself from his own vulnerability, his own deep personal and hidden concerns?

He glared at me. "Keep going; I haven't said you're wrong yet. I'll tell you when you are."

I soon learned that this was the most affirmative kind of response he could manage. As our intense dialogue unfolded, I continued to shape my comments with this awareness constantly in mind.

After a few more minutes, I realized that whenever I responded to the ideational content of his statements, as contrasted with his attitude and demeanor, our discussion would become tangled in pointless semantics about what he was saying and about "conventional" attitudes and expectations. Alternatively, if I focused instead on the messages conveyed by his physical behavior, we seemed better able to maintain a useful dialogue. From time to time, he even became animated and jovial.

"No one ever called me on my bullshit before," he chuckled at one point. "They accept it because they have to. I have the money that keeps them in line. Oh, I say the right things and I express the appropriate sentiments, but I don't really care about anyone or anything and they know it! Hey, I thought that you guys were supposed to be silent and say, 'Ah-hah!' Got you out of your cage, didn't I, doc?! Hey, I'm good at that." (Having noticed that I had affected him, he quickly reversed it and saw it as his having affected and controlled me—an interaction of dominance and submission.)

Listening to these remarks, it seemed evident that this patient's need to be seen and validated, and to have a powerful impact, spoke to a deeper hunger to have his existence confirmed. At the core he felt worthless. Without the money and the ruthless control he imagined it gave him over others, he would be unmasked as a cipher, a non-entity as worthless as everyone else. When he looked at other people, he was seeing the mirror-image of his own feared true identity!

Although this man displayed a sometimes appealing sense of humor and some other positive traits, it seemed evident that his more positive qualities were constantly being overwhelmed by his need to reassure himself that he was powerful and in control. This compulsion resulted in his fairly constant sadistic devaluation of others as a threat to his tenuous self-esteem.

The sessions were difficult, but during our first twelve meetings, we were able to sustain this form of dialogue. I was hopeful that a more meaningful connection might develop with this man, even though his manifest attitude remained scornful and sarcastic. Again and again, he made the kinds of denigrating and undoing comments about our interaction. I felt that he was hoping to provoke a confrontation that might allow him to self-righteously terminate our relationship. When I wondered aloud about this, he said, "No, you're not special. I'm this way with everyone." Was I perhaps in the category of people who had to put up with his bullshit because of his money and power; perhaps the relationship of mutual exploitation that he often spoke of? "Well doc, could be. I do think everyone is a whore."

I did my best not to directly counter, engage in, or be deflected by his belligerence, all the while trying to examine it's meaning. Simultaneously, I was finding ways to directly examine his aggression. However, I did not foresee the wearing nature of his hostility and contempt. I believed that the leavening introduced through shared humor and its implied joint recognition of his troubled behavior was leading to a deeper engagement.

When we met for our thirteenth appointment, however, I was struggling with a bad cold. As we sat down I reached for a tissue and blew my nose. He responded instantly by becoming furious. He insisted that I wouldn't be able to concentrate, and that I would be exploiting him by charging my usual fee for the session. He immediately stormed out in a rage and, despite my urging, would not return.

Was there any way I could have prevented this negative outcome? In reviewing our sessions, it seemed that Blake had liked those early encounters in which I'd paid close attention to his physical actions and their possible meanings. Encouraged by that early response, had I unwisely relaxed my awareness of other dimensions of his experience? His response to my cold told me that I had paid too little attention to his obvious fear of showing his vulnerability and expressing his needs and yearnings. Most importantly, had I failed to reach the level of authentic empathy necessary to genuinely grasp the deficits burdening this man?

Too often, I'd been so caught up in my own uncomfortable reactions to his denigrating commentary about others that I'd failed to imagine how he must have been experiencing our interaction. Here was a man who felt required by his spouse, one of the people he most denigrated, to rise early in the morning in order to pay a virtual stranger to speak with him about his behavior and feelings, some of the most denigrated aspects of himself!

Why should he, a man of his success and professional accomplishments, be forced to sit in a roomful of worn furniture, talking to a man with a bad cold about his anger and his disdained, denied, and shameful yearnings for connectedness?

In the end, doing those things must have represented too stark an admission of need, which this man could not bear. It was such an affront to his defensive narcissism and its attendant shame.

After the breakdown in communication occurred, I realized that I had not been adequately attuned to the shame this patient must have felt. Each time he arrived at my less than pristine office for another session, he brought with him his sense of being demeaned. My lapse in empathy had prevented me from understanding how hard it was for him to go to such lengths in order to talk about his needs, feelings, personal losses, etc., when everything in his own life seemed to deny the importance of genuine feeling.

I had continued to be startled and a bit awestruck by the undiminished intensity of his rage. How could he express such continuing fury, in session after session? Somehow, I had allowed myself to be so blown away by this manifestation of his character that I'd lost sight of his disavowed core self. For me, there was an almost awesome quality to that level of continuous outrage. Had I failed to fully examine the issues that his fury touched within me? Or had I allowed myself to be distracted by the rage, while failing to stay focused on the deeper fears it masked?

I couldn't help wondering if I had made an inner choice to turn away from Blake because of his great intensity of feeling. If so, the fault was mine, for all he had done was to bring in his ordinary character for examination. And that was all any therapist could reasonably have asked of him! The fact that he seemed uninterested in examining his character merely represented an initial problem requiring careful work.

As I reviewed this treatment history more deeply, I recognized that some of my distraction had allowed me to play out a character in his life drama—the "convention-bound person" who denies his own aggression. Meanwhile, my false role allowed me to remain unconsciously superior by virtue of my different manner. (I was patiently listening and responding, after all, to his hate-filled devaluation of people and relationships!)

In hindsight, it seemed clear that if I had been better able to focus our attention on his powerful feelings of anger, and if I had challenged his characterization of himself as "merely honest and not bound by false convention" (qualities, his position implied, that his therapist clearly lacked!), I might have succeeded in reducing the emotional distance between us. Instead, many of my responses had tended to confirm his perception that I was bound by conventions both false and superficial.

With further reflection, I concluded that I had, indeed, let him down. I had not challenged him with the insight that he was a bully because he feared being the opposite: a powerless victim. Why had I failed to confront him? Why had I failed to probe as deeply as I could into the dynamics of our relationship during the treatment hour, which is more my usual manner? After a great deal of painful introspection, I sensed that at some level this angry man had become the feared and hated Nazi of my childhood. In the end, the loneliness of his isolation was not addressed because of an issue in me. I had withheld some aspects of my usual self to punish the Nazi. Normally, I identify and clarify the Nazi/bully openly for examination.

The struggle with Blake was sharp and at times emotionally violent. In most cases, treatment unfolds much more slowly, and without as many direct confrontations. Nonetheless, the therapist will inevitably be required to work hard at maintaining empathy as the treatment unfolds.

My work with "Florence" provides a good example of how these less dramatic but still challenging enactment scenarios often take place. Florence was a middle-aged woman and a highly regarded health administrator with many honors and advanced degrees. As she explained it, she had decided to enter therapy because of her inability to form lasting personal relationships and her continuing loneliness.

Since she regarded the need for assistance as evidence of a personal deficit, Florence was controlling of our interaction and viewed any comment or possible issue that I raised as something she had already considered and discarded. Sensing her distress, I expressed curiosity at her observations or experiences, wondering with her what factors she felt might be contributing to her circumstances. Therapy proceeded and after several months, she seemed to feel less demeaned by the process.

I recognized gradually that two key issues were beginning to dominate our sessions. First, in spite of my directness, I tend to speak very softly. Second, the patient had a moderate hearing deficit. Most of the time, I compensated by speaking more loudly and keeping my hands away from my mouth. Florence also compensated at times, usually by pulling her chair closer to mine.

During one session several years into our work, I realized that I had been speaking less audibly to her, while also bringing my hand to my mouth. I wondered why I had done so. Then I realized that during that hour and the previous one, the patient in some subtle way had grown more emotionally removed and intellectual. These two sessions followed a period of many weeks of more involved work. Unconsciously, I had responded to her withdrawal by trying to pull her in closer to me by speaking more softly. I felt left behind by her and missed the more involved relatedness of our recent sessions. Having become aware of my enactment, I told her what I had observed in myself, and my sense of a difference in her. She was pleased to hear of my feeling and reaction and teased me briefly. We could then explore the difference in her emotional presence.

UNDERSTANDING PART-OBJECT RELATIONSHIPS

Adult intimacy requires a particular form of trust on the part of both individuals in the relationship. In order to be close with another, we must trust in the other person's desire for (and concern with) understanding our experience and perspective. Likewise, we need to have a similar concern for the other person. Only then, in the context of a mutual sense of shared concern and awareness, can we allow ourselves to volitionally lower our defenses.

But such intimate relatedness requires a high degree of a sense of wholeness or completeness in both parties. Part-object relationships, in which a portion of the person is taken for the "whole" person, mitigates against adult intimacy.

The intimacy of childhood, namely that of the child with his or her primary attachments (parents or their substitutes), is predicated upon a child's sense of the parent having that concern for the child, who remains the center of the parent's interest. Only later, when specific emotional development has occurred within the relationship, can the child tolerate a sense of the parent's separate life, needs, and interests, while recognizing that these co-exist with the parent's genuine concern for the child.

People entering therapy are at various points in the developmental continuum of "relational trust." Blake, the angry man described before, was at an early stage in this continuum and needed many assurances of my presence. But Florence was at a different point; her laughing and joking with me about my observation of my response to her, affirmed her sense of perspective about our working relationship, while also signaling the pleasure she took in being genuinely noticed and engaged. What happens when an individual cannot manage such trust, and instead insists on controlling all aspects of his or her relationship with another?

Driven by a primal anxiety, a fundamental mistrust of others, such people are precluded from experiencing the intimacy that we all crave (Khan 1964). In this unhappy situation, the mistrustful individual cannot take the risk of permitting others to enjoy spontaneity and freedom in the relationship. Instead of interacting freely with another, and thus being able to gradually integrate a realistic sense of that person's character, these individuals cling to a few rigid presuppositions about the character of the other person.

This fundamentally paranoid framework is built upon a core belief that the individual does not contain a loveable self. Thus it becomes necessary to defend against the potential consequences of such a shortcoming—primarily abandonment—by controlling the involvement of others.

The presuppositions mentioned above function as preconceived "inner models" that substitute for the rich, full-dimensioned reality of other people with whom patients of this kind form relationships. These inner versions of the other members of the relationship contain some accurate, partial observations, which give them at least a partial grounding in reality.

This is the dynamic of the part-object relationship, in which the patient treats his or her partial view of the other person as if it represents the entire person. This distortion allows the individual to avoid a sense of fear/anxiety about the unknown other. Through this mechanism, the threatening unfamiliarity of the other is removed. The other is now a "known quantity," and "there's nothing to be feared here."

The part-object "substitution" is based upon a fabricated sense of the other person, rather than upon a more gradually constructed reality in which first impressions are altered through experience. Because it serves a protective (defensive) function, people[1] who use this mode to a significant extent must vigorously defend the substitution. When this phenomenon occurs in therapy, a struggle will often develop between the patient and the therapist—a battle in which the patient works steadfastly to validate the preconceived assumptions about the therapist contained in his or her partial view of the latter.

This is a familiar pattern. First, the patient makes a quick assessment of the therapist's persona, in order to fit the latter into one of the few basic personality-models that the patient uses for the part-object substitution.

Once this ersatz identification of the therapist with the model has been accomplished, the patient's anxiety diminishes because the risks of dealing with an unknown person have (presumably) been reduced. Anything introduced by the therapist that challenges the fictional identification is then treated as an attack, criticism, denial, defense, or deception by the patient.

Patients who have spent most of their adult lives interacting with others in this way are usually quite skilled at accurately identifying partial

---

1. We all may use variations of this mode. The issue is how much does this predominate and whether we are flexible enough to keep adding to and altering this sense of the other in light of more experience.

Figure 1
Borderline Patient: Schematic Representation
of Part-Object Relationships

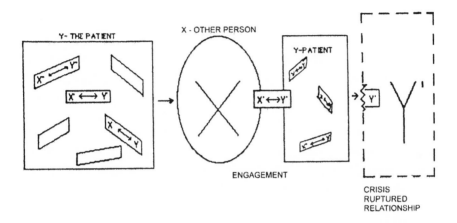

aspects of personality structure in others. With great consistency, they will be able to demonstrate some congruence between their presuppositions about us and the reality of our characters. They will then point to that congruence and insist that their rigid, partial construct of us is wholly accurate.

The diagram above (Figure 1) illustrates some of the complex dynamics that are frequently at work in part-object relationships:

In the sequence of drawings above, the square on the left represents a borderline patient's thin ego shell. The numerous rectangles within the shell contain partial views of the self (Y) and others (X). The bi-directional arrows linking the Xs and Ys symbolize the preset, rigidly controlled, relationship style, in which the two part-objects (self and other) interrelate.

When the borderline patient with this disorder engages another person (the oval X) in a relationship, he or she makes a quick assessment of X and notes a few characteristics. Then the patient activates whichever internal part-object relationship seems to most closely resemble the other.

From this point on, the patient will treat these partial structures as if they contained the entire personality of the therapist. But great difficulties arise whenever X begins to display aspects of personality that are not contained in Y's narrow, petrified view of his or her partner in the relationship.

When that happens, the patient will almost invariably experience feelings of betrayal and abandonment. In these instances, a spontaneous or unanticipated aspect of the therapist will often trigger a sense of rupture, in which the patient's projected partial sense of the other is overwhelmed by threatening and unanticipated new aspects of the therapist's personality.

In such moments, the alarmed patient will experience a loss of the fragile sense of self that is imprisoned in the rigidly organized partial relationship. The result? In many cases, the patient who has been deprived of these projected, partial views of self and other will experience the panic that accompanies loss of self-identity.

These ruptures between patient and therapist form the "crises" that periodically threaten to overwhelm most borderline patients.

TREATMENT

As illustrated in Figure 2, the treatment of patients struggling with this disorder requires a great deal of time, energy, and emotional engagement. Both patient and therapist must weather numerous crises. With the therapist's involvement, the patient and therapist work to make sense of each enacted crisis (mini-drama), and these mirror the episodes of betrayal and abandonment that occurred earlier in the patient's life. Such inner distortions of the sense of self come in the wake of those repeated early experiences.

The hope is that the patient will achieve both some perspective on these familiar situations and a growing understanding of the earlier traumas and their distorting effect. Such understanding and perspective (the capacity to stand aside and view oneself) will foster a coalescence of the fragmented internal "self and other" into deeper, more cohesive internalized versions of self and other without the preset relational template.

Figure 2
Part-Object Relationships

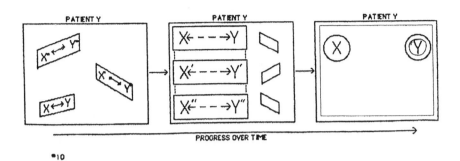

•10

Eventually, these rigidly preformed relatedness patterns (the bi-directional arrow) can be abandoned and the perilously thin ego shell[2] will be allowed to develop into a more adaptive, resilient container, interfacing with the outside world in a more flexible and spontaneous manner.

The glue that holds the process together is the maintenance of a stable treatment situation over time, with the therapist demonstrating again and again his or her willingness to "stay the course" through the often painful process of internal object coalescence.

THE THERAPIST'S STRUGGLE

While the patient labors to integrate the fragmented self, the psychoanalytically oriented therapist confronts a considerable challenge: the exquisitely complicated task of remaining "in the soup" (otherwise known as Paul Russell's "Crunch") with the patient while keeping perspective on his or her own interior landscape, and thus avoiding destructive reactions.

---

2. The change in ego-shell thickness comes from many aspects of the work. One aspect involves the capacity to have perspective: namely to hold a view of oneself, to stand apart and observe oneself, and to make less distorted observations of self and other. Another is the capacity to stay in a relationship and work toward this evolution of the ego.

Specifically, the therapist must recognize his or her internal im-balances—and especially the easily provoked sado–masochism that can be triggered by the patient's reenactment. By remaining continually attuned, the therapist keeps the lid on these inner reactions, while simultaneously striving to become aware of the nature of the patient's pre-consciously and unconsciously orchestrated ensemble of part-object defenses. Ultimately, the object is to bring them into the light of con-sciousness.

As this process unfolds, it's important to remain mindful that the patient actually *wants* to be shown that his or her world-view is distorted and unreal. However, in order to have this occur, the inner dynamics of these conflicted individuals require them to work furiously at proving the validity of their distortions. In their mind it is the therapist's job to disprove them! At the same time, the patient, hoping desperately to avoid being deceived and disappointed, will use every means at his disposal to prove the therapist is deluded, dishonest, or wrong whenever the latter does not agree with the patient's painful view of the world and human relations!

As therapists, we cannot take on the responsibility for changing the patient's view. Instead, while trying to hew a middle course of involve-ment, exploration, examination, engagement, empathic interpretation, observation, and steady presence over time, we demonstrate our willing-ness to be with these patients in a way that helps them question their premises and reach a new sense of the possibility to feel safe with themselves and others. We continuously comment upon our sense of what is occurring and being demanded of us and also upon possible meanings our interactions might have for the patient.

What's required is a form of psychological jujitsu, in which we don't accept the full force of the demand upon us. Instead, while deflecting it slightly, we seek to examine its apparent origin and purpose. All the while, we must struggle to keep our balance and remain firmly in the relationship.

There's no doubt that this sort of interaction can be exhausting. It helps to consider the struggle from the patient's point of view. Caught like Odysseus between the towering rocks of Scylla and the roaring whirlpool of Charybdis, these people must steer their frail crafts past two equally threatening dangers. If they attempt to remain safely isolated and in total control of every relationship with other human beings, who, they feel, are at every moment "seeking to degrade them" (the situation of the grandiose narcissist), they will pay a fearful price in loneliness.

On the other hand, if they see themselves as the degraded and worthless victims of others (and therefore as deeply aggrieved victims in full possession of their "victim rights to any and all compensatory or retaliatory behavior," the situation of the angry borderline or narcissist), they will then be sentencing themselves to the unrelieved misery of constant anger and victimhood. As such, they will use all means to dominate and humiliate the currently superior person (that is, the therapist), and their self-justifying anger can never be assuaged. (This pattern is seen again and again in masochistic patients who seek therapy.)

CHARACTER FORMATION: A LAYERED PROCESS?

At first glance, this rather stark depiction of the conflict-laden treatment process may seem extreme, especially if the patient turns out to be a polite, thoughtful, only mildly remote professional who has sought consultation with you because of "problems with my relationships."

How could such an intelligent, mild-mannered individual be engaged in the kind of devouring and ruthless inner struggle described above? It seems unlikely at first. As time passes, however, the therapist will begin to feel and identify the signs of part-object distortion. Perhaps they will show up in a slight sneer, or in a gently sarcastic dismissal of your observations.

Maybe they'll make themselves known in some "helpful" suggestions about your office decor, or an occasional, breezy disparagement of your questions or interpretations.

Repeatedly, I have found myself uncomfortably caught up in and surprised by the fact that I am once again "in it." Typically, this dynamic appears in the earliest phases of treatment with more characterologically troubled people, and somewhat later in the therapeutic process with patients who are more developmentally advanced.

In order to understand why the dynamic operates as it does, it's helpful to remember that character formation is a layered developmental and interactional (object-related) process. This slowly evolving and extraordinarily complex development begins with the fundamental unit of personality, the foundation-stone of character known as the core self. This entity is present in some form at the earliest moments of life.

The wonderfully complex combination of innate character, genes, physiology, neuro-biology, and interactions with prenatal experience (coupled with the earliest perinatal life experience) supplies the discrete and unique entity that is the evolving core self.

As I understand it, our work is to help the patient first uncover and then integrate the core self [(Freud, "Ego and the Id" (1923), Winnicott (1960, 1971), Loewald (1980: 226, 229)] that has been both protected and imprisoned by characterological defenses erected for survival from the earliest interactional experiences in life.

These crucially important formative experiences provide the template for later interactions. In order to begin repairing the damage caused by distortions in the template, patient and therapist must engage, via their evolving relationship, in a retrieval-and-rebuilding process that one might term "reconstructive archaeology."

This recovery of the core self and its continual reintegration is the vital goal of our efforts at treatment.

Figure 3 contains a representation of the treatment process as a multi-layered experience in which different defenses and interactions appear somewhat predictably at various levels. The model also gives a rough sense of the complex developmental layering of the individual.

Although no visual model can describe the exact topography of each and every treatment, I am attempting to present a reasonable approximation, a generic image of the unfolding process. Although everyone will present his or her own unique version of this layering, with some levels that appear to be absent or thin and others that seem hypertrophied, a general model may help one to picture the process.

Many people enter treatment at a particular level where they live much of their lives. For example, someone whose character has significant aspects of a false self or reaction formation and denial may present at Level #6, while an individual with predominant anger and self-destructiveness may present more at Level #5. An angry, demanding narcissistic person may enter treatment mostly at Level #3. And the

Figure 3
Recovering the Core Self:
A Model of Treatment

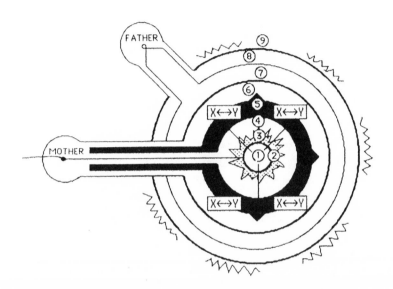

LEVEL 5-6 INTERACTION

A - AREA OF "FALSE GOOD SELF"⑥
AND "FALSE BAD SELF" ⑤

B – INVOLVES <u>GUILT</u> RELATED TO
BEHAVIOR.

C – NEEDS AT THIS LEVEL RELATE
TO INTERPERSONAL INTERACTION
AND SATISFACTION – WHAT OTHERS
GIVE AND DON'T GIVE.

D – INVOLVES ISSUES OF VICTIMIZATION
AND DISAPPOINTMENT BY SPECIFIC

E – PART OBJECT RELATIONS; LIVES IN
PROTECTIVE IDENTIFICATION DYADS.

F – PANIC AND FRUSTRATION OF EGO
DEFENSES WHEN EXPERIENCING
REAL OR IMAGINED LOSS.

LEVEL 2-3 INTERACTION

A – LEVEL OF ① TRUE "VULNERABLE" SELF SURROUNDED BY
② WALL OF MATERNAL DISGUST, NEGATIVE INTROJECT;
SURROUNDED BY ③ NARCISSISTIC RAGE.

B – INVOLVES SHAME ABOUT ONE'S CORE SENSE OF NEED,
SENSITIVITIES, VULNERABILITIES, "WEAKNESSES" -
ASPECTS OF ONE'S BEING. ACCEPTANCE AND VALUING
OF THESE SELF ISSUES BY THE INDIVIDUAL LEADS TO
EMPATHY, COMPASSION, AND THE CAPACITY TO LOVE
SELF AND OTHERS.

C – NEEDS HERE RELATE TO ONE'S OWN ABILITY TO
RECOGNIZE, VALUE, AND BECOME RESPONSIBLE FOR
THE SATISFACTION OF THESE CORE ISSUES.

D – THE NARCISSISTIC RAGE ③ IS A DEVICE TO WARD OFF
EXPOSURE AND SHAME

E – CONTAINS, IN ADDITION TO NEEDS, SENSITIVITIES AND
VULNERABILITIES – THE EARLY TRAUMATIC EVENTS,
PREVERBAL, MEMORY, VISCERAL AND SOMATIC MEMORY.

more neurotic individual whose life is more stable may enter treatment at Level #9.

During any single therapy session, patient and therapist will probably be engaged at many of these levels throughout the hour. As the treatment progresses, however, the therapeutic work will usually find its locus in one particular area. As issues are addressed, distortions examined, and conflicts resolved, the therapy will gradually move toward deeper layers.

As the psychoanalyst Loewald (1980, pp. 228–229) has pointed out:

> The analyst, through objective interpretation of transference distortions, increasingly becomes available as a new object. And this is not primarily in the sense of an object not previously met, but the newness consists in the patient's rediscovery of the early paths of development of object-relations leading to a new way of relating to objects and of being oneself.
>
> Through all of the transference distortions, the patient reveals rudiments of the core of himself and objects that have been distorted. It is this core, rudimentary and vague as it may be, to which the analyst has reference when he interprets transferences and defenses, not some abstract concept of reality and normality. . . . If the analyst keeps his focus upon this emerging core, he avoids molding the patient in his own image or imposing on the patient his own concept of what the patient should become.

These observations by Loewald cogently underline the goal of our work, which is the gradual emergence and evolution of the patient's core self. In most instances, the steps in this act of reconstructive archaeology lead from areas at the periphery of the personality toward its core.

The diagrammatic model illustrates this in the following manner. At the outermost edge of the diagram, a series of serrated lines (Level #9) demarcate the "presenting issues" that bring a patient to treatment. These issues may involve anxieties, fears, phobias, depressions, or substantial problems of various kinds.

During the first months of treatment, the fact that the individual is having his or her concerns and issues seriously considered and examined in a thoughtful, empathic manner leads to an initial sense of relief.

*   *   *

In this general model, one may then begin to hear more about a particular parent (frequently the father), who will typically be painted in stark, vivid colors, whether positive or negative (Level #8). As time passes, however, the patient will expend increasing amounts of energy discovering and recognizing other aspects of this same parent's character that were not initially noted (Level #7). Much of this powerfully emotional material will be presented in a panoply of memories and unconscious recapitulations through the patient's current relationships. Of necessity, it will also begin to play itself out through the transference.

After a year or so, the patient will often report a significant improvement in the original symptoms, and will note that he or she has gained a more balanced perspective with regard to both the focal parent and those individuals who currently serve as "stand-ins" for the parent in the patient's daily life. Quite frequently, the patient who reaches this stage will wonder about the need for further treatment. A thoughtful consideration of the possibility of stopping or interrupting at this juncture is frequently followed by a decision to continue.

The therapist will soon notice that a shift in affect tone has begun to take place. The patient appears to be working quite earnestly at considering and understanding important issues. Indeed, it seems at times as if the patient is trying too hard to do a "good job" in therapy, to be a "good patient," to the point that the therapist may begin to feel uneasy about an increasingly unreal sense. The issues being noted and examined are genuine, yet there is something quietly unsettling in the earnestness of the effort. Something feels left out, incomplete. Thus, the sense of unreality. The patient has reached the next level (#6) in the therapeutic struggle: the level of the "false good self."

This period of exaggerated display of the good self may last for months, before the dynamic changes once again. Almost invariably, the change will be triggered by one or more incidents in which the patient shows up late, forgets an appointment entirely, neglects to mention a vacation, etc.

Responding to the incident with a curious inquiry, the therapist will find himself the object of a sharp retort or an angry outburst from the suddenly furious patient (seen as the black projecting areas of Level #5).

Why are these angry outbursts taking place? At first, the patient will dismiss them as the result of simple fatigue or irritability due to some outside stress. Efforts to understand the outbursts or initial behavior in terms of deeper motivations will be brushed aside. The earlier curiosity about meaning is absent in these moments.

As the weeks pass and the pattern continues, both therapist and patient will sense an unexplained but growing irritation and distress during treatment. They have now reached Level #5: the region of the "false bad self."

Typically, the patient who is struggling through this stage will report that things are "going great" elsewhere; it's only during the therapy sessions that he or she feels miserable. Once this dynamic begins, the therapist can feel fairly certain that the locus of the transference enactments has shifted to the treatment setting.

From here on, the transferential reenactment will serve as the center stage for the drama of the patient's quest for the core self.

As therapist and patient work through associative material, memories, and transferential recreations, the clinician will gradually discern that Levels #5 and #6 are reciprocally developed from early mother–child interactions in which *behavior* was the primary focus.

Haltingly at first, the patient begins to reenact scenarios in which some behavior became the apparent source of mother's anger, blame, dismissal, or other forms of distancing and disengagement, which the patient experienced as abandonment.

As a vulnerable infant or small child, the youthful patient had no choice but to accept the mother's judgment that his or her behavior caused this response. Obviously, a child needs mother's love and understanding during the vulnerable, early years of total dependence upon her. While the child might protest, at a deeper level he cannot tolerate a consideration that she is wrong. He is too dependent upon her to be infallible.

Mother, who is the desired, needed, loved, and cherished ideal necessary for survival, is also perceived as the absolute arbiter of all right and wrong. The child cannot help but be troubled by the knowledge that he or she is the source of behavior that is offensive to mother if she declares it to be so. Inevitably, mother's view is deemed appropriate, no matter how irrational or unfair that may be to the child's core self.

"Carla," a woman with a history of childhood abuse and low self-esteem, tearfully recalled an incident in which she had been nuzzling her mother affectionately, only to be thrown upon the bed, while her mother glared at her with a look of disgust and an expression of: "Yecch! Disgusting!" As it turned out, the child had inadvertently been pawing and soiling with food and mucous her mother's neck and blouse.

This painful memory emerged after several months in which the patient repeatedly appeared in torn and soiled clothing. Increasingly depressed, she spilled a drink in my waiting room at one point, and guiltily described herself as a "dirt-ball." As her depression deepened, her irritability and hostility toward me increased. When I attempted to explore her associations regarding the spilled drink and her anger at me, she suddenly shouted, "Don't you get it, stupid? I'm a dirt-ball [negative introject!] My mother was right. I never get it right, no matter how I try. You should toss me!"

I responded, "Your mother was right? Toss you? What are you thinking?"

The patient was able to trace her associations back and recall the incident noted above where she soiled her mother's blouse, and to recall later examples of similar disgust and rejection. Because she had accepted responsibility for her actions and consequently accepted her mother's behavior and characterization of her as "dirty" and "dirt" (better a "black" sheep than "no" sheep!), she had never consciously questioned the severity of her mother's punitive rejection.

Instead, she'd tried to compensate for what she believed to be her bad self by inventing an exaggerated, good behavior-based opposite, the false good self.

She attempted to be neat and organize herself in a way that would garner mother's approval, but something always went awry. She always "messed up."[3] Unknowingly (unconsciously), she needed to embrace her mother's view in order to be sure that she continued to be seen by mother, and also because she had come to believe that the "messy self" was her *genuine* self. Thus, to continue messing up represented an attempt to not fully submit and disappear, but to remain loyal to the alleged genuine self.

The vignette described above is an example of what happens during treatment at this level, as the patient strives to enact the false good self. For many months prior to this incident, the young woman had been hard-working and careful in her therapeutic hours to try to examine each nuance of her experience. When I wondered what might be driving her to try to consider each issue so intensely, to cover all of the interpretive possibilities, her only response was that she didn't want to overlook any possibility. She seemed to mistrust that we could learn in a manner that was less self-punitive. She only shrugged at my inquiries and comments.

Then there were months of increasing depression as her internal demands for perfection seemed to exhaust her. She became less careful about her appearance and appointment times, but dismissed these changes as meaningless until the spilled drink incident. Her anxiety about its impact upon my attitude towards her triggered both a regression and the opening of a new awareness of this area of trauma in her character formation.

However, the perfection-seeking patient must also occasionally act out aspects of the false bad self in order to avoid complete submission to the internalized, harshly punishing mother. At this point, the patient strongly believes that the bad self is the authentic inner self and that he or she must carefully conceal this true self with the disguise offered by the compliant good self.

Gradually, however, the patient begins to reveal this supposedly truer self, and the treatment becomes more distressing (for both patient and therapist) as the patient seeks to provoke the feared blame and rejection. Carla enacted both the false good self and the false bad self.

---

3. This unconscious ruining of "false good self" behavior is shown in the diagram as the darkly shaded points intruding into the attempted good behavior.

This juncture of false good and bad self is a place where many treatments go amiss. At this level, it's important to recognize that the therapist's own masochism, sadism, and narcissism will be challenged, as various part-object relationships are painfully enacted, until there is finally a genuine clarification of the enacted experience. The therapist feels drawn in and wonders what he or she is doing wrong. Self-blame and confusion in the therapist mirrors the patient's guilt. The therapist may feel like a bad self.

This is the level at which painful early mother–child interactions are reexperienced. For the therapist, this part of the struggle will often include distressing wishes for control, retaliation, flight, abandonment, and dysphoric sexual involvement. As these fantasies break into consciousness, the clinician may feel inept and fraudulent. Feelings of hatred and depression will cause the therapist to wonder if the patient should not be referred to a more skilled practitioner. The therapist feels involved and worried, guilty and angry, desperate and panicky. He may come to resent, avoid, and distance himself from the patient, retreating into intellectualization and theory.

The pull towards such responses in the therapist should be regarded as a signal pointing toward enactments that need to be analyzed.

This highly demanding level of work may continue for years. If one is successful with it, the therapy will next enter Level #4 in which the patient seems to be effectively integrating the previous work. For the patient, the earlier therapeutic struggle becomes a blurred memory, and a successful integration of ego skills seems to be taking place. The work feels genuine and the therapist is called upon to be a quiet presence, an affirming witness.

After months or even years at this level, another abrupt shift will probably take place. Some mild comment from the therapist sets off an outburst of fury in the patient. But this event differs from the explosion that occurred at Level #5. In this instance, the startled therapist does not feel guilty or inept because of the patient's outburst. It's as if the practitioner has been swept into someone else's storm. The turbulence is unpleasant, but it's not about the therapist. While startled and bewildered, the therapist is not burdened with guilt and self-doubt as in Level #5 enactments.

Now the patient hurls accusations, becomes enraged, and employs exaggerated projections in an effort to clarify issues. At this point we have reached the level of narcissistic rage (Level #3), the difficult-to-penetrate barrier designed to protect the subject from the annihilating sense of shame that surrounds the negative maternal introject (Level #2).

It is this same maternal introject, of course, that has been mistaken for the core self during the early stages of the child's development. And it is this misidentification which lies at the very heart of the patient's snarled and malfunctioning system of inner defenses.

If the therapist can work within this level of narcissistic rage in a gentle but present manner and the patient can resist the temptation to flee, material will gradually emerge to clarify the mistaken sense of self that defines Level #2. This is the level at which the patient has internalized mother's projected negative sense of herself (negative introject), which the mother then attempted to control within the patient.

Typically, mother had seen the child/patient as the embodiment of her own "shameful self" and had communicated this view. The patient had then internalized this as his or her sense of self. Recently, a patient who had labored successfully for many years in therapy while dealing with just such a negative internalization came upon her mother's diary written during her first year of life.

The patient, who had successfully raised her own family in a genuinely loving and warm manner, and had worked responsibly at a job and in her community, found a note written when she was six months old. Her mother had written, "I can see in her eyes that she will be a manipulative and controlling person."

In fact, that description had been accurate—as a description of the mother. It was a projection. As the diary incident revealed, patients caught in this situation must come to terms with an exceedingly painful realization:

> *They must realize that the self-condemnation of Level #5 was based on "unacceptable behavior," but the terror at Level #2, the cause of the maternal rejection, was not behavior but the very existence and presence of the self as perceived by the parent. What is at issue is not some behavior that the child can change, but the child's very being, which is seen as unchangeable, and therefore unloveable! It is not what I did,*

but who I am that was deemed unacceptable! Is it any wonder that this level is surrounded by a defensive narcissistic rage?

Because the injured child's feelings of potential annihilation at Level #2 (the negative introject misperceived as the core self) are shame-based and not guilt-based (behavior-based), they cannot be eradicated by mere changes in behavior.

Thus there is the need for the intense narcissistic defense of Level #3. This defense has a quality of extreme intensity. It is hard but also brittle. The preceding description indicates why it must be so strong.

As the therapeutic struggle unfolds over time, the therapist who stays in the soup, while refusing to make judgments and remaining calmly empathic, will begin to see a profound impact on the patient. Again and again the patient will present the negative introject (Level #2) as "self" and will question the wisdom of the therapist's refusal to react as the mother had. Slowly and painfully, this refusal to reject the patient begins to raise questions about the patient's "true self."

Now the core self (Level #1) emerges, bringing with it more repressed memories, instincts, and creative energy. There is usually much grieving as the core self disengages from the negative maternal introject. (Only rarely will fathers play this role, a fact that comes as no surprise, given our knowledge of the mother's crucial importance in early child development.)

Clinicians should remember that although this diagrammatic model of treatment can be used to help locate oneself in various stages in the unfolding therapeutic struggle, it can provide only a rudimentary outline of the fascinatingly complex and interwoven steps that take place during effective psychotherapy.

A further explanatory note: The lines radiating from the core self to the periphery in the drawn model indicate that there are always aspects of the core self showing in the character.

5

Enactment and Intervention

This chapter further explores the dynamics of transference and countertransference interaction, with a focus upon the communications that take place between patient and therapist during each encounter. The discussion includes the issue of disclosure. What are the factors involved in deciding whether to disclose or not disclose? What are the functions, purposes, potential outcomes, and impacts upon the treatment of such disclosure? And how does it affect the therapeutic framework? Under what circumstances might a therapist decide to disclose countertransference-related information to the patient? Several case studies illustrate.

Having noted some of the ways in which distortions within early life relationships can leave people struggling with psychological deficits and distorted perspectives on their own characters and relational possibilities, we can more easily understand the dynamics at work in those patient-orchestrated mini-dramas that so often erupt in the psychotherapeutic process.

As the previous chapter attempted to point out, these unconsciously motivated scenarios often represent an attempt to force the clinician to experience painful feelings similar to those troubling the patient. By acting in ways designed to trigger the therapist's own inner issues, the patient is hoping to gain the reassurance of knowing that the clinician is authentically present and actively experiencing the painful dilemma being continuously relived by the patient.

Referred to by psychotherapists as enactment, this process of or-chestrating mini-dramas has been described by McLaughlin (1986), who defines enactments as "events occurring within the dyad that both parties experience as being the consequence of behavior in the other" (p. 600).

How can the analyst best respond to such enactments, in order to provide the most helpful insights for the patient during the treatment hour? According to McLaughlin (1993) and Jacobs (1986), the therapist must self-analyze effectively in order to uncover early unresolved con-flicts that have been reactivated during these mini-dramas.

The process of living through and examining these painful and troubling inner conflicts and then working to usefully integrate them into the treatment setting in a creative way is in fact the process of "living in the countertransference."

RECOGNITION OF THE PHENOMENON

One aspect of this process involves empathy on the part of the therapist and its role in countertransference. Buie discussed this dimen-sion of treatment at a 1979 Tufts University Symposium and in an article published in the 1981 *Journal of the American Psychoanalytic Association*. On those occasions, Buie was careful to note that empathy is not the result of an affective bonding between therapist and patient. Nor does it involve an innate capacity to understand a patient's feelings. Instead, suggested Buie, the clinician who authentically empathizes with a patient responds affec-tively to multiple signals, both overt and subtle, and then allows these to resonate within his or her own experience.

McLaughlin agrees and further suggests that the therapist focus carefully on clues provided by the patient's voice, posture, and physical movements, in order to best understand these reenactment signals.

It is not that the therapist feels what the patient feels, but that through a multiplicity of signals he feels something in his own experience. Gradually, he comes to understand that this affect somehow mirrors what the patient feels. As I noted earlier, the more extreme resonant states may even feel like a "foreign" feeling has been placed inside the therapist. Although they do feel foreign, these situations actually involve the re-awakening of something in the therapist's own life experience.

In a related discussion on projective identification, Ogden (1979) noted that the receiver of the enactment process "has the characteristics of the projected aspects of the self." At some level, the patient has sensed and targeted something in us akin to his or her own experience. The recipient, here the therapist, only *seems* to be controlled by the person who projects.

"In fact," notes Ogden, "the influence is real, but it is not the imagined absolute control by means of transplanted aspects of the self inhabiting the other; rather it is an external pressure exerted by means of interpersonal interaction [the coercive element described earlier]."

Buie attempted to clarify the nature of empathy further by delineating four basic components:

1. Cognition: The therapist accurately comprehends the content of the patient's communication.
2. Self-experience: The clinician recognizes that he or she has experienced events or situations similar to those being described by the patient. Because of the similarity, the alert therapist should be able to summon related memories containing cognitive imagery, along with associated affects and meaning.
3. Imaginative capacity: In situations where the therapist has not directly experienced something described by the patient, he or she nonetheless possesses the ability to imagine such a situation and its impact upon the patient. In part he imagines the feelings and responses he might have, and he uses his understanding of the patient to inwardly depict how such a situation might impact on the patient. This imagining draws upon evoked images, feelings, and experiences of the therapist.
4. Resonance: Describing this powerful phenomenon, Buie quotes Furer, who has defined it as "a primitive form of affective communication." Furer also sees resonance as a "contagion in which a strong affect in an individual simply stimulates the same affect in others." While Furer's words describe the feeling evoked in this situation as a "contagion," Ogden more accurately

points out that individuals in the treatment setting do not have the ability to "implant" new ideas but only to trigger psychic elements *already present* in their psychotherapeutic partners.

I would amplify Buie's description by suggesting that resonance experiences can be dramatic or subtle, chronic, acute or low-level. They are also quite fatiguing and require constant self-scrutiny, and yet they can form a major component of the treatment. When one manages to successfully live through these resonances and reach an understanding of their deeper meanings, the results can be markedly positive.

Among the potential benefits for patient and therapist are a new-found capacity to achieve authentic insights into oneself; the ability to recognize the origins of earlier interactions, and the emergence of new premises about the meanings of one's experiences. With these gains may come freedom from the repetition of incapacitating character traits. By recognizing and analyzing their defensive responses to the enactments (Jacobs 1986, McLaughlin 1986), therapists can clear the ground for these understandings, while also gaining a new openness and availability to the patient.

In many instances, multiple, subtle, discrete communications from the patient will gradually evoke a subtle affective alteration in the therapist. These affective shifts may gradually lead to increasingly powerful feelings of discouragement, annoyance, despair, depression, boredom, and anger in the struggling clinician (Maltsberger and Buie 1974, Kernberg 1984, 1986).

The painful stress of these negative affects will frequently tempt both participants to engage in a kind of quiet, nearly invisible collusion in which disquieting issues are avoided. This dynamic may present in a number of ways: as a "pseudo-idealization" of the therapist and therapy; as an emotionally empty and merely intellectual discussion, or as a sense that the work has reached an impasse and can go no further.

By constantly monitoring shifts in one's own mood, behavior, interest, energy level, associative direction, fantasies, and other affect-linked internal states, the therapist can learn to recognize the inevitable repetitions and interactions that are triggered by enactments.

To summarize: Patient–therapist enactments usually involve some predictable elements, including the following:

1. These countertransference mini-dramas, to some extent, occur in every treatment. Their impact on therapist and patient alike is often quite powerful.
2. Countertransference, or the therapist's response to both the patient's transference and his or her own inner conflicts, has a positive function. Appropriately understood and addressed, it can serve as a vehicle for communication between both treatment partners, and as a source of clarification in the treatment situation.
3. It is the therapist's responsibility to recognize the existence of an enactment and its affectively experienced impact. He or she then attempts to analyze and understand his or her own issues that are being activated. After that, the clinician seeks to learn how these responses may be related to the current situation with the patient. While maintaining a sense of his own responses and their possible relevance to the treatment, the therapist may choose to quietly sit and observe the possible relationship of his ideas to the current work. He may ask related questions, or even introduce them as possible understandings of the treatment.
4. At the same time, the therapist must be careful not to burden the patient with his or her own personal material.

Another way of picturing these dynamics is to place them inside a different meta-psychological frame, and to view the process as one in which the clinician enters an encapsulated, part-object relationship with the patient.

Most therapists have been through the experience of being partly defined by a patient in ways that seem familiar and consonant with some aspects of themselves, even when these definitional categories also feel dystonic and uncomfortable.

The congruence of a patient's projective identification with one or more of our inner facets will often leave us feeling that something foreign and alien has been implanted within us. It is precisely here that the therapist may find a rich opportunity for therapeutic clarification. If the analyst can manage to contain the discomfort, while also examining and understanding it, then the underlying experience can be metabolized and reintroduced into treatment, often with striking results.

Following this, the process can move forward, since there is now a greater awareness of self and other. Authentic relatedness has been enhanced as a direct result of the therapist's refusal to merely react to the patient's orchestration, and his or her insistence upon integrating the enactment at a deeper level of relatedness. This may lead to a more thorough clarification of the interaction.

In summary, by staying with the resonances triggered by the patient's enactment, the clinician in this situation stands a good chance of discovering and then being able to work with the patient towards effective understandings that can have a major impact on treatment outcome.

EXAMPLES

Like those mentioned previously, the examples that follow first describe dramatic, direct interventions. Later chapters include more subtle forms of countertransference reactions.

Soon after completing my residency, I began working with "Sarah." At that time, she was a young woman, successful, single, and well-established in her career. She had entered treatment because of depression brought on by a series of failed love relationships.

During the first months of treatment, she seemed thoughtful and polite, but also guarded. Most of the time, she did her best to keep the discussion safely abstract and speculative, as she sought to "figure out why men are that way," and why they had disappointed her so often.

In this early phase of treatment, I was struck by the fact that her overt attractiveness produced no evocative impact on me. This left me wondering, what was being touched? Sarah was extremely controlling, in terms of the inquiries and observations that she would allow during the hour. Her descriptions of events in her life and of interactions with others seemed devoid of self-reflection. She saw herself as the recipient of externally orchestrated events over which she no influence. There was a hardness to her manner.

Sarah was unable to consider that her own actions might have played a role in these troublesome events. She also tended to regard any comments or questions about this possibility as threatening criticisms.

The more she spoke, the clearer it became that her difficulties with men actually pervaded all aspects of her life. Constantly suspicious of colleagues of both sexes, Sarah saw herself as the victim of endless intrigues, both at work and at home. Forever proving her "worthiness" by taking on difficult tasks, and then attacking herself with perfectionist fervor, she lived in dread of failure and ridicule. Yet her successful accomplishments failed to lessen the intensity of her need to continually prove herself. Where had all of this painful turmoil come from?

As treatment unfolded, it became clear that her internal object world was dominated by a continuously critical and perfectionist maternal voice. Again and again, the patient described the disparaging inner monologue that accompanied her as she worked. While this excoriating voice was not a hallucination, it did remain a steady inner companion and a hostile presence.

On those rare occasions when she experienced warmth and ease, it was usually connected with experiences involving her father, a well-meaning but ineffectual man who had always been submissive and compliant in the face of his wife's continuous demands and criticisms.

The patient relentlessly disparaged her own yearnings for care and comfort, experiencing them as weaknesses linked to the influence of her ineffectual father.

Later, as she learned to better tolerate her own needfulness, she was able to articulate her disappointment in him and her rage over his use of her to gain the affection denied him by his wife.

The treatment hours soon revealed that the men this young woman chose for herself were like her mother: self-centered, exploitative, cold, critical, demanding, perfectionist, and devaluing. The patient often fantasized that if she could only be perfect enough, she might win them and be accepted as worthy. Through these surrogates, she would be winning her mother's recognition. At the same time, she would be pleasing her mother by offering a male substitute for her own inadequate self.

The patient knew that her mother deeply regretted her own inability to produce a second, male child. There had been an intense competition within the mother's sibling group to produce a male grandchild in order to win status from the authoritarian grandfather. During the patient's early years, her mother had openly lamented her failure to provide this yearned-for male offspring.

As treatment proceeded, the patient recognized a constellation of similar character traits among the men she had previously dated. Becoming more confident, she moved from her parents' home to live in her own apartment. She then became preoccupied with new anxieties that had emerged after the move, and with some other inner distortions, such as a compulsion to check doors and windows. She fretted endlessly about what her new neighbors thought of her, and she tormented herself with nagging questions: Would an elderly neighbor approve of her? And what might that neighbor think, if a man stayed the night in Sarah's apartment? Would the apartment look presentable when her parents came to visit? Although Sarah had gained a measure of independence, she was forever experiencing a sense of judgment from internal and projected sources.

By paying careful attention to her continuous sense of injury at the hands of others, she began to recognize how rage lurked perpetually beneath the surface of her consciousness. Prior to this, she had seen her anger as merely situational, reactive—and justified! Although this patient's life seemed to be improving externally in many ways, the treatment hours became increasingly dominated by her expressions of rage, both direct and indirect.

As this phase of treatment developed, Sarah began to make harsh, venomous comments with increasing frequency. Glaring angrily, she would announce, "I should have known better than to think you'd know!" Or she might say, "A lot of help *this* is!" Any inquiries about these negative remarks were met with intellectualizations regarding the "understandable limitations of therapy," coupled with denials of any ongoing negative feelings towards me, or the treatment. These mild characterizations of her outbursts were offered despite the violent anger that was so often evident in her comments.

During this period in treatment, I began to feel either excoriated or a grinding tedium that was wearing. Increasingly, the sessions seemed to have become obligatory rituals of abrasion. Clearly feeling victimized and disappointed, Sarah exploded when I dared to ask if she thought I'd let her down in the process of our work. Was I really so condescending as to think she might need me? I must think she was some kind of "wimp" or "mush" who needed those "goddam tissues" sitting on the table beside her! When I attempted to explore these volatile comments, she quickly dismissed them and me as irrelevant—as simply a nettlesome distraction.

As the hour passed, she frequently became angrier and angrier. But when I noted her increasing wrath and wondered out loud what was affecting her, she erupted. She insisted that I was of no use and no help, just like everyone else in her life. Increasingly, the sessions seemed to be recreations of events she had described at home and at work. Yet we could find no way to step back and examine them together. How could it be otherwise, when she insisted that I was "just like everyone else," useless and worthless?

For the first time in her life, she developed ulcerative colitis, which she blamed on her treatment. At first, she insisted that it was the direct result of the anger I had caused. When I questioned this assumption, she shifted the blame. She was ill, she said, not because of my anger-inducing comments, but because of the way I'd forced her to confront her own inner rage.

Although she was struggling hard, this patient had managed to make a clarifying distinction between seeing the locus of the issue within me (via projection), and understanding that she was struggling with her own, inherent anger, which she now recognized was not a reaction to external factors. It was now *her* anger, even if I was somehow wrongfully responsible for making her feel it. Her need to blame me gave her an ongoing sense of our still having a connection. However, the underlying injuries that had triggered the anger were still out of sight.

But what did this patient's recognition of her inherent anger actually mean to her? It meant that she was imperfect, bad and, eventually, "shit." One could easily understand her need to project these negative qualities into someone else and then see herself as the victim of others: of their criticism, attacks, indifference, etc. They were telling her that she was shit; that message was not coming from within! This unquestioned premise about her own value was at the heart of her self-hatred.

The dynamics at work here were quite complex. Because Sarah chose to see herself as the victim of others' low opinion of her, she felt self-righteously entitled to attack her persecutors. After all, she was only defending the alleged good within from an unfair assault! As she saw it, any suggestion that the locus of the "bad anger" might be internal implied that she was worthless, a failure, and therefore unlovable. Thus, with me, she oscillated between depressive self-hatred and raging attacks on others, much as she had in her life outside of treatment.

When I again tried to explore her disappointment with me, it left her feeling that I saw her as defective, since she could not possibly have been "disappointed," unless she had needed me in the first place! Similarly, if I saw her as needy, then I must surely regard her as worthless. She was also certain that my ostensible interest in her only served to mask my disgust. We lived in a world of constant projections, a labyrinth of mirrors that seemed to offer no escape.

By now the sessions had become exhausting. For mixed reasons of my own, however, I was determined to keep struggling with this patient. For one thing, I felt a certain narcissistic challenge; she would *not* defeat my efforts to understand and help. And so we struggled on and on. Was I also trying to prove my own worthiness through her? Would her pathology defeat me, forcing me to face uncomfortable limitations within myself? I was clearly caught up in this in some personal and unhelpful way.

Struggling with these negatives, I also felt compassion for a very desperate part of her. I sensed that she was trying to ward me off, while hoping I would not let myself be pushed away. More than once, I felt an identification with a lonely child who knew that she had to figure it all out by herself. It was part of my feelings noted in the previous paragraph.

As our sessions continued, she began to describe her bloody bowel movements in great detail. She spoke of herself as disgusting and blamed me for it. When I challenged that characterization, she withdrew the complaint against me but continued to define herself as a "disgusting" person.

At one point she said, "You probably think I'm rubbing your face in it. I'm just trying to say what's there." Here were recognition, projection, denial, and defensive rationalization, all taking place in a single moment. This level of complexity was exhausting, especially given the fact that all attempts to review her comments were seen as traps and met with derision and defensive mockery.

By now, we had each noted that her bloody bowel movements occurred almost immediately after experiences of rage during treatment sessions. As the months passed and the struggle continued, I felt exhausted. I did my best to keep perspective and understand her tormenting inner rage. But it was difficult, since all my inquiries, clarifications, and correlations seemed to provoke nothing but scornful hatred.

Increasingly, I struggled against my own hatred for the hours spent with her. I often saw her as someone who tortured me and confronted me with my own failure. At the time however, I did not fully understand these inner resonances and resisted their recognition.

Later, I would come to see that my determination to work it out was based on my own need to deny my rage and impotence in what had become a grueling power struggle. At the same time, and on a more conscious level, I was convinced that her attacks had a basis in reality—I wasn't helping her. She was getting more physically ill. I began to harbor fantasies of working in my father's lumber business, an arena in which I felt competent and successful. At the same time, I frequently doubted my competence as a therapist. Was I a fraud? The fact was that I felt awful when I was with her. Hoping to extricate us from the impasse, I suggested that we seek a consultation. Sarah agreed. She disparaged the first consultant, an older woman, but agreed to see a second.

This second consultant, also a woman, was a senior analyst and a former teacher of mine. She recommended that we stop the treatment because the patient's borderline rage, heightened and focused in the treatment, was too intense and was disrupting her life. She pointed out that we had accomplished significant work in the sessions, including interrupting the patient's pattern of serial, devaluing, and exploitative relationships with men. The patient had also been able to geographically separate from her parents, and to reduce the number of self-destructive disputes that flared up at work.

The consultant further recommended that I now work in an ego-oriented fashion to strengthen these reality-aspects of the patient's life; henceforth, she said, the two of us should avoid intensification of transferential material.

While this consultation allowed me to reflect on the work more dispassionately, I remained convinced that the gains would disappear if the patient were deprived of these painful sessions with me. I felt sure that she needed to continue enacting her rage. If we interrupted our work and the therapeutic relationship, however turbulent, she would almost certainly begin to recreate these negative interactions elsewhere with others.

It seemed to me that we had merely relocated them to the office, which allowed other areas of her life to become relatively conflict-free. If we stopped here, I feared two potentially destructive outcomes. First, the recent behavioral gains might very well evaporate. Second, it seemed likely that I would be repeating her earlier experience with the inept and abandoning father of her childhood, whom she had eventually rejected.

Some of the motivation behind her fury was now becoming clearer to me. As I mulled over my anger, I reflected on the fact that I was simultaneously receiving both the rage she felt for her father and the original painful criticism from her mother.

I also recalled how I had offered her several interpretations along these lines in the past, only to have them disparaged, ridiculed, and ignored. She had never been able to consider them on their own merits.

One day, as I opened my office door and stepped into the waiting room, I saw her features shift to form the all-too-familiar mask of rage and disgust that haunted our sessions. I felt myself chill at the prospect of the ensuing hour. I felt small and defenseless. I wanted to hide, but had no place to run. Duty compelled me to remain there and endure the unpleasantness that surely lay ahead. Before the patient had even seated herself, she began a high-pitched, screaming denigration of me for my failure to understand something that had been said during our last hour. In spite of my anticipation, I was shocked and surprised by the virulence of her fury. I held up one hand and said:

> *Therapist:* Stop it! I hate it when you treat me this way. It gives me a feeling of being small and frightened and worthless. It feels like I'm being torn apart. I hate being with you when you treat me this way. Is this what it was like for you when you had to stand naked in the tub with your mother screaming at you and no place to go?
>
> *Sarah:* (startled, she began crying. Then she screamed back.) YES! You're supposed to hate me. No one can love me.

(Then, crying harder:) I didn't know that I was doing it, but with your saying it, I knew I had to get you to feel it!

Therapist: To feel like you?

Sarah: Yes! You couldn't understand it from just my telling you. Words aren't enough!

Therapist: So I played you, and you were your mother to me?

Sarah: (Still crying, she continued shouting:) Yes, you had to feel like me. I didn't know I was doing it, but when you began talking today, I knew that I had to get you to feel like me. No one can love me!

Therapist: (Very softly but emphatically:) No one can love you? You said that a moment ago and now you repeat it. Why is that? Why can't anyone love you? [Sensing a shift, I persisted.] Is that what this has all been about?

With these exchanges, the tone of the hour shifted dramatically. All at once our communication felt quiet, peaceful, reflective. I sensed that we might now be able to begin exploring a fundamental issue: her continuing sense of worthlessness and a fundamental unloveableness.

Instead of endlessly reenacting this constellation of painful beliefs, the patient could now begin to consciously explore them.

With further reflection, I saw that my unresolved need to deny my anger had compelled me to tolerate her abuse in ways that were inappropriate. All of that ill-advised tolerance had only increased her despair and sense of unworthiness (Maltsberger and Buie 1974) as I enacted my own hatred.

In order to help this patient recognize and integrate the dynamics issues that lay buried beneath her enactments, I had been required to confront my own masochistic idealizations, and to admit that they were a cloak for my own rage and sadism.

Eventually I came to understand that surrendering to her abuse had been the means by which I painted myself as "good," while at the same time exposing her "badness" as an abuser who felt compelled to bully others with aggressive harangues. Only after this recognition had taken place was I able to bring the archaic connection that had been masked by the enactment back into the hour. After that, it became possible to appropriately reintegrate it as part of the treatment.

Clearly, my denial, resistance, and shame about my hatred had interfered with our ability to examine and resolve what was occurring in the hour. Such fencing is a significant issue in psychotherapy, and this case reveals some of the negative effects that can occur if the therapist fails to recognize, examine, understand, and resolve the issues underlying his or her affective responses to the patient. The experience with Sarah and several other people early in my career forced me to examine many of these issues within myself. This work allowed me to recognize and respond more quickly to similar circumstances in a freer and more genuine way. While I still tend to wait and gather material to understand more thoroughly what seems to be occurring, I find the greater comfort comes from recognizing how my own aggression and hatred have aided in understanding and responding appropriately.

I am still cautious about "shoot from the hip" countertransference responses. Although they may demonstrate the authentic presence of the therapist, they can also involve arrogant intrusions of one's own interpretations and unanalyzed reactive expressions of one's own affect.

At the same time, as this case demonstrates, resisting the affective experience and its meanings can cause treatment impasses or harm. Had I been able to recognize the full extent of my responses earlier and examine them more deeply, I could have introduced them more effectively and more quickly.

When confronting enactments, I have found it best to become aware of my own emerging affects and issues before responding. *I also believe it crucial to link my response to a potential genetic explanation of the enactment that puts it in the context of trying to understand the meaning of this interaction in terms of the patient's life experience.* Merely responding affectively carries a very real risk of emotional reinjury for the patient. On the other hand, linking one's response to a possible genetic issue or dynamic helps both participants in the experience to understand that both are seeking to interpret the enactment phenomenon as a coded message. The focus upon the message and its understanding says to the patient, "These responses on both sides have some meaning that we are both seeking. We are not just reacting to each other."

In the preceding example, taken from my earliest work (and during a time when such responses were considered "wildly unprofessional"), I waited too long to respond, thus prolonging the distress of the patient.

After I corrected my error, however, the patient and I went on to spend a considerable amount of time reflecting upon the source of her distorted self-image. Sarah soon recognized her mother's negative self-projection, which she had absorbed as a negative introject, a false image of herself. She later came to understand how she had mistaken this image for her genuine core self. There had not been sufficient time or maternal environment for her to emerge and flourish.

Sarah's mother had clearly viewed the patient as an extension of herself, and as visible evidence to the world of her own worthless, shameful, and imperfect self. Her constant criticisms were actually attempts to perfect her flawed daughter/self. During the enactment, I had become the devalued, failed, and unseen child.

This unfolding dynamic represented a formidable challenge for me, because it touched directly on some of my own impossible childhood tasks. Like the patient, I had accepted certain obligations in the hopes of being seen and valued. The patient's rage, like my own and that of my parents, frightened me badly. In order to cope, I would deny my own anger and quell hers.

In this way, I was once again left alone to solve the problems of both parent and child. As I recognized this archaic personal paradigm, the guilty inhibitions that subtly controlled my behavior became apparent to me. After more self-analysis and personal treatment, I saw that I had not been able to stand the intensity of my anger. It threatened to push aside my capacity to feel love and affection. Like the patient, I had felt a compulsion to ward it off.

Once I became clear about this reactivation of my inner dynamics, however, I could speak of my hatred without fearing that it would overwhelm either of us. And she seemed to be confirming this insight when she pointed out that she had not succeeded in getting me to hate her, but only to hate *being with her when she behaved in this way*. (As it turned out, she hated being with herself during those times as much as I did!)

Together we inhabited an encapsulated experience initiated by the patient's projections from her internal object world. For her, I had become the devalued, failed, and undeserving self-child, even as she enacted the role of the harsh, demeaning, endlessly critical maternal object.

The topography of our struggling relationship became even clearer as we explored how the patient's maternally identified part-object felt victimized by the inadequate and shameful child (the part-self enacted by me). As victim—aggressor, this maternal part-object felt entitled to revile and degrade me. In this kind of dynamic, the aggressor actually experiences the situation as a victim whose aggression is fully justified by his or her awful plight.

Only when I was able to feel and then identify the aspect of myself that was in collusion with this unfolding dynamic could I step out of the encapsulation. This necessarily painful reflection allowed me to metabolize the experience and then bring the relevant aspects back into the work for joint examination.

In the early years of this work, interactions of this kind often left me exhausted and concerned. I felt convinced that more training and experience would allow me first to anticipate and then to avoid these enmeshments, which I assumed were the result of my own inexperience. I still harbored a fantasy of the idealized senior analyst whose internal resolution of conflict and accumulated wisdom would completely eliminate such painful floundering.

Although I managed to learn how to avoid the sado—masochistic prolongation of this transference interaction and to become more skilled at recognizing when I was being drawn into such an enmeshment, I soon discovered that it was impossible to anticipate the arrival of the countertransference dynamic during therapy.

Gradually, I began to understand that the countertransference was in fact a necessary and vital component of the treatment process. It could not be avoided for the sake of my own comfort without short-circuiting the treatment. Each countertransference eruption was unique, and could be recognized as such only after I had become enmeshed in it.

With the passage of time, however, I did become more aware of my own tendency to withdraw or become pedantic and retaliatory, whenever threatening enactments took place. I also saw that my own sense of failure and doubt actually served to signal that the process was underway.

Indeed, these painful feelings during therapy could be regarded as helpful indicators that almost invariably announced the emergence of the countertransference enactment.

The preceding phenomenological descriptions and examples illustrate many familiar psychological issues, including:

—deficits in early bonding,
—defects in the holding environment,
—the development of negative introjects,
—the problems of separation / individuation,
—lack of self-soothing and self-containing internal objects,
—the inability to move beyond the "paranoid-schizoid position," and
—the range of meta-psychological descriptions for early narcissistic injuries and their sequelae.

Kernberg describes the helpful aspects of the countertransference, by describing how it can assist the therapist engaged in the process of intensive psychotherapy:

> The analyst's exploration of his own emotional reactions to the patient under the condition of stalemate may be crucial to the diagnosis of both chronic countertransference distortions (which are more pervasive though less obtrusive than acute countertransference developments), and subtle but powerful transference acting out. . . .
>
> In this regard, the analysis of the analyst's total emotional reaction is a "second line" of approach when the first line of approach, direct transference exploration, proves insufficient. (1975, p. 233)

As the example of Sarah suggests, my feelings of failure, powerlessness, and worthlessness, along with my painful sense of being trapped and devalued, were of considerable help in allowing me to better understand this patient's childhood experience. I had to recognize my own rage and failed narcissistic grandiosity, however, before my vision cleared enough to let me see this recreation from the patient's life with useful clarity.

Merely understanding the message contained in the patient's enactment was not enough. To be most effective, I had to bring the experience back into the treatment in a way that could lead to useful understandings. This complicated and challenging process unfolded in the following manner:

1. By clarifying and then disclosing the feelings the patient elicited in me, I affirmed that she and I both existed and affected each other. I did not reveal the personal issues her enactment had touched in my own life. Instead, I spoke only in terms of our interaction.

2. I outlined a possible genetic linkage of this experience, then proposed it as a hypothesis that *might* explain the psychodynamics of our mini-drama. To have simply declared my feelings would have burdened and injured the patient, while also making her responsible for my feeling state. To avoid that hazard, I restricted myself to suggesting that her enactment might have been intended to help me understand something new about her inner life. In this way, I managed to hold the countertransference securely in the psychotherapeutic frame. Describing the crucial importance of this kind of circumspection, Hoffman (1983) points out that it is arrogant for clinicians to assume that their experience, crystallized in moments of seeming clarity, can be equivalent to the richly complex set of experiences that the patient has spent months attempting to clarify and communicate. Instead of making such potentially harmful assumptions, the therapist would do better to present enactment interpretations as possible clues offered for mutual, open-ended consideration.

3. I waited a considerable length of time before introducing my responses to the patient. And, although I waited too long in this instance, it was obviously important to carefully examine and analyze my inner landscape, in order to avoid premature, injurious, or self-serving responses.

4. When such urgent declarations of personal responses and possible genetic origins are appropriately introduced, the result in most cases is an almost immediate cessation of the enactment. In this instance, we were quite fortunate because we were able to

define the part-object and part-self representation, while also clarifying the pre-determined interactional dynamic and identifying the functions of the repetition. The words used at these critical junctures must be carefully chosen. In an example presented earlier, Little (1951) said to the patient who was threatening to smash a flower pot, "I'll just about kill you if you smash that pot!" Here the phrase "just about" clearly means "almost." This phrasing seems to convey a sense of Little's ongoing struggle to maintain an empathic tie with the patient. Her remark also delineates the situation of being on the verge of annihilation as a consequence of an impending action. Was that a basic concern for her patient, and was she actually reassuring the latter that annihilation would not in fact follow as the result of merely smashing a pot? It seems evident, in this example, that the therapist's judicious (and perhaps fortuitous) choice of words played an important part in defusing a potential rupture in the treatment.

As Sarah recalled years later, during termination, "Even then, I couldn't get you to hate me. Instead, you just kept saying you hated being with me when I treated you that way." The judicious choice of words allows the therapist to clarify one's actual responses and to avoid suppression and destructive acting in.

In summary: A crucial consideration in working within the countertransference framework is the understanding that it represents an underlying hope for a human connection that is being played out in the dynamic interaction. In essence, the patient is saying, "Although I feel alienated, worthless, etc., some part of me is counting on reaching some part of you, so that we can have a bond in which you will genuinely understand me and I will not be so alone."

This formulation contains great hope. It embodies the yearning for the sense of an early maternal bond in which one felt cared for, accepted, understood, and loved. Yet it also includes the anguish of the now anticipated abandonment, along with rage-filled fantasies of retaliation based on deep sadistic wishes to cling to another human being and be felt, even painfully, in order to have one's existence validated. These kinds of intense transference enactments usually indicate the presence of the paranoid–schizoid position in the adult, as delineated by Klein.

For the therapist, the fatiguing nature of the countertransference dynamic includes two significant components:

1. It usually involves a continuous psychological assault that must be contained without retaliation. Such containment requires that the clinician maintain the empathic tie with the split-off positive aspects of the patient.
2. The dynamic also requires the therapist to continually analyze his or her responses as part of the process of metabolizing the experience in order to discern the therapeutically significant elements of the patient's enactment.

One must follow both analytical vectors simultaneously, while retaining authenticity and spontaneity and also refusing to submit to the patient's model of sadomasochistic relatedness. This is an enormous challenge! Again and again, we must guard against feeling so threatened that we retreat or retaliate, for then hope will be lost and the patient will feel abandoned. These are the lapses in empathy that we experience and analyze in the treatment. The case history that follows provides a potentially useful example of a treatment situation in which I failed to fulfill this objective.

I was asked to see a patient in treatment who had already been diagnosed as having a borderline personality organization with cocaine and alcohol abuse that had continued for several decades. Germaine had been through numerous episodes of self-destructive behavior. I also suspected that she might be suffering from a rapidly cycling bipolar affective disorder. This patient was about to be discharged from a detoxification center and would soon return to work. In spite of her daunting history and her broad range of diagnoses, she presented in the office as an intelligent, albeit impulsive and driven young woman. She had worked well at her demanding and complex job, despite serious disturbances in her private life, she had great skill at disguising her lapses at work.

During a brief evaluation, I determined that we could attempt to work together, provided that she first stabilize her daily life. We initially focused upon developing a structured routine of eating, sleeping, exercise, work hours, and nonstimulating social activities. She accomplished that and we began meeting regularly. In order to assist in the stabilization process, I focused on clarifying how she made her choices and decisions. What factors, if any, did she consider before deciding on an issue such as whether or not to engage in drug-taking behavior, socializing in various circumstances, etc? My overt approach was structured and behavioral.

We also worked to clarify the role of anxiety and panic in her impulsiveness. I chose not to explore early trauma or examine defenses, except as related to issues that she made overtly apparent. Having decided not to risk affective overload by exploring early issues, I also believed that her ego-observant and affect-containment capacities were limited. In addition, I was convinced that the previous alcohol and drug use would continue to limit her abstract thinking capacity for months to come. For these reasons, I chose to focus and respond on the here and now of her daily life while listening for hints about deeper motivating issues. Although she was able to work successfully at a complex technical job that did not require abstract thinking, her personal reflections were distorted by projections of self-hatred and paralyzing depression.

Soon after beginning our work, we were able to successfully resolve a sector of conflict with a family member. For the first time in many years, the patient began to enjoy comfortable visits and conversations with this relative. Encouraged, I thought to myself, "If we could achieve a few more small successes of this kind, we might develop a more solid working relationship to build upon." Instead, she took a turn for the worse. Her resolution of a relatively small conflict with a family member resulted in her reinternalizing the self-hatred that had previously been projected upon this individual. If he wasn't really so bad, then she must be! As a consequence, she fell into a paralyzing depression marked by suicidal preoccupations. I tried to hospitalize her, but she refused and talked her way out of an emergency room evaluation. She overdosed within a day and was hospitalized. Two more hospitalizations followed in quick succession. It seemed that our work had not adequately prepared her for the impact of the loss of the projected negative object and the reinternalization of her self-hatred.

Unlike the young woman who had directed so much rage at me

during our sessions, this patient had not developed enough hostile transference toward me, and was directing most of her destructive rage at herself.

Because of her capacity to seem well-organized and competent when sheltered by a hospital setting, she seemed capable of taking care of herself. As a result, I soon found myself struggling against hospital staff who wanted her discharged only a few days after transfer from the Intensive Care Unit!

At the end of this first hospitalization, the unit psychiatrist understood my concerns but felt powerless to detain the patient because of her presentation, which made it virtually impossible for the hospital to justify her stay to the insurance company or to legally hold her. After all, she was not psychotic, disorganized, or incoherent. She also denied being suicidal and wanted to return to work.

I asked her repeatedly to explain how her situation had changed. What had she learned or understood that would protect her, once released, from becoming subject to the same rapid emotional decline and mood destabilization that had provoked the suicide attempt? But she brushed aside my question and insisted on leaving. She was discharged and overdosed again that night.

After medical stabilization, she was readmitted to the same hospital, where she soon repeated her "I want to be discharged" enactment. After an admission of several more days, she was successful in pushing for discharge, despite the lack of meaningful change. An effective split was present. The life-preserving protective role had been projected upon the hospital and doctors, and the self-destructive sadistic role was embraced by the patient. She was in a pernicious struggle with her would-be caregivers.

During her next hospitalization, at yet another facility, I attended a treatment planning conference. I listened as her history was reviewed, and I was shocked when the unit director began by introducing the subject of discharge planning. I was truly astounded. Previously, I had engaged in numerous discussions with the ward staff, had left copious notes reviewing our sessions and had pointed out the lack of any significant change in the patient's emotional status, in spite of her manifest compliance with ward routine.

Distressed by the direction the conference was taking, I interrupted, "What has changed within her? What has she learned that assures her that she will not act in similar fashion when the rage and despair manifest again? Where has she demonstrated a capacity for self-containment and self-reflection that would indicate more integrated and balanced working processes? All I have seen is angry, behavioral compliance. It's as if she were saying, 'I'll beat you people at your own game. I'll give you the behavior and words that you want, but nothing has really changed. This kind of behavior is my forte. No one really cares about what really goes on inside me—and you people are no different!' "

I concluded my remarks by pointing out, "It seems clear to me that her requests to be discharged do not indicate increased stability at all. Instead, they show her to be endangered. Her angry struggle with the staff is a form of enactment that can only lead to further collapse."

The conference consultant agreed. He spoke up and discussed the issues I had addressed in a calmer, less impassioned manner. I felt comforted, safe, and listened to, instead of feeling that I'd been left alone with an overwhelming task. I also felt that I could manage within the situation, because I now had an ally who would support more thoughtful decision-making.

As I struggled to evaluate my performance with this patient, however, I recognized a serious error on my part. Caught up in a powerful enactment of my own, I had ignored the burdensome aloneness I was feeling with her. I had assumed a determined and resolute stance, to try to stay the course with her, but its actual function was to allow me to deny my own sense of being overwhelmed.

Although I had admitted my feelings of confusion, anxiety, and anger, and had sought assistance from hospital staffers and former therapists, the fact remained that I had refused to face something in myself: a profound aloneness and a desperate feeling of having to shoulder too much responsibility. Both of these feelings had eventually become overwhelming and unmanageable.

Alone and in consultations, I tried to examine my own motivations and responses. I recalled that in the past I had worked with a number of deeply troubled patients like this one. Their struggles had been sharp and exhausting. Yet I had managed to stay the course with them, out of a deep personal concern that they should not be abandoned in the midst of crisis. The annihilating impact of such an abandonment was an old personal theme for me. I knew it well.

Among my colleagues, I had a reputation for working successfully with difficult patients. How large a factor was my own narcissistic mythology playing into my refusal to admit my fears and aloneness while treating this patient?

As I considered these aspects, I was startled by another surprising insight: the recognition that, like my patient, I had been denying my anxiety about this treatment. As a result, I had given the patient a false version of myself. I hadn't been authentically available to her because of my need to block this painful affect from my own awareness.

It soon became clear that the errors depicted by Maltsberger and Buie (1974) and Buie (1981) had infected my caregiving. Yes, I had done and said the appropriate things, and I'd been actively engaged with the patient. In the end, however, I had evaded part of my responsibility by retreating from her.

As I reflected on my fallibility, I recalled our last session, just before her most recent overdose. At that point, the patient, for the second time, had been discharged from the hospital against my advice. The hospital staff, while partially agreeing with me about her care, felt powerless to oppose the patient's wishes.

I asked the patient what had changed that might help her cope with these terrible feelings when they recurred. She mouthed some platitudes she'd picked up from a behavioral therapist: "Feelings are only feelings" and "Feelings can't hurt you; only you can."

I asked her how this advice could be usefully related to her recent, devastating experience, and I also noted the vacant, mechanical tone in her repetition of these mental-hygiene slogans. She only smiled, however, while insisting that the *other* doctors had accepted her declarations. Why was I being so difficult? Besides, she had been told that she was "uncommitable." I asked her why she seemed to perceive herself as engaged in a struggle with me. What was she trying to prove?

I now understood that a split had developed. Somehow, I had taken on the sense of danger and despair that was appropriately hers, and I was alone with it. Clearly, I had felt incapable of dealing with the resulting projections. At the same time, I recognized that our relationship had not developed to the point that it could contain the inevitable sadistic rage.

Once again I urged her to return to the hospital. I enumerated the many cues she had offered that showed how her internal state had not changed. She was entrenched, however, and denied any plans or wishes for suicide. At that point, I knew I would have to transfer her care. For one thing, we had no treatment agreement. I also sensed that my aloneness and despair required that I take some time to reflect.

As the hour ended, we reviewed the available possibilities, should her state change and her denial fail. Her words sounded hollow. I noted this but did not pursue it as I normally would have. This nonpursuit constituted my emotional retreat from her and left me with feelings of abandonment.

By retreating from the conflict and failing to press her with my observations, I was partially surrendering my therapeutic responsibility. In layman's parlance, I was simply going through the motions.

That night she overdosed and began another hospitalization. All of the reflections described above went through my head in quick succession, as the consultant echoed my concerns about the staff colluding with the patient's denial. He also recommended extended hospitalization.

As I struggled to understand how my treatment of this patient had broken down, I came upon a further understanding. My experience of distress, powerlessness, feeling overwhelmed, and bearing responsibilities beyond my capacity were all countertransference inductions that closely replicated an important aspect of the patient's own early experience.

The unhappy fact was that I had not sufficiently taken that experience in, metabolized it, or brought it back into the treatment setting. When we finally did discuss this crisis, we recognized that it had replicated a period of her life in which she had been devastated by maternal abandonment and isolation.

The patient described her mother as "mouthing empty phrases and platitudes," but never really establishing a close connection or a cogent understanding. Transferentially, I had enacted the failed mother and had then been subject to the patient's sadistic anger. In an alternating and oscillating fashion, I had experienced powerlessness similar to the patient's, and along with it, a rage at abandonment, followed by resignation and retreat. By not pressing forward with my observations of her sadism and the split in treatment, I had become deadened in the same way that she had as a child.

This example illustrates several common difficulties in treating complex characterologic issues in individuals who use actions as their primary mode of communication. Russell's "Crunch," with its attendant bewilderment, aptly characterizes the plight of the clinician in this treatment setting. Although there are many aspects of this case that warrant discussion, the most significant one involves the impact of these countertransference problems on the dynamics of psychotherapy.

One key aspect of countertransference encounters in treatment is metabolization, the process by which the therapist examines his or her experience with the patient, then breaks it down into its component parts: affects, associations, memories, images, etc. These elements are then analyzed in order to locate potentially useful understandings of self, patient, and the treatment circumstance.

After that, the therapist carefully reintroduces this material back into the treatment in a clearly articulated manner. In order to accomplish this step, however, the clinician needs to recognize the patient's projections, transferences, affects, old traumas, and conflicts aroused in the treatment, but without acting upon them. As they are absorbed, many of these enactment resonances will feel to the therapist like foreign intrusions of non-self experience. (They are in fact the intrusions in the "potential space" described by Bollas (1983).)

As this dynamic unfolds, various denied, repressed, and split-off aspects of the therapist's own life experience will be reawakened by the patient. Although the resulting projective identification may feel like something foreign is being forced under the clinician's skin, the process actually involves the reactivation of archaic but still potentially distressing issues within us. Like the patient, we understandably wish to rid ourselves of these discomforting affects. As we work to contain our own responses and analyze them, while also noting how they operate in us and where they come from in our experience, we begin to understand how they are being aroused in the treatment.

We recognize our own transferences to the patient and begin to understand possible meanings of this re-creation in the hour. The components and genetics of the mini-drama slowly become clearer. We begin to perceive our true roles and those of the patient. The meaning and the function of the enactment messages become more apparent, and the patient's compulsive need to repeat the sequence begins to clarify itself.

With the emergence of this kind of understanding within us, we may observe a lessening of our own distress and feel more open to the patient's inner turmoil. Experience shows that when this point is reached, we have begun doing the work defined by Schwaber (JAPA 1992). To paraphrase Schwaber: Countertransference is anything that pulls the clinician away from the patient's point of view. Recognizing this, she outlines the therapist's task, which calls for being able to maintain one's own perceptions of factual reality, while also noting discrepancies between the patient's perceived and experienced reality. The effective therapist will examine these discrepancies without substituting inappropriate affective content or partial insights hastily culled from one's own perspective.

For the clinician, the challenging reality is that this kind of intense psychotherapy does indeed "pull us into the crunch," while forcing us to confront and then manage our own internal dissonances in order to help the patient. As Schwaber notes (pp. 104–105): "It remains a singular struggle for us not to regard our own vantage point as holding the more real, the more correct version of what is true. Despite our best intentions, we may recognize a fundamental disinclination to shift our own perspective, particularly our view about ourselves, in order to locate that of the patient."

Once we have extricated ourselves from the enactment and regained our perspective, we can bring our hypotheses back to the treatment for joint consideration. At that point, both patient and therapist can begin to benefit from the insights generated by the clarifying and hope-instilling experience of resolving inner conflicts and moving toward creative growth.

It seems clear that working with an awareness of the complexity of the countertransference represents an enormous challenge for the therapist. And yet the useful outcome, in terms of treatment depth and effect, makes this struggle well worth the effort.

6

Subtler Forms of Enactment

Most enactments unfold slowly and without great drama. With experience, the therapist develops a sensitivity for those situations in which the reenactment is more subtly present. Chapter Six includes both dramatic and subtle forms of enactment.

The preceding case histories involved patients engaged in overtly dramatic struggles in order to protect and rebuild their vulnerable and brittle sense of themselves. Fortunately, most treatments involve less dramatic forms of enactment and countertransference. In the more common treatment scenarios, transferences develop quickly but manifest slowly. The resulting enactments take place gradually, without the devastating emotional eruptions that often occur with more severely troubled patients.

Regardless of their intensity, however, most psychotherapeutic enactments share similar dynamic interactions, as can be seen in the following examples.

"Judy," a woman in her early twenties, entered treatment for the fifth time because of depression and a chronic lack of motivation in her life. Although she had previously been involved in a number of therapies and had tried various medications, she had remained unchanged for years.

When her most recent therapist moved unexpectedly to another city after treating her for a year, she became more passive and withdrawn, living in a state of clinging dependency with various family members. She reported that she had begun to feel increasingly connected to this therapist and liked him, even though her condition had not improved significantly during the year she spent with him.

At first, Judy's attitude seemed passive and hopeless during our treatment sessions. If she spoke at all, it was to complain in a whining voice about being misunderstood and criticized by everyone around her.

"Nothing is exciting. I'm always bored and nothing makes me feel good," she often pointed out. "Everyone and everything is a disappointment. Other peoples' lives go well. They have something. But no one ever makes me feel good. Instead, they constantly criticize me." It sounded as if the vector of this patient's expectation and energy moved from the outside world inwardly; she seemed unable to identify any innate sources of interest, pleasure, or satisfaction. She felt there was nothing of value within her, and that the "missing goods" had to come from sources external to her.

I listened carefully to Judy and on several occasions wondered aloud if she were waiting for something to be given to her that would change her life. Would her life then begin? Had the clock stopped somewhere? Did she feel that she'd lost something important in her world at some earlier point? Had things ever been different? Could she recall a period of time, perhaps even a decisive time, during which her life had changed for the worse?

Her responses were predictably clouded, "Huh? What do you mean? Are you saying it's my fault? What are you talking about?" The vague and disconnected quality of these responses seemed to confirm that she was in a separate container even as we were together. My comments and questions seemed to be an intrusion into some private dissociated experience. It was as if I had interrupted her. She was preoccupied with her internal experience.

Was I truly expecting something to come from her? Didn't I get it? I was supposed to give her something, not demand that she find it within herself!

The weeks passed, and our sessions continued in this manner.

Repeatedly, I attempted to shape inquiries that would get her to reflect on how her depressed, angry state, with its attendant isolation, had evolved. As I saw that my questions evoked nothing more expressive than a shrug of the shoulders or an occasional "I don't know," I began to make more declarative comments. These described my sense of what her experience seemed like as I heard it. But it was difficult going; these attempts were met with only slightly more related affirming sounds, such as "uh-huh," and "yeah." Still, I had begun to give her something that described her as she seemed with me or others, and possible understandings of this presentation—a form of mirroring that affirmed her existence without demanding anything from her.

It was clear that Judy could not see or imagine herself as playing a personal role in the endless repetition of her unrewarding and joyless life experiences. According to her descriptions, this discouraging pattern of interactions with others reached all the way back to an unhappy child-hood, about which she also remained characteristically vague.

When I wondered aloud about her current circumstances, she explained that she felt alienated from her family, whose members complained often about her whining voice and her helpless passivity. She clearly understood that these family members were frustrated at their inability to motivate her to finish school, go to work, or engage with them.

Judy also described how friends would become furious at some of her behaviors, such as "spacing out" in mid-conversation, or absent-mindedly walking away as they spoke. These companions also expressed outrage at her for hanging up on them, or putting down the telephone in the middle of something they were saying.

Seemingly mystified by the negative reactions of her friends to these lapses, Judy complained that they were being unreasonable, "That's just the way I am. It's hard for me to pay attention when I don't care. I don't listen to what I say or how I say it. How should I know I'm whining? They should understand!" In response, I wondered aloud, "Maybe there was a time when you did care?" Judy did not respond. I knew that Judy had consulted several other well-regarded therapists before beginning treatment with me. When I inquired about them, she insisted that these experiences had not helped her in the least. They did nothing to make her life feel less empty. According to Judy, Therapist X had been "nice," but had failed to accomplish anything. Therapist Y had prescribed endless medications that brought no improvement, while Therapist Z "just kept asking me questions and waiting for me to say something."

Struggling to find an opening, I asked her if she'd ever thought about ways in which she might have contributed to the treatment impasses she so frequently described. Did she have a sense of what approaches might have been more helpful to her during those earlier, failed therapies? (Foolish questions. Once again, I was failing to appreciate that no constructive initiatives were to come from her!) As always, she responded by saying, "I don't get you. I don't understand your questions."

In spite of her seemingly impenetrable passivity, Judy had managed to graduate from college with a "B" average, and was now enrolled in a graduate program that she was failing to complete. (Only later did she allow me to know that she was actually quite accomplished in several areas of art, literature, and music.)

As the treatment continued, I noted an intriguing behavior pattern that seemed to frequently recur. Judy would arrive for each of her twice-weekly sessions on time. When I first opened the door to my waiting area, she would briefly flash an energetic smile, while making direct eye contact. This would last for a split-second.

As she entered the office, however, her facial expression would visibly and dramatically become flat and vacant. Dropping onto her chair, she would allow her arms and legs to flop carelessly, even as her head lolled forward and her eyes partially closed.

With her gaze averted, her mouth down-turned and her face devoid of expression, she would remain silent in this dramatically apathetic posture. Her responses to questions, comments, and observations sounded flat and lifeless. She was barely audible. In session after session, she offered no spontaneous thoughts, comments, questions, or reflections. Intrigued by all of this, I sensed that I was seeing a caricature of despair that had elements of being both genuine and provocative. What was that initial spark in the waiting area? There was something engaging and mystifying in all of this; a game I didn't understand but felt drawn into. While the overt display and enactment were not subtle, there was much more to this then I understood. "A game?" I was feeling teased and challenged to play, but play what? What was stirring in me? What was intriguing me? It was like hide and seek.

These hours were exceedingly difficult, but my curiosity remained high. I was not put off, not even by my own confusion and mystification. Struggling to understand and find an opening, I would note the contrast between her appearance and manner in the waiting room and her lifeless attitude once the session began. What might account for this rapid change, I wondered aloud. On other occasions, I would recall comments or issues from previous hours, only to find that this attempt at engagement produced little response.

Increasingly baffled, I pointed out, "You go to all this trouble to get yourself here on time, and you make all this effort (the display of caricatured behavior) during the session . . . and yet, nothing useful happens—just like everywhere else in your life! You just don't get what you want, or do you?" This might produce an affirmative groan or sigh, with just a hint of a teasing smile. Sometimes I said these words softly with a hint of mystery and irony. At other times, I would slip into a kind of monologue in which I made comments to myself about my inability to "get it." In a quasi-comical fashion, I would ask myself what was "going on here." Then I would wonder aloud; Did these sessions contain some clue that I wasn't seeing?

Interestingly, I soon discovered that these "monologues" caused Judy to sit up straight and pay attention to what was being said. At times she admitted that she was "annoyed" by my soliloquies, and insisted that I was inventing them solely in order to criticize her. In spite of this response, I didn't quite believe her. Then, like that seemingly befuddled TV detective, "Columbo," I would scratch my head, mutter, and suggest that I was just too dumb to "get" her coded messages. Was there any way she could help me?

Interestingly, these mildly self-denigrating parodies of my efforts often caused her to laugh. They seemed to rouse her from her torpor at the same time. Animated now, she would participate energetically in the discussion, provided only that I continued to maintain this light-hearted, semi-comic, and self-deprecating manner in which I was both wily and confused.

I noted another pattern, as well. On those occasions when I asked her what a particular posture or facial expression might mean, or wondered how she would feel if someone else used the same body language she was demonstrating in the office, she became most intrigued.

Recognizing the pattern, I began to act on it. Increasingly, in situations where she seemed not to understand, I would ask her permission to imitate gestures which she claimed to be unaware of. Each time I asked for her permission to imitate the gestures, she nodded and seemed to be entertained by the idea. Once again, she would become attentive and energized during my "imitations." Between the sessions, however, she reported lapsing back into apathy. She also seemed to forget the content of each session as soon as it ended. However, if I paused during a session to recall something from a previous hour, she would now immediately remember it, and frequently add some detail.

Repeatedly, I wondered to myself, What does this mean? Who once behaved with her as she is now behaving with me? What is this really about? Is it about being recognized? Remembered? Cherished? Affirmed? Mattering to someone?

As our interaction continued, I painstakingly gathered fragments of Judy's history. She couldn't remember much before age seven, when many of the behaviors I was observing had begun to develop. If I persisted in my role as the befuddled but persistent detective, she would permit me to help her as she recovered memories, dreams, and associations.

Often I would need to ask her to repeat something said unclearly. Or perhaps I would inquire about a tone of voice, an intonation, a phrasing, or an emphasis. It was a game in which I needed to repeatedly demonstrate that I was closely attentive and engaged. Nonetheless, she seemed to remain consciously unaware of the content or the dynamics of our halting dialogue.

As the months passed, I found myself continuing to imitate her posture or voice, or pursuing her by carefully noticing the qualities described above. Meanwhile, she began to grow increasingly aware of elements of rage and pain that were operating deep within her. She became convinced that they were dictating her behavior in some way that remained unclear to her.

Although the "Columbo" hours were often energetic and animated, many other sessions were marked by the familiar lifeless despair. Yet,

Judy began noting that she felt most alive during these treatment hours, to the point that she even began to fantasize about stretching the sessions out, and having dinner with me. She became openly resentful upon hearing that another session had come to an end and wondered why I wouldn't "just keep going." I did my best to explore the fantasies of dinner or disappointment that the hour had to end. Like the attempts to examine the sense of lifelessness in the hour and her reports of life between sessions, there was little productive response. All she knew was that my imitations of her were funny and it was "stupid" to end a good session and send her away.

> *Judy:* Yes, I see the pattern. Nothing happens in my life. But so what? Are you telling me that I'm causing it? Not true! It just happens. I just feel like this. It comes, it goes.
>
> *Therapist:* Like other events in your life? You're powerless. Your dad and mom come and go and you have no influence. [Such responses seemed to strike a flicker of connection signaled only by a quick tightening of his jaw and torso. This would be followed by a deeper slump into passivity.]

My cumulative impression of her associations, with the history we had gradually pieced together, was a clear sense that these treatment hours recapitulated the visits she'd had with her absent father following her parents' divorce. Increasingly, it seemed evident to me that she was enacting her father's role, emotionally uninvolved, while I played the part she had once played during his weekly visitations, namely trying to engage him. The difficulty appeared to be finding a way to meaningfully introduce this possibility back into the work for our joint consideration.

No matter how hard I presented such considerations, Judy seemed unable to link her behavior during the sessions to the experiences she described more frequently from her past (the rate was glacial). Yet, it was at precisely those junctures, when I struggled to help her find the link, that a permitted imitation of her posture or expression would quickly bring her to life. She had no trouble seeing her lifeless gestures and expressions when I imitated them, when I brought aliveness into the relationship. Yet, she seemed completely unable to recall or visualize her behavior until there was some graphic display. How could this be? Was it organic? What was I playing into?

Our hours together seemed somewhat more productive. She was becoming a little more aware of inner motivating states, and her life outside therapy was also improving. I felt concerned that our interaction appeared to be her only emotional contact with other people. Increasingly, I felt that I was required to bear an inordinate amount of the responsibility for lifting her out of her lifelessness during the treatment hour. If things were improving, even slowly, why was I more tired and concerned? The sense of burden and concern about keeping it all going struck me as an important piece of the transferential puzzle. I already had some sense of my own reasons for getting into this position where I take on responsibility in this manner. I also understood how I could come to resent such a burden. Still, I felt that I had not reached that juncture yet. I was intrigued by my own confusion and by my positive engagement with her.

The difficulties had me engaged. I sensed something more at work here, if only I could understand it! I did not feel in a competition but in some kind of game. The concern was whether I had the capacity to play the game. Yet, this was not the most difficult or demanding patient I worked with. What was this concern about time passing and nothing happening? Often I had the sense of pursuing something alive and desirable, but hidden, a treasure hunt in which I might never reach the longed-for objective! I believed that it must be related to her frustration at making consistent and meaningful contact with both of her parents.

Judy's expressed frustration continued. This seemed to tap into my sense of concern. By her description, the content of most hours evaporated before she even left the waiting room. Still, this enigmatic person continued to be punctual and rarely missed appointments. As I was engaged, so was she. I felt certain that she needed me to continue in the role of interested pursuer, yet I continued to feel the growing imbalance in the responsibility that each of us had assumed for understanding the meaning of our work.

Judy clearly enjoyed the involvement, but I felt that we were getting stuck in the Columbo-style gamesmanship and were not gaining a mutual sense of the deeper issues that had her stuck in life and perhaps therapy. Merely playing the game gave it no closure—and I knew that any gains would be transitory without understanding and integration.

I increasingly believed that we were reliving Judy's feelings about her involvement with both parents, prior to their separation and divorce when Judy was seven years old. Judy described her father as an energetic, warm, and playful man, who was the center of her family's life. Once divorced, however, he became bitter and withdrawn. Worst of all, he was mostly unresponsive during his visits. Judy would do her best to engage him, while coaxing him to open up to her. By the end of each visit, he would become enlivened and animated, as if somehow restored to his former self.

To me the repetitious pattern seemed clear. Why wasn't it useful in treatment? More labored questioning revealed that her father's animated vitality would disappear at the end of each visit, requiring her to coax him all over again, the next time they met. I noted the similarity between this scenario and our sessions and wondered aloud about it. Were we re-creating this dynamic for some reason? Was there something to be learned from the Columbo motif?

In spite of the clear descriptions and apparent parallel, Judy saw no such connection. We were back to, "Huh? I don't get it. What do you mean? Why do you keep saying that kind of stuff?"

I saw that my queries about the similarity usually triggered the regressed, clouded, confusional, and lifeless state that had marked our earlier interaction. What was the need for this dynamic to be repeated? There was something more important about "running the replay" than about understanding it! The activity itself was important and gratifying, but why? Feeling a bit slow on the uptake (even now, I feel foolish as I recall this while writing), I said to myself, "Why didn't I realize it? *I want understanding; she wants the experience!*"

One day, in yet another repetition of this pattern of interactions between us, I said to Judy that I would like to describe some of my responses and concerns about our work in the hope that we could understand more. I suggested that it would be helpful if she noticed any responsive chord within herself after any of my comments. I also told her that the feelings I was registering seemed quite specific to our hours and related to something she might be experiencing. These were feelings that didn't precede the hour and seemed unrelated to what was occurring in my own life outside the office. They seemed to be part of our work. She sat up.

With that introduction, I said that I felt I was shouldering a huge responsibility for fighting through the lifelessness that she so often seemed to display. I explained that I was aware of wanting to engage her in some mutual discussion, but feared she might disappear at any moment. I described my sense of anxiety that I might fail in that effort. Most powerful and inexplicable to me was my dread of feeling shut out and alone.

I talked of the distress I felt as I groped for the right words or ideas. I also described the discouragement I experienced, knowing that even if I succeeded in bringing her out during a particular session, I would have to do it all over again the next time we met. I then inquired, Was this something like her experiences with her father that she had described, or perhaps with her mother, or someone else that I didn't even know to consider?

As I presented my feelings in this manner, Judy's face changed. She became both alert and tearful. She was smiling and crying simultaneously. She replied:

> *Judy:* You've said that I was being like my father before, and that I was doing it to you, shutting you out, the way he did to me. I didn't get it then. But you never said that you felt something whenever that happened. What you've just told me is different. I was afraid that you'd disappear! (Tearfully) I loved my father. He used to carry me around and sing when I was little. But after the divorce he was different—strange, angry, formal. Those visits with him . . . I didn't know what was going on. He was everything and then he was gone. And I was stuck with her (mother). She was depressed, always depressed. The house felt terrible.
>
> I didn't know it, but I was afraid that you'd go away, and take all the feelings. Everything good was sucked out of the house.

Therapist: Oh?

Judy: Dr. [X] did [leave], and I liked him, too. Then he moved away. [I wondered, did she link her positive feelings toward Dr. X with the fact of his leaving? Was that the case with her father? Might that be another facet of her hiding her involvement with me? All of this could be explored later.] I kind of wondered when you would stop trying with me, when you'd leave me.

Therapist: Just like with your dad, the other doctors, friends, and—?

Judy: Yes, yes! I never felt alive after that. I just existed. I needed you to feel!

Her comments opened the door to many implications and possibilities for exploration: withholding herself to be in the position of the sought after one; fears of responsibility for loss; futility in life; personal defectiveness; etc.

This treatment enactment and my countertransference experience had opened a window onto the dynamics of the transference. As the therapy progressed, I had become the child who strove desperately to reach the lost father. I had also come to symbolize the bright, lively father who could be lost at any moment, if Judy relaxed her terrified grip on him.

My disclosure about the painful feelings Judy had evoked in me opened up new areas for exploration. Did she suspect that there were causal connections between her affective bonds and her losses? How did her own needs and wishes relate to those losses? What had been the nature of their earlier relationship? What form had her parental relationships taken, early and later, and how had these been affected by the divorce? In what ways had the divorce trauma altered the dynamics of her personality organization?

Gradually, the reason why she needed more than a simple clarification of the dynamics of our interaction became clear. Her recognition of her need for an affective and affirming response as the motivation for the repetition led to an increased understanding of her sense of invisibility—a profound narcissistic injury. If she and her needs and wishes were invisible to her parents, then how could her words or behaviors have an impact on anyone? Her father had come to assume such prominence in Judy's life, not only because of the developmental timing of the separation and divorce, an oedipal struggle in which she felt she and her mother had both lost, but he had been an alternative to an earlier, overwhelmed, and chronically dissociated mother, with whom Judy could not form a consistent bond. She had fears that she, like mother, had been inadequate to keep father's interest. Thus she identified with her internal perception of mother and become hopeless.

She had learned early in life that it didn't matter what she genuinely felt, thought, or needed. Only her negative behaviors could engage a consistent response, and even that was brief and aversive. Yet, better something than nothing.

There was no doubt that the descriptions of my affective response to her enactment had served as a crucial element in opening up this deepening of the treatment. In contrast, my earlier interpretive clarification of the transferential nature of the patient's repetitious behavior, along with my identification of links to earlier events, had proved to be of little use. They were only me doing my job. It wasn't personal enough. The key point: In this treatment situation, the understandings and clarifications achieved significance only after they were linked to the experience of my own affective involvement in the patient's enactment.[1]

This case history demonstrates that action-oriented, externalizing, and non-self-observant patients like Judy need to know directly and urgently that we experience an authentic affective involvement with them during treatment. At the same time, our descriptions of these affective responses must be carefully and clearly worded and connected to clearly defined elements in the treatment hour.

Why is this aspect of treatment so important? Experience shows that our felt responses, as related to particular circumstances within treatment, often provide a powerful contrast to the patient's early experience of being invisible to parents. In the end, my permitted imitations became a way of affirming that the patient was seen and had some impact. Much later in treatment, we found the same dynamic operating in a far more

---

1. Elvin Semrad frequently told us that treatment could only work when we joined the patient where he or she was. More easily defined than accomplished.

subtle voice. Periodically, Judy would respond to a clarification or comment with "right" or "got it." Her tone would be clear, but a sense of briefness and abruptness were in the words. It sounded as if she were not only ending the line of discussion with a seemingly affirmative expression, but the change in her voice sounded as if she had gone away. At first I wondered if there had been some shift. To this she responded with, "No, I understood." After several such episodes, I said, "I guess that you're telling me that I should shut up and drop that?" She laughed, and said, "Hey! You're sharp, got me on that one." The brief words and her tonal shift had signaled dissociation and closure. The laughter at my direct comment was the hide and seek phenomenon, and the excitement of being sought out and discovered. We could then explore the meanings and needs being played out. In many cases, the painful awareness of the experience of invisibility occurs when the patient consciously realizes that his or her words, actions, needs, wishes, experiences, or feelings go unseen, misinterpreted, or dismissed by the important others.

The experience with Judy seems extreme, in terms of the actions that were required by her unique style of engagement. Yet, many patients have described moments where they have had the sense of being two people—one whom they recognize as themself but who is unseen, and a second, standing close by, who appears to resemble them. It is this lookalike who is actually the one seen by the parents. Without realizing it, they live out their lives as the lookalike, full of resentment but needing a connection, albeit a false one. In treatment, they may come to recognize their anger and the underlying neediness that has led them to participate in the charade.

A man in this situation heard his mother describing him and his accomplishments to his aunt. When he told her that he had not even participated in these activities, she stopped him and said, "Nonsense, of course you did." From many such experiences, he developed a sense of what his mother wanted him to be and he tried to become that. For many years he enacted a false self, while trying to please and win her. During the process of development, many of these individuals come to view their own behavior as insignificant and lacking impact. Since it never provoked a consistently valid response from their parents, how could it be expected to affect others in any meaningful way?

Here is where the countertransference can play an important role in therapy. When a patient in this situation does manage to elicit a clear response that contains an authentic affect from the clinician, and providing that the response is mutually examined, then the patient's long held assumptions about being invisible will be usefully challenged. Declarations of feelings of concern, understanding, and involvement by the therapist are virtually meaningless, or even counterproductive in this treatment scenario. In fact, such avowals may have much more to do with the therapist's denial of negative countertransference, frustration, and impasse than with the psychotherapeutic task at hand. What the patient actually needs most during these enactment crises is evidence that the clinician has been going through something related to the patient's own felt experience of the treatment.

The key step in using the countertransference in this way occurs when the therapist successfully metabolizes his or her response, then restates it during the hour, in brief, clear terms directly related to the patient's own experience. In describing such an experience, I search for what feels like the relevant historical dynamic in the patient's experience and present it as a possibility. Even if incorrect, it emphasizes that I see our interaction as coming from the patient's need to communicate with me. It clarifies that the focus is not on my feelings, but on the patient's underlying needs that we are both searching to understand.

On the other hand, the uninvited inclusion of our felt responses to patient enactments can disrupt and distort the process of treatment. This point should be strongly emphasized: What the patient needs from us are descriptions of countertransference affects that have been internally assessed and metabolized, not the raw, spontaneous emotions triggered by enactments. In this regard, we need to keep in mind that these enactment-triggered feelings are our own, though stirred by the involvement with the patient. They emerge from our own characterologic makeup, and their sole relevance to treatment is that they can often be used to help understand the patient's experience. For this reason, we are obligated to assess our involvement and responses to enactments and to determine their origin within us, before introducing them into treatment. The clinician needs to be able to distinguish between issues in his or her life that resonate with the patient's material, and issues that are directly linked to the transferences and projections of the patient.

"Hank," a 35-year-old accountant, entered psychotherapy after a notable personal loss. He had begun therapy with a clinician who specialized in issues linked to bereavement. The work went well and Hank was able to grieve the acute loss. As the treatment unfolded, however, Hank began having a sense, an intuition, that the therapist had endured a similar loss. He wanted to know if his insight was correct, and the therapist responded by confirming it and then providing a few of the related details.

When Hank reentered therapy several years later, I asked him why he hadn't returned to the therapist who had been so helpful earlier. He said he wasn't sure, and then recalled that the therapist had moved . . . but he then associated to the incident in which he had asked about the former therapist's own bereavement. Hank recalled that "funny, something had changed" for him after the disclosure by the therapist. Continuing to associate, Hank began to recall his mother and his lifelong sense of obligation to care for her. More than anything else, he had always dreaded burdening his invalid mother with his own cares and concerns. When his former therapist confirmed her own loss, he came to regard the therapist in much the same way—as someone who had to be protected from the burden of his needs. With surprising clarity, Hank looked up and said, "Strange, I never thought about it, but I couldn't go on once she told me."

Could they have proceeded? Perhaps, if the therapist had been able to explore the associations and responses Hank was having. After the clinician's description of her own grief and bereavement, the treatment dynamic in Hank's case was permanently altered. Having seen how her revelations about loss had triggered similar feelings in him, Hank felt that he could no longer run the risk of expressing his pain during the treatment sessions. Much later in his work with me, he was able to uncover the resentment at his mother's illness and her inability to be fully available for his previously repressed needs and longings. His own needs and guilt for his own unconscious anger could only emerge in a setting where he did not feel required to re-live his obligation to take care of someone else.

While listening to one of my responses, a patient asked me why I seemed so animated about that particular issue. I asked him what my responsiveness meant to him. He explained that my vivid response made him wonder if I were reacting to something in his commentary, or to something from my own life. If my response was simply a reflection of my own experience, how could it be useful to him? He noted that I would then be reacting more from my own needs and would have lost sight of him.

Like many other interactions with patients over the years, these episodes have taught me to contain, understand, and then determine as best I can the origin of my responses before sharing them during the treatment hour. At the same time, I try to maintain spontaneity and responsiveness, even as I conduct this internal assessment from moment to moment.

The following case vignette describes a more common enactment that may be present for a long period before coming to light.

"Harold," a married man and father of two children, was a successful professional in several disciplines. He entered therapy after several losses and a serious car accident in which he had been a passenger. Following the accident and during his prolonged recovery and rehabilitation, he had functioned as if nothing had happened. Cheerful and entertaining to visitors, he amazed friends with his undaunted energy, determination, and continuous good spirits.

Having fully recovered physically, he returned to work and immediately received several rewards and a promotion for work started before the accident and completed at home during his recovery. Bright and effervescent, looking many years younger than his age, he took pride in not being bowed by his circumstances, and began a vigorous program of renewed physical activity. His recovery was a featured article in a magazine. As the months passed, however, he began to feel less energetic, developed sleep disturbances, became irritable, and then frankly depressed. His internist prescribed benzodiazepines and attributed these changes to the accident, reparative surgery, and numerous medications he had required. While the benzodiazepines were initially helpful, his symptoms outran increasing doses of medication. He was then referred for psychotherapy.

In therapy, he first presented his bright, energetic self—articulate, keenly observant, intellectually sophisticated. From the beginning, however, he worried that he might do better seeing a female therapist, in keeping with his sense that a cosmopolitan man like himself might need a more empathic person, a woman perhaps. He noted that I wore a suit and tie, was older; maybe I was too traditional. I was not as friendly and responsive as his friends' therapists, who were described as more casual. There seemed to be a steady stream of doubts and emerging criticisms in our initial meetings. I clarified that our evaluation was open to the option that someone else might be a better match for his needs. We could both consider that option.

In the third session, he mentioned that he had no sense of his own inner life. He had spent his life excelling, but feeling estranged from his own accomplishments. Somehow, they didn't feel like his own. He had always felt that he had to succeed for his parents. It was very important for them. Though long dead, he felt that his recovery from the accident was driven by the need to make them proud. Had there been room for moments of fear, dread, uncertainty, need for comfort, I wondered? "Come on doc, I was busy doing my act." "No room for other aspects of your experience," I responded.

He went on to describe his family of origin and its sense of expectations. It was soon clear that he had little sense of himself apart from the treadmill of fulfilling others' expectations. He dreaded the thought of letting go. Who would he be? I wondered, was this related to his depression so long after the losses, accident, and recuperation? With all of the accolades and the success at performing, had some dread about the emptiness of living as a performer begun to emerge? His early sessions included many references to important and accomplished people whom he knew and who admired him. Yet, despite his own successes, he felt less accomplished by comparison. They were real. He just looked good.

In a circumspect manner, he revealed that a previous therapy had ended when it became apparent that his therapist's comments were inappropriate and suggestive of a relationship outside the office. While he had found this suggestion flattering, like the suggestions of previous graduate school professors, he feared that he had charmed the man into overvaluing him and would worry about disappointing him. Again he would be performing. I wondered aloud how that might affect his considering work with me.

He responded that my being older and formal didn't give him the same sense of approval and he would like that. He also seemed offended that I did not seem as impressed with him as all of his friends and teachers had been. I did not convey to him a sense that he was special. In fact, he had been checking on me through his friends to learn what I was like. Based on this information, he had created an image of me that was conservative, solitary, and unresponsive, as opposed to his own view of himself as spontaneous, exuberant, and life-involved. During these early sessions, he continuously observed me in order to draw conclusions as to whether I liked him or not.

I responded by acknowledging his uncertainty and the sense of hurt in this situation with me, where he was not getting his more familiar affirmations. Maybe it would give us a chance to know him as he was, without the need to win approval for his performances. Perhaps we could identify his own sense of himself?

What became disquieting to me, however, was the way in which our seemingly genuine understandings of a dynamic interaction had no holding power. His impressive intellect seemed quite separated from his affective life. As his depression deepened, his demands for overt recognition and affirmation increased. His inability to grieve significant losses seemed connected to the energy invested in being a performing "self of the moment." It left him no time to grieve. That would come later. There was only this moment within which to perform. There was little enduring internal sense of deeper personal motivations, connections, and satisfactions. I also sensed that attending to loss meant accepting that something was gone forever and he would then feel the absence and incompleteness.

He was in a fairly constant projective state of anxiety, watching me and deciding how I felt about him by the way my voice sounded, how I looked opening the door, etc. Any exploration of his scrutiny was met with strongly held speculations as to what I must feel about him. Occasionally, he saw that it was he who didn't like me, mainly for withholding the demonstrations of approval he so easily received elsewhere. I clarified at such times that my simply buying into his demonstrated skills and accomplishments or responding to his capacities to engage in an entertaining way would distract us from understanding who he really was.

He would seem briefly comforted and reassured by my steadiness at these times, and we would continue for several more sessions. While I felt clear within myself about his distress and my concern for it, I was also aware of an increasing wariness within myself. With his constant critical scrutiny, he was searching for some evidence of a flaw or impropriety within me that he could use to discredit me. What was he touching that I feared?

For a number of weeks he continued his critical focus upon me and my responses. That was followed by a week in which he seemed quiet and reflective, with some understanding of the preceding hours. I then, mistakenly, started to end the session, and we both realized that I was actually ten minutes early. (The hour was not our regular one and had been rescheduled to a different time.) I could have attributed the miss-step to the change in schedule, but I found myself wondering why it had happened.

At first, he teased me about wanting to be rid of him, but then asked what might my reason be. I responded that I wasn't clear but would think about it. As I reflected, I remembered that I had been thinking that we were approaching the anniversary of his accident. I had wondered about his not mentioning it, but had decided to wait and listen to derivatives to see if it was lurking there. I had then looked at the clock. As I started to recount this to him, I realized that, more importantly, I had been fearful of disrupting the hour by mentioning the accident and returning to the turmoil of the previous sessions. I didn't want to ruin the hour (for me) by triggering something painful. I told him this, and he looked at me with a startled expression. That was exactly how he felt going into his house as a child. He feared causing some upset by making some seemingly innocent comments. He never knew what might trigger an upset. Thus he always tried to figure out what was necessary to please the important other person. That's why I was so upsetting for him. He never knew what to do in order to win my approval. He now seemed comfortable and at ease as we examined my response and the awareness that it triggered in him.

Although we had discussed a similar recognition months earlier about therapy being a place in which he could never feel "right, as in his home," he was much more engaged and enlivened on this occasion, because I had experienced a feeling akin to his. I had made a mistake out of my fear and wish to avoid something distressing that I would cause. He was jubilant.

Months later, I learned that life seemed real to him only in these resonant enactments where he could feel a connection with another. Otherwise, he was just thinking or performing to win accolades. This recognition was played out repeatedly over the years as a way to feel a living connection. His capacity to hold such moments gradually increased.

In this instance, I could have attributed my error to the change in scheduled hour, to fatigue, or to some other insignificant cause. Yet, I believe that these small errors are actually much more common that we realize. I'm also convinced that they provide the therapist an important opportunity to explore issues more deeply through the countertransference.

7

Twinship Transference

This chapter explores the dynamics of a particular, more subtle form of mutual enactment. Among the topics to be examined is the "alter-ego self-object transference" and its complex interactions with both members of the treatment dyad. Several case vignettes illustrate some of the ways in which this form of transference may unfold.

One of the more subtle and difficult to define treatment enactments takes place when a patient feels so alone and isolated, and yet so threatened by intimate contact, that he or she must establish an "alter ego," which is then projected onto the therapist. By relating to this inner projection rather than to the clinician *per se*, the patient unconsciously hopes to rebuild an early, injured part of his primary narcissistic-object relationship. This is a necessary step in the interrupted development of a cohesive sense of self. This aspect of the developing self was damaged in his or her earliest primary object attachment, usually with the mother, when there were repeated and persistent empathic lapses. This complex treatment dynamic has been explored by Kohut (1971), who defined it as "alter-ego self-object transference," or, more simply, "twinship transference." According to Kohut, this form of enactment often occurs in patients struggling with painful feelings of loneliness and estrangement from others that developed in their earliest relationship and has been masked by more superficial adaptations.

The dynamics of twinship transference can be seen in the case of "Frank," a senior hospital administrator who entered treatment at the urging of his wife and colleagues. Frank obviously possessed intellectual brilliance and professional skill. Yet his brusque, abrasive manner was increasingly alienating many of the people in his life.

After a few treatment sessions, it became evident that Frank was experiencing psychotherapy as a punishment for what seemed to him to be minor expressions of frustration with incompetent subordinates and children. These initial consultations were a source of shame. They were a narcissistic injury. He saw himself as a prominent person at the pinnacle of his professional career, the leader of an internationally acclaimed medical center; yet he found himself talking to a virtual stranger about personal issues that he would never have deemed worthy of discussion with anyone. How foolish! Might this attitude explain the fact that Frank remained uniformly hostile and condescending throughout the hour? Indeed, he often communicated his scorn for the psychotherapeutic process (and for me) with his tone of voice, with his devaluing words, and with his physical gestures of dismissal: "What use could you be to me? You sit in a small, odd-looking office, just talking to people all day long, while I must confront urgent issues and make complex decisions that affect thousands of lives. I don't know why I come here!"

I responded by agreeing that his question about the usefulness of psychotherapy was a reasonable one. Might it also contain his wish to find some value in our endeavor? I then suggested that we might try to explore and understand those situations and difficulties that inexplicably seemed to jeopardize his accomplishments. Frank's doubts about therapy often sounded like some of the same devaluations and criticisms he had leveled at others for whom he worked! These subordinates seemed not to understand his needs and how, through their ineptitude, they left him exposed and vulnerable. By framing our initial work in this manner, he could cognitively focus upon something important to him, namely managing frustrating situations in a way that protected and enhanced previous successes.

I was also concerned that too early in the process I might also fail to him in this way. While I knew that empathic lapses would occur and become significant issues, I wanted to find a way to initially build some successful experience in the treatment. Did I have a blind spot that prevented me from seeing the lonely, isolated position in which he felt trapped? I suspected that beneath this haughty self-importance, he feared being exposed as a fraud who only looked accomplished. I had seen this with many other people like him. Certainly, Frank's angry reactions to family, acquaintances, colleagues, and subordinates showed me his sensitivity to any suggestion that he might feel vulnerable. Yet the intensity of his angry rejection of others only served to increase his isolation. No one could get near this suffering man. Reflecting on his situation, I thought of the story of the roaring lion with a thorn in his paw. Like the lion, Frank's painful thrashings about warded off even would-be allies.

On several occasions, for example, he told me bluntly that I was "probably afraid to get out there in the real world and mix it up with real people! Staying in this little office protected me from the real give and take." I suggested that he might be able to use me because I was so different and removed from his world. Perhaps he could use me to reflect upon and examine his work and involvements, away from the fray. Even soldiers in combat needed time away from war to restore their fighting edge. These carefully chosen references to "using me" and being a soldier needing "R and R" sat well with him.

Despite his steady expressions of disdain, Frank attended the sessions regularly. On many occasions, he spent the hour describing his endless difficulties with numerous people—medical staff, insurers, government agencies—all of whom seemed intent on damaging him or otherwise frustrating his "reasonable objectives." They were all idiots and nincompoops! Only he had the clear vision.

I listened carefully, then suggested that it might be helpful for him to examine these situations carefully, in order to enhance the clarity of his perceptual lens. I also wondered out loud about his approach. Would he be more successful at gaining support for his ideas if he tried to convince with the facts, instead of constantly trying to prove that he was right and others were stupid?

Early in our work, Frank talked candidly about a dilemma that he was experiencing during the sessions. He explained that whenever he found my comments or inquiries useful, he would immediately grow fearful that my effectiveness might give me power over him, "I could wind up needing you," he said, "and then where would I be?" This was quickly followed by, "Don't worry, doc, I won't let it happen!"

I saw these exchanges as the beginning of his willingness to risk a more open engagement with his own needs and vulnerabilities. I agreed that from his point of view, he was indeed caught up in a painful predicament that stemmed directly from his view of the world. If life were nothing more than a power struggle, with some people dominant, the others, ruled from above, bitterly resent their submission. Then he could hardly afford to value understandings gained during the hour. Why? It was simple: If Frank found me useful and valued my participation, then he would have to face the danger that I use my alleged power to control him. On the other hand, if I seemed ineffective and of little value, he could not gain from our association. In that case he would feel foolish and exploited, since he would be participating in a useless endeavor. He nodded, smiled, and said, "You've got it!"

Were there, however, other possibilities? A deeper and more personal view that might serve him here? What if he considered the idea that he was in fact lonely and needed safe involvements with others, even if he couldn't trust that they actually even existed? In such a situation, the real danger might actually come from his own needs and not from the possibility that I would misuse him!

Frank's disclosures made it clear that he regarded his need for other human beings as the source of a dangerous vulnerability. Because he feared the risk of experiencing his existing needs and vulnerablities, he felt doomed to remain lonely, isolated, and helpless. He consciously denied and unconsciously affirmed his need for people by entering into an endless series of adversarial relationships. Thus he was simultaneously engaged with others, even as he held them at arm's length. We were already doing that in our rational clarifications.

When I outlined these key aspects of Frank's treatment dilemma, he nodded affirmatively and then turned away. Briefly, his facial expression changed.

His associations and preoccupations repeatedly confirmed that he lived in a world of dominance and submission at home, at work, everywhere; in constant struggles, he was never alone. In his mind, he was always replaying and anticipating new struggles and arguments. For him, such unremitting conflict was ordinary and usual. Wasn't that how life was for everyone, he inquired?

Of course, Frank understood the idea that other ways of living might be more peaceful and less painful. But that possibility remained only an abstraction for him. It had nothing to do with his own experience, which had been significantly devoid of understanding, care, respect, and empathy.

Repeatedly he expressed mystification at his wife's apparent affection for him and at her own easygoing self-acceptance. He marveled at her humorous but accurate caricature of his self-centeredness. Her ease in life contrasted sharply with his own continuous state of tension and his fighting endless fantasy-battles with opponents at work, with other drivers on the road, and even with other shoppers in the supermarket checkout line. This man lived in a world where he was continually at war without a single ally.

After five years of psychotherapy, Frank's provocative behavior at home and on the job had diminished significantly. Gradually, he had come to be regarded as a senior consultant and the voice of reason at his hospital, rather than as a brilliant but volatile "loose cannon." Frank saw these changes taking place in his behavior, and he linked them to his therapy. Yet, he was unable to see the connection between his changes at work and the issues we examined, primarily because, by his own description, he never remembered what was said during the treatment hour.

Intelligent and thoughtful, Frank cognitively recognized the need to scrutinize his emotional life carefully. He valued the changes in his behavior as important. But he also saw them as superficial, because he felt unchanged within himself. He predicted that these behavioral alterations would sooner or later evaporate in a full-blown emotional crisis, unless he were to change his inner landscape in some fundamental way. Although he was living better and feeling better, he sensed that he had not truly changed, and that he still had not achieved the kind of self-understanding that would be required for a comfortable life.

In our seventh year of work, I began noticing a pattern of repetitive interactions. On several occasions, Frank would describe conflicts within the medical care delivery system. He described these outrages clearly and compellingly, and I felt a rising personal fury and disgust at the reduced quality, to say nothing of the diminished availability, of the less-than-optimal medical services he discussed.

It was evident to me that my personal feelings on this subject were synchronous with his. I, too, felt a sense of moral outrage at the appalling stories of medical mismanagement that he so frequently related. My internal affective responses were frequently powerful, but I said nothing about them. Instead, I kept the focus on Frank, and on his responses, fantasies, and associations. I did my best to help explore the meaning of these incidents for him.

On one occasion when he raised this issue, I called his attention to some of his earlier discussions and then asked him if he knew why the topic had come up once again. He responded with a laugh and said, "I know what really gets you! I can tell. It gives me a chance to digress, get away from whatever we're talking about."

He went on to explain quite openly that whenever he felt he'd succeeded in making me angry about these medical issues, it gave him the feeling that he'd gained power and control over me. Yet his comments on this particular occasion lacked their usual hostile and devaluing tone. I wondered to myself: *Why the difference in affective quality?* After thinking about this question for a few minutes, I noted that he seemed genuinely pleased to know that he could affect me strongly by describing these problems. I also asked him what he thought the shift in tone might mean.

Frank blanched noticeably at my remarks, then fell silent. After a bit, he explained that he had felt "distracted" as I was speaking. Then, in a soft voice, he went on:

> *Frank:* I know that you care, and I need you to care. But I have to control it. When I bring up these things, these medical issues, I see that you feel outraged by them, just as I do. It's like I can control your feelings. I can affect you at will.
>
> *Therapist:* And if you find that you and I do have similar feelings about certain issues, what happens then?
>
> *Frank* (responding quickly): It feels close. Like we're standing beside each other. (When he spoke again, it was through tears.) I want

to be close, but I'm afraid it will do something to me. I'll lose control—with you, with my wife. . . .

As we continued to explore the different facets of this interaction, it became clear that Frank needed a focus external to himself, a safe psychic space in which he could share mutual feelings and understandings with another. His strong opinions and feelings about medical care gave him that space. It was a safe topic, and he knew that if he kept the discussion focused on the flawed health care delivery system, he would be invulnerable to attack, disappointment, or exploitation. We were both looking at an external issue that we both cared about. Anything more intimate than this predictable and stilted kind of interaction was extremely threatening. If he admitted his hunger for intimacy, he knew this disclosure would leave him feeling weak and needy. It would also reignite his fears of being dominated, while triggering the despised needfulness and shameful vulnerability that lay at the heart of his defective sense of himself. What he feared most, he said, was that his needs would lead him to become a "Wuss," a limp sycophant who would be endlessly humiliated and scorned, most of all by himself.

For the first time during our seven years of work, Frank cried and associated to his powerful, frightening, and violent father. A passionate man, the father could also be dangerous and irrational at times. His mother, for her part, had been cold, distant, compulsive, and controlling. As a child, Frank had yearned to be held. But he felt safe with neither parent, and could not take the risk of asking for more intimacy. Instead, he had always externalized such yearnings.

He and his father had shared a passion for music. As long as Frank's emotions could be focused on an external object in this way, he had felt protected from his own vulnerability. Was it any wonder that he depended on a similar external focus—our shared passion for good medicine—to provide a safe framework for our treatment interaction? By lambasting the negative aspects of bad medicine, he could be sure to direct the anticipated attack away from himself. In this way, I could be the longed for, caring father whom he "stood beside." At the same time, however, he could control the father's potentially dangerous aggression by focusing it elsewhere. For this lonely man, making certain that my emotional experience exactly matched his own was a key aspect of twinship transference. Yet he never asked if I shared his feelings about the importance of high-quality medical care, and I did not overtly confirm the correctness of his perceptions about this issue.

As we examined this enactment together, other dimensions of his past experience were revealed. He began to see how our shared focus on good medicine allowed him to feel that he was achieving authentic intimacy with another person. That insight led to a desire for professional allies with whom he could feel safe. At the same time, Frank was also beginning to understand that his longing for emotional comfort was linked to fantasies of fusion with his mother, and that these were rooted in an original, shame-laden core sense of himself that had been repressed and then defended against by his narcissistic disdain and hostility. Often extremely subtle, these kinds of mutual transference enactments can sometimes trigger treatment scenarios in which the therapist's hopes and wishes for the patient will become part of the unfolding therapeutic dynamic.

Such a scenario took place with a patient named "Richard," a 45-year-old physician who had been treated by a female colleague for many years before beginning to work with me. As the colleague later recalled, Richard had a history of engaging in excessive work, while also shouldering other significant responsibilities. He would then sink into periodic episodes of depression. His endless striving for success and the admiration of others seemed to mask his essentially masochistic character. An established physician who was enjoying a successful clinical and academic career, Richard lived within a longstanding, stable marriage. He had two adolescent children with whom he appeared to be deeply involved.

After several years of intensive psychotherapy two and three times a week, Richard had uncovered and resolved much of his repressed aggression. He understood that his unconscious (and for him, unacceptable) hostility and anger had been feeding his guilt and depression for many years. In typically neurotic fashion, Richard felt exceedingly guilty about his unconscious hostility, as if it were being consciously expressed in his actions. Small errors on his part would often cause acute and severe depressions, gloomy eruptions that served as evidence of the dangerous forces he sensed at work within his troubled psyche. On some occasions, however, the depressions would be relieved by unconsciously orchestrated "accidents"—a fall, a bump, or perhaps a bruise. Invariably, these mishaps were self-caused, and it soon became apparent that Richard's aggression was being directed against his own person.

This patient's distorting guilt had been masked and compensated for by his excessive work, and by his exaggerated willingness to assume responsibility, while endlessly proving his reliability. In short, he had spent much of his life struggling to consciously eradicate his own unconscious but unacceptable wishes.

Early in his treatment, Richard recognized his enmeshment with (and his struggles against) his frightened, fragile, and controlling mother. She had sought to cope with her own fear of the world by regarding him as a fragile person, a narcissistic extension of her sense of herself, who required extra care and protection. Richard felt controlled by her. At the same time, he felt obligated to reassure her by denying any of his own needs that seemed to be separate from her wishes. Richard felt intruded upon by his mother. Yet, he also feared the same world that had so terrified her. He had spent a great deal of time alone with her as a child and had felt the burden of comforting her while also having to suppress his own wishes and needs. This behavior had earned him praise for being "good and responsible." The unconscious rage that this controlling behavior mobilized within him required endless vigilance and perpetual "undoing" through good and responsible actions. His episodes of depression and overwork were overt manifestations of the inner conflicts produced by this painful relationship with his mother.

Richard's unresolved conflicts had been further exacerbated by his recurrent colitis. Coincident with the onset of his own illness, his mother had developed a chronic disorder that left her with mild facial asymmetry. Both of their illnesses persisted for four or five years. On many occasions, the two would find themselves at home, attacked by illness. Or, they would set off together to consult their various doctors. These continuing ailments only deepened the enmeshment and further muddled the already poorly defined boundaries between mother and son.

During his early adolescence, Richard had escaped from this regressive relationship by avoiding his home. He disdainfully distanced himself from his mother's intrusions, while treating her with a neutral civility that barely masked his hostility. He also engaged in counter-phobic and counter-dependent activities that included an intense denial of risks. This abrupt separation and the resulting high-risk behavior helped Richard develop a number of adaptive capacities. It also allowed him to gain a high degree of skill in various sports and other risky, outdoor activities. Concomitantly, these skills were paid for with an accumulation of physical injuries.

During this period of adolescent separation, Richard was accident-prone for several years and frequently required medical attention. At one point during treatment, he blithely remarked, "It [getting hurt frequently] seemed like the price I had to pay for getting away." Closer scrutiny revealed that, paradoxically, these same chronic injuries served to keep his mother connected to him, since she felt compelled to assist him in obtaining necessary medical care. He also remained aware of the fact that his mother was always thinking and worrying about him, and that the accidents perpetuated her continued concern. Thus, his apparent separation from mother was only superficial; he continued to hold onto her by perpetuating her worry about him.

As these unconscious conflicts and motivations emerged into Richard's consciousness during therapy, he began to recognize his anger at his mother for treating his wishes and his feelings as mere extensions of her own tangled inner life. He recalled experiences in which she coughed and would then insist that *he* take medicine because he "must be sick." Gradually, Richard came to understand that his initial sense of guilt for hurting his mother by leaving home had disguised a deeper unconscious wish to hurt her because of her emotional unavailability and self-centeredness.

He now recognized that he had experienced a painful disregard for his true self by endlessly responding to her excessive concerns about non-existent physical dangers. This dynamic, along with the endless and unrealistic worrying about him that had dominated her life for many years, prevented her from actually seeing her son. Somehow, his genuine worries and concerns never really became visible to her. As Richard and his therapist continued to explore this relationship, he became aware of a persistent fantasy that he had "exhausted" his mother with his colitis. After all, she was always tired and depressed! He concluded that his chronic illness had become the center of a battleground on which he sought to wear her down in order to find the longed-for "good mother" within her. Furthermore, he saw that his wish to "find" her also included a wish to injure her, and to make her tolerate and love his "shit."

As the treatment unfolded, he realized that the concomitant emergence of his mother's illness, so soon after the onset of his own colitis, only served to confirm the destructive power of his unconscious anger. Trapped in this powerful dynamic, Richard had no choice but to try to contain his "badness," while also performing an endless, guilt-driven penance for the "injuries" he had caused his mother. An unconscious conclusion was that his power to reach and affect her was destructive. Thus, understandably enough, he was uncertain about his capacity to be a loving person. This continuing theme of "undoing injuries" would later prove crucial in his decision to become a physician. It would also inspire his immense dedication to the task of developing better care for the needy and the indigent (whom he regarded as society's "damaged and injured").

Later in his treatment, Richard discovered an involvement with his therapist that appeared to recapitulate an aspect of these maternal issues. Over the years of their work, he noted that whenever he would consider launching new ventures or making life changes, his therapist would explore these aspirations with him and then raise questions about various aspects of the proposed endeavor. All too often, however, Richard experienced these questions as signs that she found him foolhardy or once again over-committed to some momentary enthusiasm. Like his mother she must be "too" worried about him.

The parallels between the therapist's concern for him and his mother's intrusiveness seemed obvious, but Richard steadfastly denied that he was experiencing the clinician's inquiries in the same way he had once responded to warnings and cautions from his mother. Each time this treatment scenario occurred, Richard did his conscious best to weigh the issues dispassionately. The results were mixed, however. On some occasions, he merely tried to reassure the therapist that his plans were prudent and safe. On those occasions, he felt he was acting out of mere intellectualization and obligation, as a responsible individual who wanted to be a "good patient" (like the "good son" he had once been).

At other times, Richard went ahead and took the risk in spite of the therapist's purported worries, although he was careful to cloak his actions by contending that they had been necessary and unavoidable. There were also some occasions on which he postponed or even shelved a planned risk on the advice of the therapist and then wound up feeling resentful and controlled as a result. None of these complex internal interactions was discussed, although Richard felt them sharply and also felt convinced that they were having a significant impact on his treatment.

But then a change occurred. During a painful confrontation with his distrust for women, Richard consciously addressed this maternal trans-ference repetition with his therapist. He reported that he now found himself reacting to any explorations or inquiries from the clinician as if his mother had been indirectly cautioning him by raising questions. (Even when she *hadn't* raised such questions, he had assumed she was thinking them and doing her best to restrain herself!)

While he understood that there might be legitimate reasons for the therapist's questions (namely, the destructive tendencies he had displayed both in his past and in his more recent behavior), he felt annoyed, guilty, and also excited by his sense of her involvement. He yearned to be seen by her as reasonable and responsible. On the conscious level, he did not wish to make his choices reactively, nor was he interested in shelving his more challenging projects. Instead, he wanted to reach decisions that were his own, and free of conflict. At the same time, he wanted to hold onto his exciting sense that the therapist was urgently involved through worry. For her part, the clinician wondered if the patient might be concerned that their relationship might not survive his achieving independence. Did he need to keep her attached by "worrying" her, even half-teasingly at times, as he had once alarmed his fretful mother? While examining this possibility, the therapist asked if his responses might have been different had she phrased her inquiries differently, or introduced them in some other manner. Richard responded, "It wouldn't matter. Your voice, your eyes, your posture—something would have given you away."

He went on to describe his growing suspicion that he *needed* to draw her in, and that she could not help responding because of who she was. Somehow, he needed her to give him the kind of attention that his mother had once provided. In fact, he still hungered for those same cautions and queries that he had formerly resented and rebelled against (but had also clung to as his only familiar and reliable form of attachment). Richard was surprised at the clarity of these perceptions, and he also recognized that he had subtly enacted this scenario with his therapist on many different occasions.

As the two of them explored this dynamic and examined his secret fantasies of omnipotence (beneath which lay his authentic wish for a more mutual relationship), Richard enumerated the various instances in which she had cued him in this way. He was now able to see that her concerns were about him as she knew him. As she later told me, he was correct in this. In many instances, she had been concerned based on his past behavior, and many of her questions were related to past experiences he had described in therapy. They also explored their separate perspectives on his underlying mistrust of participating in any but this familiar dynamic. Richard wanted to work out relationships differently, yet he found the compulsively repeated sequence of enactments describe above to be strongly rooted within.

While treating Richard, the therapist had always been careful and reserved. Fortunately, his capacity for self-observation and examination eliminated the need for a more active style on her part. What he needed most was for her to simply be present, in the manner described in Winnicott's "The Capacity to be Alone" (1958). Nonetheless, this keenly observant therapist recognized the accuracy of Richard's description as soon as he offered it. She quickly began to identify instances of this behavior in herself, even during periods in which she had looked on silently, saying nothing.

As Richard continued to explore his distrust of women, based now on his newly perceived recognition of this maternal transference, he speculated aloud, "To me, you're like a mother, maternal and caring. I hope that you don't take offense. You do seem to want the best for me. It must be a fine line for you. I guess I would see anyone who cared as trying to control me, or else I would try to see things through their eyes and not mine. All I can tell you is that, for me, that care and control seemed intertwined. I'd like it to be more separate."

The enmeshment of care and control described above was particularly difficult for this patient, and understandably so. Richard needed to feel cared about; but the price for such caring was high, since it required him to tolerate what he resentfully experienced as a feeling of "being controlled." Examining his dilemma in a transference-countertransference context loosened the painful inner straitjacket in which this double bind had placed him.

As Richard continued the work of psychotherapy, he moved on to explore his past relationship with his father, who had been replaced by the medical doctors of his adolescence. (These medical men became the sought-after allies in the struggle to disentangle from mother during that period of his life.)

Although briefly outlined here, Richard's story illustrates a subtle but powerful dynamic in which the therapist is drawn into an enactment, and then plays a role for the patient. His struggle raises an important question: How are we to keep attuned to our natural wishes for the patient's betterment, while also making certain that these aspirations do not interfere with the therapy?

Was it a mistake, in this case, to somehow lose sight of the fact that the therapist was feeling like a protective mother and then subtly enacting that role for the patient? Or was her performance actually a necessary part of the treatment enactment?

The subtlety of this interaction can be seen in the fact that even when the clinician had stopped questioning Richard's choices, the slightest pause or hesitancy was enough to convey her concern. Did she in fact needlessly extend this enactment process through her "good wishes" and thus delay the recognition and elaboration of the dynamic?

Or did the patient have an urgent need to relive these experiences in the less charged and more open atmosphere of the treatment hour? In hindsight, it seems clear that this patient did need the kind of complex interaction that gradually unfolded during these many sessions.

This form of subtle and mutual transference enactment occurs more frequently than any other, and seems too little examined.

8

Unsolicited Personal Disclosures: Useful Strategy or Therapeutic Mistake?

Occasionally, personal historical disclosures by the therapist can be helpful to the patient. In many other situations, however, such uninvited disclosures can interfere significantly with treatment. When should a therapist disclose personal information to a patient? The author's recommendations are illustrated with case studies.

Although the preceding chapters have included numerous examples of personal disclosure by the therapist, it should be made clear that these revelations involved transferential responses that played an integral part in the therapeutic process. They did not provide personal historical detail of the therapist's life, but consisted of descriptions of affective responses and possible meanings triggered by enactments within the treatment setting. These disclosures, if chosen appropriately, can often be quite useful in helping the clinician to clarify issues currently being played out in the treatment. The clinical situation changes markedly, however, when the information to be revealed by the therapist involves personal information taken from his or her own life.

Experience shows that the risks of interfering with treatment and perhaps even harming the patient are substantially higher when the material to be shared consists of such unsolicited biographical data. All too often, in that scenario, this new and undigested information only serves to further complicate the patient's already formidable task of sorting out feelings and motivations. It should also be noted that the impulse on the part of the therapist to reveal something personal is most often the signal of a countertransference event in which the clinician is attempting to avoid, end, or circumvent some difficult issue.

In spite of these clinical risks, however, there will undoubtedly be occasions on which the therapist feels a strong inclination to introduce such unsolicited materials into treatment. These are moments in which one feels tempted to say, "Yes, I've been through that," or perhaps, "I certainly understand, because of what happened to me."

In my own case, these kinds of urgings often arrive with great force. But experience has taught me that I need to resist them. Instead of acting on them, I have learned to carefully scrutinize my own transferences, in order to see if I can learn more about the actual origins of this sudden impulse to "tell." My approach to this issue is based upon my experience that when I *have* made such disclosures, I've usually found them to be unhelpful, or even counterproductive. Quite frequently, the revelations merely reflected something about my own feeling state during the session that I wished to avoid. Later, after the session ended, I would often discover that my alleged compassion and concern were actually masking my own negative and unanalyzed feelings of powerlessness and frustration, exclusion, competitiveness, or anger as I listened to the patient.

In an earlier chapter, I described the paralyzing effect on treatment when a therapist revealed during a session that she had experienced a personal loss similar to one experienced by her patient. In that instance, the latter had asked for the biographical information, which the clinician then supplied. In several treatment situations, however, I was confronted with a sudden, spontaneous impulse to reveal personal information that at first seemed directly related to the patient's own experience.

In one such instance a middle-aged woman named "Susan" was struggling to cope with a severe illness in one of her children. The child's health was deteriorating and the mother had become increasingly despairing that no treatment could save the youngster.

Susan's sadness and despair were profound. As our treatment sessions continued, I found myself inclined to point out that I had some experience with this same illness. Superficially, my motivation seemed apparent. I knew the patient well, felt distress at her plight, and wanted to gain some credibility. Hence I felt a strong need to encourage Susan in her struggle to remain closely involved with her ailing child.

My impulse to mention my own experience with this illness was quite urgent; I yearned to tell her that, in some way, I understood how "unbearable" her situation really was. I managed to contain this urge, however. Instead of acting on it, I did my best to examine its inner meaning for me. I soon realized that Susan had begun to withdraw emotionally from the child, and that I wanted to strongly encourage her reengagement.

Further reflection allowed me to see that I was identifying with the abandoned child in this situation. This meant that I was also distancing myself from an empathic understanding of the mother's distress. In fact, I was detaching myself from the anguish that had led her to withdraw and defend herself against what appeared to be an inevitable loss.

Quite simply, I was angry at her "abandonment." Why? Because it recapitulated certain events in my own life where I felt that I had experienced maternal abandonment while ill. All at once, I saw that I was in danger of doing to the patient exactly what she was doing to the child. In my transferential identification with her child, I was retreating from Susan's emotional distress!

After unveiling this hidden side of my motivation, I was able to rejoin the patient in a more genuine connection, and to be more capable of being fully present with her while she described the endless medical procedures, the nights of helpless anguish, the dashed hopes and failed treatments. I was also able to hear the anger she felt for medical doctors (including me) because of the limitations in our capacities, and her anger at the child for leaving her. Freed in this way to experience, express, and examine her anger and her powerful grief, the patient was able to rejoin her child emotionally, so that the two of them could live out together their mutual fear of losing one another.

This case illustrates the importance of carefully scrutinizing any impulse to make personal disclosures to a patient. But several earlier treatment experiences also underlined that point for me. On two different occasions before treating Susan, I had tried to offer reassurance to patients who faced approaching surgery. Because I had already undergone the surgical procedure, I assumed that I could ease their fears about it.

With both patients, I waited until we had spent some time examining their concerns and associations linked to the surgery, then mentioned the fact that I, too, had undergone this operation. In each instance, however, my comments proved essentially irrelevant. In fact, I had erroneously assumed that my experience equaled theirs, and that I could somehow reduce their anxiety by pointing out, "See, it went fine for me!"

Later I wondered: What if the surgery didn't go well for them? Why was I equating my experience with theirs, anyway? What was it I didn't want to know about their personal concerns, as the surgery approached? Were these operations bringing something up for me, some inner discomfort that had led me to want to tune out their worries? And why had I assumed that I understood the meanings of these surgeries for the patients involved? Fortunately, pausing to frame and then reflect on these questions allowed me to put my own experience aside and reengage with the patients.

A similar treatment episode occurred with "Roger," a middle-aged businessman who had entered treatment for anxiety and brief depressions. A self-made financial success with a working-class background, Roger had put himself through college and entered a world of affluent and influential people. He had married into an economically established family for whom he had mixed feelings. He felt himself to be the "not-quite-accepted outsider" from the "wrong side of the tracks" who would never fit in. He compensated for his projected inferiority by emphasizing his street-smarts in the real world and devaluing "those smart college kids."

His wife, who accompanied him during his first few appointments, presented herself as a polished sophisticate who wished only to be a source of help to everyone in her world. That was her explanation for her appearance at the early sessions; "to help." In fact, her behavior showed an angry manipulativeness based on a need to control and remain distant from people. Having been emotionally abandoned as a child, she trusted no one. As long as her husband felt inferior to her, he was constantly trying to win her. Over the years his growing anger at her rejection and control was revealed in his depression and denial of the clear messages she sent about her wishes to avoid him and be left alone.

Early in Roger's treatment, his wife announced that she wanted a divorce because "he would be happier with someone else." Gradually, it became evident that with the children grown, she wanted to separate and lead a private life apart from anyone. Getting him into treatment had been a way of getting him cared for by someone else.

As the divorce proceeded, Roger described himself as frustrated and furious at what he saw as the inequities of the legal system. For this patient, the unfairness of the "system," along with the painful feelings of angry impotence it aroused, had triggered several related childhood issues.

I listened carefully to Roger's angry complaints about the legal system. But my efforts to point out the similarities between these frustrating judicial procedures and his childhood experience (to say nothing of the sense of powerlessness he had often described in his marriage) seemed to produce little effect. Again and again, Roger insisted that his powerful feelings of rage and disgust were entirely the result of his present situation, even if the descriptions he used included the same words and phrases he'd employed when describing similar confrontations during his childhood and later in his business struggles. There was no link, he insisted, between these prior conflicts (and his ensuing rage) and the events that were unfolding now.

As his anger mounted and his fantasies of intemperate action increased, I cautioned him not to act on his angry impulses. At the same time, however, I felt a strong temptation to intervene and help him plan strategies that might effectively address his situation, so that he would not act self-destructively. Proceeding cautiously, I examined this urgent impulse on my part. Was I getting caught up in this patient's sense of powerlessness? Was that the hidden source of my need to help develop alternative strategies aimed at "preventing" his imagined actions?

Clearly, I had no real power to alter his proposed course of action. Nor could I realistically help him beyond exploring the basis for his fantasies and affects, while also encouraging him to scrutinize his motivation. Why was I even thinking about being powerful?

Inwardly debating these questions, I soon realized that joining in to help with "strategic planning" would essentially amount to confirming his own sense of the irrelevance of our work to his "real-life" situation. In my affective state, I was preparing to confirm that our endeavor was as meaningless as he had felt himself to be in his early family constellation. I would be confirming that words were fine in the abstract, but when the situation became "real," life was only a desperate conflict in which one had no choice but to react. Roger's problems were in large part the result of his self-hatred and his sense of personal failure at not making his marriage and everything else perfect! His secret hope was that this would undo and erase his childhood sense of failure and defectiveness.

The struggle over the divorce was only a surface manifestation of his lifelong struggle. It was a way to resist seeing how he had tried to use the marriage to ward off his early sense of failure! My getting involved in "strategy" would keep the focus of attention on the current-life events, and ignore the hidden but powerful dynamics and symbolic re-creation that lay beneath them.

Of course we had also learned during many similar struggles that even if Roger won this particular battle, he would soon need to find another wrenching conflict in which to act out his archaic feelings of rage and disappointment in others. In fact, his endless struggles actually represented a desperate attempt to deny the grief of his early losses, even as he did his best to accept the bitter fact that he was "unlovable."

In short, my urge to "help" via strategizing would confuse the focus and allow me to avoid examining the frustration I felt in trying to uncover connections he was resisting. What I actually needed most at that time was to understand my own motives and how they related to what was being enacted in the treatment.

Reflecting further, I examined my own experience of feeling powerless during treatment sessions and my responses to this patient's rage. I sensed that his continuing fury, intensely linked to his current struggle with his spouse, did in fact recapitulate childhood experiences in which he had turned away from his own emotional vulnerability and his need for others. He had shut down, while saying, "Fuck it, I don't need anyone!"

If I failed him here—if I proved to be demonstrably unhelpful—would his anger lead him to abandon me with a similar pronouncement of, "Fuck Wishnie!" I sensed the anger for me that I was trying to side-step by ostensibly "helping him with strategy." I feared being the useless failed parent and didn't recognize that I already was in my feeling of strategizing.

At some point in his early life, Roger had abandoned his sense of vulnerability and had begun constructing an angry, narcissistic shell around his emotions. All at once I saw that my joining him in strategizing aimed at improving his external situation and diminishing his rage would amount to little more than a repetition of the earlier abandonment. Caught up in the externals, both of us would then be ignoring, even betraying, the vulnerable core of authentic (if wounded) selfhood that lay hidden beneath the surface of his rage and frustration.

By pausing to examine my own emotional responses and impulses, I was able to reengage with the patient and to refocus our work in the direction of his earlier self-abandonment. In fact, he did eventually discover these very same issues from which I might have diverted him, had I engaged in the ill-advised strategizing. Previously repressed memories and images flooded into his awareness; images of himself as vulnerable, which he had earlier despised and rejected. Again this close call made me wonder how often I had been unhelpful in this manner in the past with others.

When confronting treatment situations like those described above, I learned to first try to recognize and then carefully examine the urge to introduce personal historical information into a session. I also learned something about the hazards of making consultative recommendations of any kind.

Gradually, I have come to see that these disclosure impulses have more to say about my personal responses to a patient's affect (or exclusion of me) than they do about the work at hand. The blunt fact is that my own narcissistic needs for recognition and inclusion may tempt me to speak up in the hope of winning some temporary feeling of value and presence—usually at the expense of learning something useful about the patient's own inner struggle.

This being said, it should also be pointed out that there are many instances in which a patient will happen upon information about the personal life of the therapist. We are often observed with our families in restaurants, at schools, or perhaps in a theater line, or a patient notices something in the office or hears something from an acquaintance.

Obviously, there are going to be times during treatment when a patient notes that such personal information about the therapist has come to light. On these occasions, the therapist needs to remember that acknowledgement of these bits of biographical data should serve primarily as a means to learn more about the patient's responses and reactions.

In such circumstances, acknowledging factual material of this kind directly will often serve to show that the clinician is not interested in maintaining secrecy about his or her personal life for mysterious reasons of "the professional role." Instead, keeping the focus upon the patient's responses and associations can reassure them that you are with them in their quest to make sense of themselves, rather than seeking to protect your secret self for some mysterious reason.

Naturally, the therapist is also going to have some internal responses related to feeling exposed or having something known. Such reactions are simply another aspect of the therapist's internal work assignment. What does this mean to me? What do I feel has been exposed and to what effect upon me and my self-image and my sense of myself in the transference? What is the source and nature of my discomfort, pride, etc?

A brief, neutral acknowledgement frequently allows the therapist to focus attention towards learning what this new information has stirred in the patient. If the patient asks for more biographical information out of mere curiosity, however, I usually find that I'm reluctant to respond openly without further exploration of the source and meaning of the curiosity.

As always, the therapist must remain thoughtfully concerned when it comes to assessing the advisability of making personal disclosures to patients who may or may not be helped by them. The risk of self-serving rationales on our part is ever present.

In one such instance, I had been working with a woman for several years. Although successful in the advertising world, she was guarded, distant, and isolated. In treatment she was also careful and controlling during the sessions. Although she was willing to consider issues intellectually, one could never be sure what she did with the unfolding material. Highly self-critical, she saw the growing length of her treatment as proof of her incompetence as a person. On several occasions over the years, she had experienced treatment hours during which she became quite agitated as she urgently identified what seemed to be a possible window onto her hidden emotional life. I learned that she would not consider asking for an additional hour at such times. Yet she always seemed pleased if I offered to look for one.

One day, at the end of a session in which she had begun to genuinely examine a repetitively occurring and distressing situation, I thought of offering an additional hour. I felt an excitement at the prospect of possibly going deeper into its genetic origin. At the same time, however, I became aware of some highly unpleasant feelings of exposure, foolishness, and shame on my part. I said nothing about them, but wondered greatly about the basis of these painful affects.

Why was I ashamed of my desire to offer her an additional hour? Wasn't it up to her to claim ownership of her own treatment by making the choice to ask for more time? Had I become too involved in this wish for her? Was I caring more than she did? Why? Yes, that was close to the feeling in me. Yes, something in me felt shamed by exposing my wish to move forward. But why? I wasn't sure.

At her next session, she was once again her intellectually dispassionate self. I asked if he'd had any further associations to the last hour? No, nothing came to mind. After a period of time, I explained that I'd had a response to our last hour and wondered if it might be useful for us to think about it together. I told her that it seemed that she'd had more immediate access to her emotions and had seemed excited and more emotionally present during the previous session. I told her that I'd been thinking of asking her if she wanted to schedule an additional hour before our next regular appointment, when I noticed a sense of being ashamed of my inclination, a sense of exposing something about myself, and that I had held back. I explained that it was unusual for me to feel this way and wondered if it might relate to anything she'd experienced during the hour. Without a pause, she said, "I've been sitting in your waiting area for weeks thinking, "I have to tell him I want to go deeper. I just couldn't bring myself to tell you.""

I was struck by the relevance of her response. Still, I could not fully understand the dynamics that were at work. Over the ensuing months, however, the therapy did indeed move to a deeper plane.

In this situation, I revealed a personal response to our work in the hour. It certainly was about me. Did it help? It did seem to give him the freedom to reveal his own wish for more for himself. One positive aspect, surely, was the confirmation that I felt authentic responses to him and was urgently involved. Although we did not examine the basis of my own feelings of shame, he went on to reveal much more about similar feelings of his own.

There's no doubt that some considered countertransference disclosures can be quite helpful in therapy. However, from my own experience as a patient, I was aware of not wanting to hear my therapist or analyst reveal much about his or her life or reactions. For me, such information can feel intrusive. Instead, I've often felt the need for the therapist's simple presence as I muck around in my internal responses and transference. Questions, comments, and interpretations have felt fine. But personal comments felt like unwanted facts that got in the way of my sorting things out and confronting issues. As a patient, I'm aware that I need the therapist to help me work on my issues, rather than becoming self-absorbed.

Still, there are many different moments and phases in treatment. Some responses offered at a particular moment may help or hinder. Example: Another patient was reviewing her prior therapy and also her therapy with me, as we terminated a lengthy treatment. She described how a former therapist had told her, in a friendly fashion, of some life changes he was going through. She had sensed that there was something similar occurring with me during our treatment, but was grateful that I'd kept it to myself. She had felt burdened by the former therapist's revelation. While she thought something similar might have occurred in my life, she had not wanted me to tell her. Now that she raised it, we were able to examine her reluctance to raise it earlier; what that meant to her; whether there were other suspicions and concerns that she had side stepped; was she protecting me or herself; or avoiding issues in the transference? We were able to see many of these issues as recapitulations of her childhood experience.

This patient had watched me carefully, it seems, and was reassured that I had seemed attuned to her. She simply didn't want to know if her "guesses" about me were correct! Would such information have been useful to her? Did her treatment suffer because she felt compelled to "secretly check me out," rather than openly and freely ask me about suspected personal changes? While we did productively explore her associations and fantasies in this area much later, did we lose something by not doing so in the moment? As with so many similar reflections, we can't know. A different therapist, with a different sense, might have appropriately dealt with the same circumstance very differently.

Weighing and deciding what to reveal, and when, is a unique challenge each and every time it occurs. We need to be able to examine the effects and outcomes of such disclosures from many perspectives. For me, a cautiously open approach seems to work best. And yet, there are moments where I may spontaneously reveal or respond with personal information. I am currently seeing several people who raised questions early in treatment about my family size, my age, training, personal origin, beliefs, values, etc. With both of these people I chose to respond with some information directly but in a limited fashion. They were both afraid of treatment and strangers and unable to examine these concerns. Providing the information and subsequently examining their responses and reactions allowed us to get into treatment and examine their personal concerns. It also seemed to me that anything factually learned about me could have been gleaned elsewhere. Our interest was not in the facts themselves, but in their meaning to the patient and the patient's curiosity in them. What function did the initial interest serve?

So, while I do not make it a regular practice to spontaneously include personal information, there are times where I may do so or respond to a request for such data. The focus, however, remains centered upon the meanings, use, and sensed need for such information, and the impact for the patient of my including it.

9

Erotic Countertransference: A Response to Frustration, Despair, Loneliness, Loss, Anger, Denial? When is Eros really Eros?

While presenting several extended case studies, this chapter explores some of the dynamics of the erotic transference. One such dynamic occurs in situations where an erotic countertransference is triggered by an emotional state such as frustration or hopelessness. This erotic response can also occur when a treatment seems to be bogged down and repetitive, or during periods when the sessions seem futile and devoid of progress. In addition, the erotic countertransference can be provoked by unexamined losses occurring both inside and outside of the treatment situation. In other treatment scenarios, this phenomenon can result from a therapist's wish for control or influence, after the necessary focus on understanding and exploration has been sidetracked. It is also helpful to recognize that the experience of erotic countertransference is not unusual. Rather than denying its reality, the task is to guard against destructive enactments that may emerge from the dynamic, even as we examine the emotional underpinnings of this form of transference in order to further the work.

Destructive enactments originating from within the therapist can result from such conditions as: depression, psychosis, aging-related mental impairment, alcoholism, and love-sick illusions fueled by illness. Clinicians must also guard against the kinds of character deficiencies and blind spots that might allow them to rationalize professional transgressions. As in most areas of medical practice, a wide range of life experiences can often help the therapist to avoid pitfalls in treatment and allow the practitioner to provide the best possible care for the patient.

A 30-year-old, unmarried lawyer named "Kate" was referred for treatment after a brief hospitalization for an overdose. This incident had occurred at the end of an affair with her boss. Kate had believed that the man would leave his wife and marry her. After deciding not to separate from his wife, the boss explained that he wanted to resume a more formal work relationship with Kate, and to break off their intimacy. He pointed out that it would look "unseemly" if he were to leave his wife in order to become involved with someone in his office. Kate felt enraged and abandoned. She traveled to another city, rented a hotel room, and overdosed.

She came to our first few sessions clad in a formal business suit. She carried a leather briefcase, which she carefully placed between us, rather than beside her chair. As she sat, I was struck by the side-slit in her skirt, which showed a little too much leg in a manner that struck me as intrusive and aggressive. Already, I was feeling a number of responses. Her clothing and demeanor as she entered gave me a sense of someone who was armored. The briefcase loomed between us as a barrier she had imposed. The skirt and leg seemed contrived, forced—so much so, that the effect was off-putting, not enticing.

I began by asking her what she was hoping she would gain from therapy. She responded quickly, by suggesting that she needed to understand where she had "gone wrong." Given the hardness of her exterior and the tone of her words, I wondered if her decision to come for a consultation might indicate a deeper longing that she could not yet admit to herself. Her harsh demeanor, along with her angry caricatures of men, might belie a fear of her own needs and vulnerabilities. While the suicide attempt could be construed as evidence of a severe attack upon her vulnerable self by her narcissistic rage, the method and mildness of the overdose might indicate other forces at work within her.

We met for several evaluation sessions and then agreed upon treatment. Ostensibly, she wanted to know why she kept engaging in unsatisfying relationships with men—relationships that all too often resulted in depression. My initial sense was to move slowly and gather history. I felt that her need to maintain an aggressive controlling demeanor indicated a kind of brittleness, and I attributed my own sense of carefulness in this early going to my perception of her possible vulnerability.

As treatment began, I learned about her childhood and family life. Kate had a sister two years younger. Her father was a prominent lawyer in the southern city where she had grown up. Her mother had been a graphic designer until the patient was born. But Kate had only the scantiest recollections of her childhood and of her mother, a fact that I carefully noted. Her father had been preoccupied with developing his law practice while she was young. Later, during her adolescence, he had taken up golf; a pastime that also tended to keep him away from home. Initially, Kate would accompany him and play golf or swim at the club pool.

When she was fifteen, however, her parents divorced. Kate was shocked and spent the next several years both bolstering and internally devaluing her mother. She and her sister had never been close, but now they shared the "burden" of caring for their mother. Kate remembered telling herself that she would never wind up in her mother's position. Whatever else might occur, she would never let "that" happen to her!

As her later adolescence unfolded, she dated frequently but maintained the persona of the cool, aloof, hard-to-get young woman. She competed with men in sports, drinking, and sex. Outwardly she appeared to be having a wild adolescence. Inwardly, however, she felt cold and calculating, while telling herself, "No one will get to me; the danger is caring for someone." Listening to her, I couldn't help wondering if the real danger she faced might not be the inner need to care for someone, while being loved in return. Was her brittle armor a way to suppress the longing that made her vulnerable, as she believed her mother had once been vulnerable?

The first interruption in our work occurred when I took a week off.

She treated the scheduled break as a minor event, after pointing out that she, also, needed a break. The interval would allow her to "get some work done."

At the end of our last appointment before the break, she bent over to adjust her shoes and her jacket and her blouse fell forward, revealing that she was braless and fully exposing her breasts. I was a little surprised, as well as pleasantly enticed, and I wondered if she always dressed this way under her severe business clothes. I noted this question and thought about it for future consideration.

When I returned from vacation, we resumed our sessions. Kate began by detailing a "wild weekend" at her beach home that had taken place after our last appointment. She said that she had been walking on the beach and had met a neighbor, a casual acquaintance. They walked along for a while. Kate explained how she had consciously decided that she wanted this man and how she had seduced him. I thought about our previous appointment. Kate went on to describe an attempt at intercourse on the beach, but said that for some reason, she could not tolerate penetration. Instead, she'd engaged in oral sex with him. She pointed out that this arrangement was "probably better," because she felt more "in control" that way.

I asked her to elaborate, and she made some associations. I asked if the encounter on the beach had been a unique experience for her. She replied that she had not engaged in such behavior since adolescence, then explained that she felt as if she'd "been on vacation" during the episode. "Vacation? How so?" I inquired. She didn't know; it just "felt that way." I mused aloud about the uniqueness of her experience, and her sense of "vacation"—from what? To myself, I noted her point about having desired intercourse, and her subsequent inability to allow penetration. Oral sex, yes—but penetration had not been possible. What might this tell us?

I also wondered, Was there a link between these events and our work? Our activity was also "oral," and seemed at times to fall short of a full engagement. Yet her words and her behavior during the sessions made it clear that she wanted something closer, something deeper. As the hour proceeded, she described similar assignations in her past. I wondered, How much of this was designed to seduce me? And how seduced was I feeling? My initial carefulness about her had diminished, but it was still present. While there was some sense of attraction, I was still registering an empty feeling and a kind of unpleasant shock, each time she described engaging in one of her impulsive and aggressive behaviors.

With these reactions in mind, I wondered aloud about possible connections to our work. The interruption of our sessions had been a vacation of sorts; perhaps it had freed her from some constraints. Did she feel constrained by some things in her life? She responded that she knew life was full of rules for behavior and that people were required to live (or at least "appear" to live) in a certain way. She hated that. She chafed at the regularity of therapy; Why couldn't these sessions be more spontaneous and less formal?

I responded by wondering if these observations might relate to something that I had noticed at the end of our last hour. She looked at me quizzically. I said that she had bent over to fix her shoe (which to my view didn't require fixing) and her jacket and blouse had moved, revealing that she was not wearing a bra. Far from being surprised, she laughed out loud. "You noticed!" I smiled and nodded and went on to suggest that I was curious about this difference between her outward, professional appearance and her inner "wild self." What did these two dimensions of her tell us, and why did they seem so opposite?

As we spoke she became more spontaneous and joking. Yes, she had decided not to wear a bra that day, thinking that it was to be her last appointment. She had wanted to "give you something to remember me by." No, it was not her usual mode of dress. Yes, she felt that law was a humdrum occupation and that like many other lawyers she knew, she was actually a wild and unconventional person outside of work.

I returned to her comment about giving me something to remember her by. Was she concerned about being forgotten? What made her think that her sexual attractiveness represented her most memorable aspect? These questions, which ended the hour, led to an opening of the treatment. The months that followed were filled with her history of sexual escapades during adolescence, and her growing recognition that sex was an effective way to get and control men. As we spoke, questions about her sense of herself as a person emerged. Her father's pursuit of younger women and his abandonment of her mother, both of which had occurred as she was becoming an attractive young woman, were seen as intertwined issues. The pain of her father's inattention and abandonment of her became profoundly painful. Months later, she saw elements of that in the feelings that had been evoked by my vacation. She noted that she had looked up information about me and my family on the internet, and was furious at realizing that she could have any feelings about me.

Along with this recognition, she recalled that she had seduced her father's younger partner. For her it was "showing him something." What was the "something?"

She blurted, "That I'm someone, too!" She grew sad once again. Then, a bit later, "You, Wishnie—you were such a formal shit! I had to almost get undressed to get you to notice me" (referring to the episode before the vacation). As we talked more about that, she described my careful manner early in our work and explained how it had left her feeling held at a distance. As she talked, I recognized how fearful I had been of that "too much leg showing." The truth was, I had feared her aggressiveness. How much of that had actually been anxiety about my own desire?

She said she had been hurt by my manner, by my discomfort with her presentation. I acknowledged her response. I saw that the more we explored her life experience, and the better I got to know her, the less formal I became. Once I was on familiar ground and felt safer, I could see the pain and loneliness that underlay her dramatic and aggressive presentation. Sex for her was merely a controlling gambit in a game. Her inner life was actually far more affected by the loneliness she often felt and by her lack of important relationships than by the erotic energy contained in these brief assignations. As I became more comfortable with her in the treatment hour, our work became more fruitful.

Years later, having explored her early losses, along with her yearning for her mother and the dynamics that fueled their turbulent relationship, Kate felt herself to be a different person. Calmer and more comfortable, while enjoying some genuine friendships and authentically intimate relationships, she chose to settle down with a man. She continues to live with him. Eventually it became clear that her early sexualizing of our relationship had more to do with fear and anxiety than with any genuine sexual feelings for me. My erotic response to her also diminished and changed over time. Our work began to feel more mutual in the exploration and understanding of her losses and deficits. In the end, I found her to be an attractive, sensitive person, and a person who no longer wore the harsh, sexually aggressive armor that had made me so uncomfortable at the start of our sessions together.

As the previous chapters attempted to make clear, countertransference is an inevitable part of the psychotherapeutic process. Sooner or later in most treatments, the therapist will respond to the interaction with transferences based upon the clinician's own inner conflicts and issues. As noted throughout the preceding chapters, the thoughtful practitioner endeavors to avoid acting on these affects until he or she can gain a clear sense of their meaning and relationship to the work. Then these affective response materials can be woven back into the treatment.

In some cases, this "weaving" process serves to validate some aspect of the patient's experience. In this way, it can help clarify feelings that have arisen during the sessions. Many times however, we find ourselves in the circumstance of piecing together the interaction, and long after the fact. In many of these situations, it can take weeks or even months to work through the complexity of the transferences, related affects, and antecedent events that are usually linked to an enactment. When it comes to sexual enactments, however, we don't have the luxury of retrospective understanding. Here the boundaries around actions must be maintained more stringently, no matter what the affective invitations or desires.

One of the most complex and powerful types of countertransference occurs when the therapist responds to the treatment situation with an erotic transference to the patient. From the earliest days of psychoanalysis, this phenomenon has troubled, puzzled and intrigued investigators. Witness the case of "Anna O," (Freud 1893) which became a classic study of the dynamics involved in erotic transference, countertransference, and therapist flight.

Describing that case, Freud went to great lengths to place the responsibility for such transferences with the patient. The social and political context of the time is reflected in these writings. Yet he also warned his fellow-clinicians to scrupulously avoid inappropriate behavior during treatment, while pointing out that sexual indiscretion by therapists could prove fatal to the fledgling psychoanalytic movement, to say nothing of undermining the treatment of the patient.

The persistence of this thorny issue has been repeatedly demonstrated in recent decades, with many authors and groups deploring the numerous instances in which erotic relationships developed between experienced and otherwise respected analysts and their patients. Until quite recently, these misuses of the therapeutic relationship were felt to be so threatening that most analytic societies were loath to discuss them in any open forum.

However, the last twenty years have witnessed a significant reexamination of this issue, along with a great deal of discussion about the role of boundaries and their violation by therapists. This dialogue makes it clear that the vast majority of analytic therapists regard sexual activity between clinician and patient as a violation of the ethical and working principles of psychoanalytic psychotherapy.

At the same time, there is a greater understanding of the complex interpersonal and intersubjective nature of our work, and of the risks that we are all subject to. If we accept that overt sexual involvement with a patient is excluded, we can then consider the role of erotic feelings and fantasies in the treatment.

What are the meanings of the fantasies and erotic affects that so often erupt in the clinician during treatment? How do we understand and use these internal responses in the context of treatment, once we recognize them? If we flee[1] and deny these responses, the result will usually be an

---

1. In one instance, I was consulting to a clinic which primarily worked with seriously character-disordered men. Many of the therapists were young women with modest clinical training. One day during a case review, one of the more experienced therapists described her work with a 30-year-old man with a history of drug use and some non-violent criminal behavior. They were meeting one or two times a week in the evening. She was an attractive woman dressed in a very youthful and stylish manner. I asked her what her sense was of the transference. She responded that they didn't do that kind of work in the clinic. I commented that given her age, appearance, and manner of dress, they might want to reschedule their appointments for daytime and not evening hours and that she consider that some of his disruptive behavior could relate to erotic transference feelings for her. She again assured me that the patients in this clinic understood that there were no such possibilities. A year later I received a call from the clinic director for another

avoidance and restriction of the treatment and its examination of issues. Enactments short of frank violations can also result in behaviors that compromise legitimate treatment objectives. How should therapists examine and then work with these internal experiences of affect and cognition, without either destructively enacting them or destructively refusing to acknowledge their frequent presence in the treatment dynamic?

Tansey has suggested an approach to the problem that seems helpful. In a 1994 Symposium on *Passion in the Countertransference* (Psychoanalytic Dialogues), he described his own struggle with an erotic countertransference. While avoiding personal disclosure, Tansey examined the feelings evoked in him during a lengthy treatment.

A careful reading of his description shows that he began to play an unconscious role in a patient-orchestrated enactment well in advance of the erotic countertransference becoming manifest. Tansey suggested this, while recounting how his patient would often sit sobbing in the waiting room, but then remain stiffly formal throughout the session. His intrigue with this unexplained phenomenon may have been the beginning of the erotic interest.

Tansey's efforts to understand his patient's demeanor during the hour were endlessly rebuffed, and he gradually became paralyzed and despairing. His role, he soon recognized, had been reduced to that of an "advocate of hope," an active role wherein he took on the responsibility to enliven the patient, rather than exploring their situation. Meanwhile, he made virtually no progress in understanding the inner dynamics that were making it so difficult for his patient to communicate during therapy. What must it have been like to be both powerless and an alleged advocate of something that was not real between them?

While describing this treatment impasse in detail, Tansey recalled a 1979 observation in which Searles had suggested that therapists who become sexually involved with patients do so out of frustration, after they realize that they are unable to help the patient. While Tansey did not

---

consultation. This therapist and two others were involved in sexual relationships with patients. One patient was blackmailing the therapist.

become sexually involved, he did note the emergence of erotic feelings. These occurred three years into treatment, after the process had become stalemated and he had become the mere advocate of an ephemeral hope. Tansey describes one of the most common circumstances within which these issues arise.

As Tansey struggled within himself to understand why his own erotic senses had come forward, the patient's demeanor began to change. Sensing the possibility of a breakthrough in communication, he leaned forward in his chair and made strong eye contact. The patient instantly became terrified and experienced the first in a series of recurring panic attacks that alternated with her earlier "stiffly formal" manner.

Observing this intense behavior, Tansey began to feel (as he later described it) like an "unwilling rapist." Moving quickly, he assured the patient that he recognized her vulnerable state and would never violate it. He also did his best to help her recover her emotional equilibrium, by encouraging her to return to certain safe, encapsulated affect memories during their next few sessions.

What was happening here? According to the countertransference dynamics outlined earlier, Tansey had been drawn into the patient's mini-drama long before he realized it. He had felt compelled to come up with a clear understanding of her different affect states. Increasingly frustrated, he had struggled with a series of questions he couldn't answer:

> Was the patient's "formality" in the office a form of withholding, and was he required to breach it in order to discover the distress beneath?
>
> Was her sobbing in the waiting room a "tease," a signal that there was pain and grief to be explored, but that he would never be allowed to confront it?
>
> Were his own paralysis and resignation more than therapeutic impotence in the face of an intractable patient? Were they actually a defense against feelings of sexual aggressiveness that he only later recognized in himself?

Tansey had no answers for these difficult questions, at least not at first. All he could do was recognize the erotic countertransference he was experiencing, while also struggling to untangle its complex dynamics. The situation began to clarify itself only when the patient brought in some of her distress. But this new openness was also puzzling for the therapist. Why had she suddenly begun to admit these feelings? Did she sense from him that he was fatigued and frustrated, and perhaps approaching exhaustion? Did she fear that she might have pushed him too far away? Did his playing out of the "advocate of hope" role finally convince her that she could trust his desire to engage her? Did he lean forward to engage her out of frustration at a time she was beginning to change? Did that piece enact some earlier experience of hers?

For unexplained reasons, this patient brought a more responsive expression of her distress into the sessions. And the therapist did his best to engage her, by sitting forward in the chair and making eye contact. This time, however, the results were much more productive, and the patient began to show more openness during treatment than ever before.

A close reading of Tansey's account of this case suggests that he had begun participating in a reenactment of the patient's life-drama, long before the erotic countertransference. Would a personal disclosure of his erotic feelings have helped this patient? Based on the terror she expressed from mere close eye contact, it seems unlikely that such a disclosure could have been useful in the patient's struggle.

Tansey's experience in this case has become familiar. Responding to such fantasies and feelings, I try to note when and how they occur, while asking myself, Why now, and why with this person? What is going on in my life that might be contributing to these erotic urgings? Have they been triggered by age, injury, the growth and distancing from my children, changes in my marital life, losses, etc? What is the status of my own intimate relationships, and how might it be contributing to these feelings? Am I experiencing a similarity between this treatment situation and deeper issues and experiences from my own past?

Although I recognize the fact that a transference of this sort has a specific relationship to the treatment, I also understand that it requires me to carefully survey my own life. And I also need to remember, as Tansey and others have made clear, that the erotic countertransference most often emerges when the therapist is struggling with feelings of powerlessness, after treatment has reached a temporary impasse. If I can review my own state and the treatment status, in all likelihood, I will find the sources of this response. This form of countertransference is also frequently accompanied by a longing for some prior period of treatment in which things seemed to go well and the therapist felt successfully productive.

These awarenesses have helped me to understand that treatment impasses are in fact a necessary part of the process. In most cases, they simply reflect the enactment of some defensive need. Recognizing this, I have found that I can remain open to my own feelings and fantasies in this realm and curious about the dynamics behind them. This curiosity about the meaning has often reduced the intensity of my erotic wishes.

There are also times where the patient introduces erotic issues and behaviors independent of our interaction. Such instances do not necessarily stem from an impasse. They may arise as a diversion, or because of a need to be recognized as a desirable person, or as a defense against fears of feeling insignificant. But these motivations are usually less interactive and more related to basic feelings that patients experience inwardly. Thus they are usually easier for the therapist to recognize. This was true with Kate in the initial example in this chapter. Her own sense that her sexuality was a device to engage and control was present initially and heightened by the sensed rejection in my "carefulness" and formality. Both of our character defenses interacted in an initial enactment. Discussing and exploring the pre-vacation exposure, vacation activity, and her response to me moved our work into an exploratory mode out of enactment.

Grappling with the inner meaning of an erotic transference can be a formidable task. As Messler Davies (1994) and others have pointed out, every relationship involves some issues of power and control. At the same time, therapists are certainly vulnerable to the kind of narcissistic injury that can occur when a treatment impasse triggers feelings of worthlessness, frustration, and failure. These negative affects can easily lead to a painful sense of rejection and impotence, for which the erotic countertransference then becomes a kind of emotional compensation. Such compensation, when unrecognized or misunderstood by the analyst, can be the basis for destructive enactments.

One of the most appealing aspects of erotic fantasy, perhaps, is the way that it seems to offer the fantasizing subject feelings of self-affirmation, power, control, and value. Considering this, I usually respond to such treatment-related urgings by asking myself, Am I feeling less effective? Why? Why now? What do these fantasies represent in the treatment? Why am I focusing on my own needs right now, instead of the patient's? Don't these erotic wishes represent a retreat into myself?

—Am I abandoning my patient emotionally at this juncture because the patient forced me to confront a limitation within me, or perhaps in order to re-experience some previous discomfort in my own life?

—What does my countertransference tell me about the patient's experience?

—Am I actually reliving some emotional aspect of the patient's experience as the result of a less visible enactment?

Concomitantly, I consider what might be occurring within the patient that has triggered a need for the diversion or affirmation offered by erotic fantasy. These questions are of course variations on the kinds of issues that have been raised by other authors, Searles, Winnicott, Gabbard, Jacobs, McGlaughlin and Tansey, to mention a few.

Fleeing from the experience of erotic countertransference is not productive. If suppressed, denied, or ignored, it can become a serious obstacle in treatment, or the basis for destructive acting out by either or both participants. The theme here is clearly, "You can run, but you can't hide!" Dealing with these phenomena is simply a requirement of our work. Careful scrutiny of these treatment experiences in ourselves, and in the context of the treatment, will often provide insights that can open a useful window on the interpersonal dynamics of the treatment dyad, and also on the unconscious experience of the patient.

In earlier chapters I have mentioned some ways in which a therapist might try to introduce possible understandings gleaned from countertransferential experience back into treatment. Often these considerations will prove useful in developing understandings of, and dealing with, impasses. How does this process work when the insights emerge from an erotic countertransference? During the Symposium *Passion in the Counter-transference*, mentioned above, Messler Davies explains her view on this issue. Her introduction to the topic contained a compelling argument in favor of including such erotic countertransference material in the treatment.

While quoting Searles (1959), Davies (1994) was careful to point out:

> To the extent that a child's relationships with his parents is healthy, he acquires the strength to accept the unrealizability of his oedipal strivings, not mainly through the identification with the forbidding rival-parent, but mainly, rather through the ego-strengthening experience of finding that the beloved parent reciprocates his love—responds to him, that is, as being a worthwhile and lovable individual and renounces him only with an accompanying sense of loss on the parent's own part. [Searles 1959, pp. 301–302]

Davies goes on to summarize Searles' opinion that the analyst's awareness of this dynamic is enough and that a direct acknowledgement of it during treatment would only serve to disrupt the therapy. After that, Davies proceeds to review the work of Kumin (1985, p. 155), who views the analyst's erotic desire, and his or her resistance to it, as interfering with the development and understanding of this transference state. Davies (1994, p. 155) also explores the insights provided by Wrye, who regards the flight from acknowledgement of erotic countertransference as a refusal by the analyst to participate emotionally in an essential phase of treatment.

Supported by this material, Davies next describes the recent shift in our understanding of therapeutic dynamics. That shift tells us that therapy is a two-person, intersubjective experience, rather than an encounter in which a patient interacts with a perfectly objective, detached clinician. Indeed, there is now convincing evidence to show that the older model, which insisted on "emotional distance" and "perfect neutrality" on the part of the therapist, may actually force the patient to reexperience earlier traumas in which he or she was left burdened with shame and guilt for desires that could never be openly acknowledged.

Davies next points out that many contemporary clinician-theorists have struggled with this issue. How can the therapist encourage the emergence of these unconsciously internalized and very powerful visions of self and other during the treatment hour? And how should the clinician go about the task of creating a transitional area in which such inner imagery can be reshaped by the experience of therapy, but without re-traumatization through either flight or boundary violation? That question becomes especially urgent once the therapist recognizes that aversion or resistance to erotic urgings in treatment will surely be communicated nonverbally, and will probably re-create the same pain that one hopes to resolve through the therapy.

In the next section of her discussion, Davies presents a clinical vignette. She describes the slow evolution of her own internal experiences with a patient, and then details a particularly frustrating impasse that led her to acknowledge the existence of her erotic countertransference, along with its relationship to issues within the treatment that had been previously unclear. Her candid description of her own dread and anxiety, along with her fears of boundary violation via such acknowledgement, and her terror of being judged for her feelings, make compelling reading for any practitioner who has grappled with these issues.

After these admissions, Davies raises the important question of whether such disclosures should be part of the design of psychotherapy, or whether they should be used only as a last resort, when all other means of inclusion have failed.

To support her contention that erotic transference disclosures should be a considered part of therapeutic practice, Davies makes one of her most trenchant points. She asserts that our assumptions, about an evolutionary line of psychological development from "primitive" awareness of the purely physical aspects of experience to the development of a more idealized, intellectual symbolism (through words and concept formation), have harmfully prevented many of us from learning effectively through our own sensed physical experience.

The history of the psychoanalytic movement attests to the fact that clinicians have always struggled to avoid becoming the chasmic, all-absorbing pre-oedipal mother. All too often, however, this very struggle has tended to create a chasm in our capacity to stay with the patient by remaining unaware of or denying our own physically sensed experience.

Years of clinical experience have confirmed for me the accuracy of one of Davies'(1994) key points on this subject:

> There is a physiologically based and somatically encoded substrate of experience that runs parallel to, but remains in most cases essentially dissociated from, the cognitive, verbally encoded operations. . . . As the child reconfigures her experience of what it means to live within her own body, as she comes to understand the separate subjective experience of the other, there will be a moment to moment, virtually uninterrupted flow of bodily states, in specific relation to each experience of self and other as they become increasingly more organized matrices of self and object representations. [p. 159]

Thus, as Davies reminds us, we are constantly feeling and registering physical responses to our interactions, fantasies, memories, associations, etc. These physical senses have a powerful and continuous impact upon our conscious cognition and state of relatedness, shaping our perceptions and subjective sense.

Like Davies, Loewald is convinced that archaic, libidinal-aggressive drives in the undifferentiated phase must divide themselves into instinctive-affective life and cognitive functions. Yet the underlying, archaic state will, of necessity, remain functionally present, and will continue to influence both instinct-affect and cognition-perception.

This insight provides the theoretical foundation for Loewald's (1980) assertion that:

> The therapist, in order to work analytically with patients with narcissistic disorders, must rely on his ability to reactivate archaic levels of mental functioning within himself, at given moments within the treatment. In other words he needs the flexibility or mental agility to suspend, when required, his ego boundaries for a long enough period, if he is to understand the patient's experience and then interpret it to him. (1980, p. 215)

> . . . because levels of relatedness, involving both patient and analyst, come into play that are far less familiar to most of us than oedipal and postoedipal levels. And furthermore, verbal interpretation itself, the

mainstay of psychoanalytic intervention, takes on connotations and aspects of meaningfulness—of which analysts need to be aware—that
derive or hark back more directly to that "magical" power and significance
of words which plays a predominant role in the preverbal and early verbal
period of life and the resonance and responses of the young child to
parental verbal material. (p. 217)

Loewald's understanding of the power of these pre-oedipal, paraverbal experienced senses, and their impact upon our moment-to-
moment involvement in the treatment process, combined with the work
of Mahler, Winnicott, Searles, Kernberg, Kohut, Semrad, and Adler,
speak urgently to the importance of understanding the dynamics of these
archaic, somatically experienced re-creations within treatment. To be
effective, we as clinicians need to sense and attempt to discern the effect
of these somatic states upon both participants in the treatment dyad. We
also need to work toward usefully including our understandings and
senses of these somatic re-creations in order to promote the work with
our patients.

What are the most appropriate ways in which therapists can effectively employ their perceptions about the powerful but often evaded
impact of somatically sensed interactional experience on treatment?
Davies (1994) attempts to answer this question on page 161 of the
Symposium: "As patient and therapist reimmerse themselves in specific
object-related experiences of the past, the physiological substrate experience described will certainly reemerge. As a full participant in the
analytic endeavor, the analyst must be willing to feel and process her own
somatic states accompanying the interplay of self and object in the erotic
countertransference, as well as recognizing those states inherent in the
patient's unfolding erotic transference."

In the above quote, Davies clearly defines the necessity for clinicians
to remain keenly aware of these powerful and impactful responses. If we
accept the premise that we are working in a two-person, intersubjective
field in which the therapist must inevitably experience somatically based
reactions during treatment sessions, is it appropriate to disclose erotic
transferences to the patient in order to avoid re-traumatization that could

be triggered by emotional withdrawal? For Davies, the answer is a qualified "yes."

Gabbard (1994), in the same symposium however, makes a convincing case against such disclosures, by noting in his own commentary: "When she openly acknowledges her sexual fantasies about the patient, a symbolic realm has been concretized, and the potential space closes [a reference to the "transitional work space" of treatment]" (p. 205).

Although I recognize the need for clinicians to be aware of the erotic countertransference and its potential meanings for the patient, I believe that Gabbard is correct. Much of our work occurs because of the construction of a carefully balanced symbolic space which allows intense involvement and is maintained by a series of boundaries at various levels of complexity. Revelations about our own erotic feelings and fantasies will too greatly burden the patient, and they complicate treatment because of the many unspoken feelings and fantasies aroused by such revelations. For the therapist, careful examination of such responses in supervision, peer-group consultation, and personal treatment may provide helpful insights in this multidimensional situation.

Examination of the timing of the emergence of such responses in treatment, their possible meaning, and relationship to the process through the therapist's internal examination would seem to be a preferred way to work with such material. While this approach will not answer all of the questions about the impact on the treatment of therapist resistance to erotic transference, it seems to offer the only viable strategy for grappling with them and usefully including them in the psychoanalytic process.

Surely it is a form of hubris for us as clinicians to assume that we can monitor own instinctual drives, conflicts, traumata, and physical desires so effectively that we could disclose them and still avoid making errors that could injure patients engaged in enactments! In my view, disclosures about erotic countertransference significantly elevate the risk of such injury, and should thus be avoided. Are there instances where one might acknowledge the existence of such responses in a general way? Yes, but rarely. Even here, one is on uncertain ground that requires vigilant observation and exploration.

While arguing otherwise, Davies warns against the dangers of silent re-traumatization, which can occur when a therapist refuses to recognize erotic transferential responses. Here I would agree that the therapist needs to recognize and examine these responses within him– or herself. But the problem of how to use them most effectively is still the key issue. In instances where the therapist feels erotic desires and flees the requisite inner awareness and self-examination, the patient runs the risk of having to shoulder an inordinate sense of responsibility for wishes that will be experienced as forbidden and shame-laden. This is clearly an authentic and urgent treatment issue, which needs to be addressed. But the solution is not an automatic, open acknowledgement of erotic responses by the clinician. The point is that both extremes, the refusal to inwardly acknowledge and the automatic disclosure, are counterproductive and even destructive in treatment.

Erotic countertransference awareness and disclosure remain a vexing issue for most psychotherapists today. Hopefully, our increasing awareness of this within the professional community, along with our growing willingness to examine it, will allow for greater comfort among therapists who must grapple daily with the deeply complex issues generated by patient enactments and their own responses. Perhaps this expanded "comfort zone" will also ease some of the tension that inevitably affects therapists who confront the issue. As the therapists are more comfortable experiencing and examining these states, this increased sense of comfort may be sensed by the patient, since the therapist will presumably be more open to raising questions, while sending fewer aversive signals.

The more the therapist recognizes that there are opportunities to gain understanding outside the hour, the less stress he will bring to the patient. At the same time, a greater willingness to examine these issues within the professional community could also begin to diminish the pernicious and secretive acting out that has so often plagued our work in the past.

The following treatment history provides an example of a situation in which I partially acknowledged an erotic impulse, after concluding that my limited admission would help the patient. Later, when I came to reconsider the impact of my acknowledgement, I concluded that it was an error.

*   *   *

A woman in her early twenties, "Ruth" had entered twice-weekly psychotherapy because of her depression and her poor academic performance. Ruth was intelligent, energetic, and athletic. Yet she suffered intermittent episodes of depression and social isolation. During several years of therapy and introspection, she had gained an understanding of her various internal conflicts. She had also completed her graduate school training, and seemed reasonably content with her life.

Apparently feeling better, she began ending therapy sessions with a flick of her hips and a flippant, smiling farewell, "Fuck you!" When I asked her about the meaning of these odd, provocative departures, she responded, "It's the '80's—everybody talks this way! Stop trying to analyze everything, I'm just being friendly." I nodded, but then went on to ask her about the meaning of her "friendliness" and the words she had used. "There you go again," said Ruth. "Not everything has meaning!"

During the ensuing months of treatment, she refused to respond to inquiries about her flippant farewells, but frequently continued to end hours in this manner. One day I responded, "Well, it might be a pleasant idea, but it's not going to happen."

At the start of our next session, she quickly stated: "Do you know what you said, last time? How can you say that? You said that it could be a pleasant idea!" I nodded, confirming her recollection of the exchange, and then reminded her of my complete statement. I added that when two people work together in such a personal way, any number of feelings and wishes could emerge, including recognition of the fantasy pleasures that might accompany physical intimacy. As with other feelings and wishes, however, we would not act on them but could examine them. After these comments had been delivered, the patient became calm and reflective in a manner that had been absent from her for many months. During the next two weeks, Ruth revealed that she had always believed her therapy would culminate in our sexual involvement. This assumption had been conscious on her part, but withheld during previous treatment sessions. Soon after this admission, Ruth recalled an incident in which she'd been alone, on a vacation with her father, and had noticed condoms on his dresser. Made fearful by the discovery, she had then locked the door to her adjoining room.

We explored these memories and her associated beliefs during the following sessions. Ruth described her ideas and her experiences with men. She reflected on boundaries, and on her need to control others through humor and teasing. She also examined her belief that therapy would lead to a sexual encounter, and certain parallel fears that she had earlier experienced about the challenges of growing up and leaving home. Our discussions were wide-ranging, but they did not reveal the desires that were hidden within her fears. Ruth eventually ended the treatment with a general sense of personal growth and improvement in her life.

At first, I concluded that my spontaneous remark about a "pleasant" possibility had been useful, and had helped to clear an impasse. On reflection, however, I came to feel that my response had been partially triggered by my own frustration and anger, and that it was also responsible, along with some other factors, for preventing her from discovering her own longings that were hidden within her fears. In discussion with some colleagues, two women felt it had been useful and appropriate, and five men felt otherwise; an interesting dichotomy. I remain convinced that it allowed her to examine her fears but obstructed investigating her desires. In subsequent years, I have discovered ways to raise the same issues with patients, but without finding it necessary to disclose my own frustration by being so provocative.

AVOIDANCE OF EROTIC TRANSFERENCE
AND COUNTERTRANSFERENCE

Although open disclosure of erotic countertransference by a therapist can produce volatile reactions in treatment, avoidance of the issue can also produce negative results, as illustrated in the following case history.

*   *   *

A 30-year-old woman named "Grace" entered treatment after experiencing several serious depressions and a hospitalization. A successful business professional, Grace had relied on her aggressive behavior to reach the top of her field. Yet, she had emerged from the climb feeling painfully isolated and suspicious of fellow workers whom she perceived as envious and sabotaging.

The only child of an aggressive, successful mother (whom she consciously despised) and a passive, compliant father, Grace had denied having any longings for care and affection. In her continuing suspicion of her subordinates and colleagues, I believed that I heard the yearning for attention from an unavailable mother.

As I tentatively began to approach this area of the patient's experience, however, her dress and demeanor became more sexualized. She began to wonder aloud if she was attractive even to me. When I sought to explore the meaning of such comments with her, she reflected ruefully on the fact that she was growing older. She also ruminated on her previous hospitalizations, and on the attractiveness of the younger staff.

When I speculated that her needs to feel physically attractive might also contain wishes for other kinds of appeal, namely a sense of being included and personally liked for who she was as a person, and that she might be vulnerable to such longings, she became furious with me, "You are unwilling to see me as a woman. Every time I wear an open blouse or lean forward, or my hemline rises, you turn your eyes. You want to see me as a needy little girl, not a sexual woman! Is it me? Am I old, or are you having a problem?"

Grace's observations of me were accurate in many ways. Her attractiveness and demand for interest on my part had both intrigued me and led me to unconsciously retreat. As I considered her statements, I recognized the warded-off sense of excitement and danger, as well as previous fantasies that had been at the periphery of my awareness. Defensively and avoidantly, I had preferred to focus on her dependent longings as a way of ducking her assertive sexuality. I only began to see the full extent of my evasion, however, when I realized that on several occasions I had prematurely (and preemptively) interpreted some remark or incident in the treatment, when waiting and exploration might have been more useful. Each time I did that, I had the sense that I was side stepping something.

In most other situations, I felt comfortable noting a person's behavior and its sexual connotations and have found ways of mentioning it for consideration. Yet, in this case I had not done so, but had instead enacted an avoidance that disturbed the patient. Over a period of days in which I was puzzling over this dynamic and my responses, I had an erotic dream involving the patient. I recognized her in the dream, and abruptly awakened myself in order to end this forbidden involvement. Immediately upon awakening, I understood some elements of my avoidance. I realized that my "premature interpretations" were also ways of interrupting the patient, just when she seemed to be reaching an exciting crescendo that I found too stimulating. Just as I had stopped the dream, so had I stopped her at these moments in the hour.

While I did my best to examine these inner feelings privately, Grace and I were able to productively examine her perceptions of and responses to our treatment interactions. Our discussion of those occasions on which she had felt me turning away from her, along with some exchanges about her motivation to provoke me into seeing her as a desirable woman, opened up aspects of her early relationships and her self perception. As I became more comfortable with exploring possible meanings, instead of instantly fleeing every erotic affect, I was better able to inquire about what seemed to be the aggressive elements in her presentation. Did her need for force and control belie her powerful fears? Over time, Grace was much better able to tolerate her own dependent longings and needs, even as she grieved her early childhood losses. And while it was true that these longings had been present from the beginning, she needed an affirmation of herself as a desirable adult woman before it was safe to examine deeper longings and vulnerabilities.[2] My attempts to circumvent this affirmation had interfered with her progression!

As our sessions unfolded, it became clear that my effort to avoid the erotic stimulation and my fear of her consuming aggressions had reen-

---

2. While Grace did not have a borderline personality, the dynamic here is a common one in many borderline patients. Having little that they value in themselves as people, they attempt to attract the needed involvement through use of physical and sexual attractiveness, as if to say, "This is best I have to offer." With these people, I usually find that any sexual attraction feels hollow and brief. Their deeper emptiness and neediness pervades the physical presentation.

acted one of Grace's early fantasies about her mother's and father's relationship and her role with them.

What happens when the patient is the primary orchestrator of the avoidance of an erotic transference? The following case history illustrates some of the complications that can then ensue.

"Fran" was a 35-year-old married woman who worked as a designer. She entered therapy after a lengthy treatment with a therapist whom she experienced as having a feminist agenda. Fran believed that her former therapist had been too involved in wanting her to divorce, for her reasons, not Fran's.

Fran presented herself as a complex mixture of mature desires, intellectual awareness, and childlike impulses. She could shift from one state to another rapidly. Although socially and professionally outgoing, her intimate behavior with men was masochistic. As she described her childhood, this orientation became clearer. While both of her parents were successful professionals, her father had seemed to her an alluring and unstable, mercurial figure who could be both seductive and frightening. Her mother, the organizer and stabilizer of the family home, had been overtly compliant with Fran's father.

We spent many sessions examining these family dynamics and their influence on the patient, both during her early years and in her current life. As we clarified some of these issues, she divorced her abusive and exploitative husband. Yet she went on to struggle with a series of less overtly destructive, but emotionally similar men.

After several years of regular sessions and without being specific, I said that while many different feelings and fantasies had been articulated, some key feelings still seemed to be lacking. Fran quickly responded, "Oh, that! I'm not going to allow myself to fall in love with you. That's supposed to happen, but it won't. I won't let it happen!" The salient absence of erotic-affectionate mutual transferences, along with the presence of humorous sparring during the sessions, had alerted me to the presence of some resistance. At the same time, my own apparent lack of a full range of transference affects and a sense of a harsh boundary hidden beneath her humorous interactive style pointed toward a hidden issue. It felt as if there were some controlled distance in her work with me.

While I thought about the absence of negatives in the unconscious and her possible reasons to need such conscious exclusion, we explored these remarks. On several occasions during this period, Fran became agitated and left the session without offering a reason for her distress. After some time, she felt that she understood a trigger to her upset. With a sense of incredulity and anxiety, she described being afraid of being in the office when I wore my winter boots. At first she said it was "stupid." However, her associations brought her back to previously repressed sexual abuses by a neighbor.

Fran had never told her parents of the abuse, because of her fear that the perpetrator would make good on his threat to kill them if she spoke out. As a small child, Fran had been charmed and "in love with" this neighbor, who had lured her into his basement. After that, her fears of erotic excitement and death had contributed heavily to her developing pattern of masochistic submission to controlling men, while remaining aloof from genuine involvement. Over several years she explored this hidden transference dynamic and resolved much of the early trauma and its sequelae. Fran went on to find and marry a more appropriate partner, with whom she then raised a family without the controlling emotional distance or masochistic submission.

In this particular treatment, my recognition of the transference resistance in the form of emotional distance and a lack of warmth, and my decision to patiently gather data and experience until Fran could safely confront the issue helped us both to move on to deeper treatment issues. In this example, the marked absence of experienced sensual feelings and fantasy became a crucial factor in identifying the patient's transference.

Over the years, I have come to identify some particular treatment circumstances in which I was usually able to anticipate or recognize erotic transferential states. I have noticed, for example, that many borderline women patients often first present in a dramatic or sexualized manner of dress or demeanor. Frequently there will be something slightly exaggerated in their dress, makeup, gestures, or words. These aspects will prove to be transiently erotic for me. But within minutes of meeting these individuals, I will be struck by the power of their underlying emptiness and vacancy, which has been so carefully wrapped in the shell of superficial appeal. At that point, their initially striking appearance loses its engaging quality and instead arouses a kind of sadness within me for the energy that has gone into this lavish preparation, which only seems to advertise a devastating emotional bankruptcy, an absence of the sense of the person.

As treatment proceeds, eroticized behavior will periodically re-emerge. For these individuals, such acting in is often a way of defending against deeper pain and grief. It's as if the patient is telling the therapist, "This is all I have to offer; don't ask me to struggle for a deeper sense of self by looking within."

These enticements do not usually arouse my own erotic fantasies, however. In most cases, I find that I'm more engaged with the painful emptiness they reveal. A female patient who had been sexually involved with a previous therapist seemed to recognize this fact, when she said after four years of work with me, "I'm going to stop trying to get you to sleep with me. I can always get a man to sleep with me. I can't always get a therapist."

A subsequent examination of this statement revealed her fears about herself, along with her vision of therapy as a form of "necessary exploitation." Although I had not been engaged in an erotically influenced transference up to that point, I noted the emergence of greater warmth and sensual feelings on my part as the patient became a more centered and fuller person during the next four years. This seemed a more natural and non-disturbing aspect of the work, as the two of us became more equal collaborators in the work. I have seen this a number of times. As the work intensifies and the focus shifts to a greater understanding of the patient's deeper experience, I am more prone to have sensual, mildly erotic responses. I have also noted over the years that additional erotic transference and fantasy will sometimes emerge for me as treatment reaches closure and I'm anticipating the imminent loss of the relationship with the patient.

Such erotic affects signal my own responses to loss and a wish to hold on, and they occur most frequently where the work has been long and intense, and has culminated in a good result. This has occurred with men, where I feel like a friend is moving away and I notice a sensed sadness, or with a woman, where an erotic fantasy precedes the sense of loss. Early in my work, these dynamics prolonged some treatments, until I came to recognize and understand my own responses and my resistance to them.

There have also been some occasions on which I noted the intrusion of unwelcome erotic thoughts about a patient after the treatment reached a painful impasse. In those situations where I felt obstructed and frustrated, or where I was caught up in a struggle with the patient and felt powerless, I experienced intrusive erotic fantasies that were unwelcome and annoying. I would wonder, Why this person, and why now? She doesn't appeal to me. She can be so difficult. Eventually, I came to see that these erotic wishes had been triggered by my own anger and my desire for control and effectiveness. Recognizing this helped me to reexamine the treatment.

I have not dealt with the area of homoerotic countertransferences. Over the years I have wondered about this. Am I too repressed? Possibly. It isn't consciously an awareness. I do note that when termination approaches with some men after an intense and positive treatment, I sometimes wish I were younger as they are or had a more robust physique. As with many of my other responses, however, these go to more fundamental issues of attachment, separation, and loss. Some women colleagues have told me that they have more frank homoerotic fanatsies and feelings with their women patients.

There is a vast range of possible emotional responses possible within the therapist. When considered in thoughtful ways, they have the potential to extend the effectiveness of our work. Experience has shown that these erotic feelings and responses, when thoughtfully assessed and understood, can indicate a wide range of subjective and intersubjective states. With careful examination, they will often contribute to our understanding and to the furtherance of our clinical work. Our increasing openness to these inevitable transferential reenactments will help us to perceive their dynamics more effectively. Hopefully that will promote a greater ease among therapists, who will then be able to work toward a greater understanding of this complex and challenging area of psychotherapy.

As many of the examples in this chapter have demonstrated, "Eros" often has far less to do with sexuality than with finding a distraction aimed at helping us avoid painful issues and conflicts during the treatment hour!

10

Countertransference and Psychopharmacology

Writing this chapter has been especially difficult, because it raises some wide-ranging and conflicted issues for me. I described previously my sense that the goal of psychotherapy is to help the individual to find his or her core self; what then is the impact of exogenous neurobiologic alterations on this objective? Do they aid, impede, or accelerate the process? Do they temporize, providing only transient relief, or do they allow better reflection?

For years, conditions like schizophrenia and autism were explained by observed familial psychodynamics, including such alleged factors as "schizophrenogenic mothers" or the supposedly remote, emotionally uninvolved mothers of autistic children. In more recent years we have found neurologic and biologic understandings that are far more compelling, and some of the dynamic "explanations" have come to be seen as descriptions not of the causes, but of the effects of neurobiologic limitations on patients, and responses to these within the family. Even though social and relational/interpersonal psychology remained crucial, in the treatment of these conditions medications were now a central feature. The question then arose, Would medications eventually play the same

191

role in the treatment of less severe emotional conditions? Today we are told that many conditions (alcoholism, depression, and obsessive compulsive disorders, for example) are genetic and biologic, and yet in many instances these disorders have proved more responsive to interpersonal interventions than to pharmacology. Where is the elusive boundary between psyche and neurochemistry? Again the questions loom: What does it mean to include biologic agents in the process of psychotherapy? Where do the two helpfully interact? What are the limitations of each? Where might they be mutually exclusive?

Complex and intimidating, these questions at first seemed to lie beyond the scope of an inquiry aimed primarily at exploring the clinical interactions between patient and therapist. Upon reflection, however, it became evident to me that such decisions as when or whether to prescribe an antidepressant, an anxiolytic, or a mood-stabilizing agent for a particular patient are, in fact, significantly influenced by the dynamics of the countertransference as they unfold week by week during psychotherapy sessions.

The decision to attempt this chapter came directly from a clinical experience with a patient and a teaching hospital, not from an abstract consideration of the issue. In the end, the struggle to work through a crisis with this patient served to underline several significant issues:

1. In many treatment situations, knowing when to prescribe medications (and when *not* to!) is essential.
2. Without a respectful relationship between the parties, any useful medication effect may be lost.
3. The prescribing physician needs to be aware of his or her motivations in prescribing an agent, and of how he or she is perceived by the patient.

Darlene, and a decision

Darlene was a woman approaching mid-life, with a history of many years of severe anorexia and ritualized compulsive behaviors. She had worked with a number of therapists, pharmacologists, and dietary specialists in the years before she began treatment with me. During our first several years of psychotherapy, which felt grueling and intense for both of us, Darlene and I struggled to make sense of her secrecy, her need for "magical control," the function and cost of her rituals, and her tendency to remain distant in relationships.

After several years of intense work, we were able to see her rage as a constant presence that drowned out her daily life. Rituals, driven by a fierce fury, made each day the same as the one before. It seemed clear that her relentless anger was the energy source for several strategies aimed at denying the passage of time. To accomplish this would allow her to remain forever a little girl living in a particular moment. While Darlene consciously conceded that it was impossible to "stop time" in this way, her endless rages and her commitment to her rigidly observed rituals seemed to suggest the presence of a psychotic component in her terror of change. I wondered, was her "frozen-in-time" behavior the chief obstacle preventing us from moving through her rage to the pain hidden beneath?

As a result of some recent psychotherapeutic work, Darlene gained weight. Suddenly, her increased bodily mass and her altered shape were confronting her with tangible evidence of change. Obviously, time had not been stopped after all, and her distress was palpable. Darlene's desperate struggle to avoid facing the temporal changes that affect all of us stemmed from her refusal to grieve several early losses and subsequent self-inflicted losses accrued during her many years of ritualized absence from life. As these two issues became the focus of our work, a regression to constant rituals ensued.

Darlene found herself enraged at the changes wrought in her body by the weight gain, and also by the physical abuse that years of stress and obsessive exercise had visited upon her. Tormented by these two realities, she demanded to know why she couldn't have everything that she wanted, the way she wanted and imagined it to be.

Over the past two years of our work, I had prescribed antidepressants that had produced only mild effects before losing their potency. Mood stabilizers had worked fairly well, although they triggered intolerable side-effects. We finally achieved a moderate reduction in her suicidal preoccupations with the use of antipsychotics, although they left her feeling "unreal." These latter compounds seemed to shroud her sense of time and her awareness of life in a dissociative haze that made open communication difficult. In fact, the antipsychotics promoted biochemically her illusion of "timelessness."

Darlene's struggle was a desperate one. She had only recently resumed eating; she had gained the weight as a result of repeated confrontations in which we labored to understand what she was doing to herself. Eventually, we came to see that one aspect of her behavior was the request that I witness her destruction and even collude in it by focusing upon details extraneous to the true objective of her behavior. I responded to this realization, "You want me to fiddle while Rome burns? I won't be a party to that!"

I went on to explain to Darlene that I was powerless to change her. I did not have any such magic. A radical transformation wrought by me was both impossible and not my job. I could work with her to understand and struggle with her pain and distress, but she had to maintain her own well-being as a precondition for our work. If she would not do that, I also had a choice: I could refuse to play the role of a passive witness whose presence tacitly approved her self-destruction. Why, I asked her, might she want me in that situation? I also pointed out that although I was intent on understanding what lay behind her painful choices, the two of us had to reach a clear understanding about her responsibility for her safety before we could proceed. In these discussions, I was aware of the intensity of the connection our prior work had given us, and hoped it would sustain us this time. But I knew I had to make clear where this boundary lay, or the work would certainly fail.

Darlene responded to my observations angrily, insisting that she was committed to our work, but her comments made clear that she could not let go of her magical controls. In our sessions, I pointed out that she was acting on her impulses whenever she disengaged from eye contact, went off into fantasy elaborations, changed her vocal tone to remove herself from the intensity of our discussion, or resorted to other evasive behaviors. Her struggle to engage, evade, and control were continuous. She was trying simultaneously both to be involved with me and to remain in her fantasy world. This fence-straddling was another retreat from genuine engagement, as she hid in fantasy and only feigned her partial involvement with me. I characterized this as a pseudo-involvement in therapy, similar to the way she lived her life outside of it. By continuously noting changes in her state of involvement, we were able to stay productively at this interface.

While these behaviors seemed to be an expression of her fury, might they also, I wondered to myself, be evidence of her terror at facing the deeper pain of her losses? I went on to state that I would be just another failed therapist full of windy theories and mawkish worries if I didn't challenge her behavior. Even while I presented these issues to her, I acknowledged that I was powerless to do more than state what I observed. I could not truly understand the basis for her rage and hurt, unless she took the risk of telling me about them directly, and chose to examine them with me, not enact them.

Our sessions proceeded at this level of active involvement. I wondered constantly: Who was I in the transference? I felt many different responses during these tumultuous hours. I felt powerless and incompetent, forceful and clear, a pursuing lover/parent. At times I was also a rejected friend and an incompetent. Had I become for Darlene the disappointing parent who failed to understand something she needed? Had I become some sort of an unknowing adversary? Was I the object of a wish—the source of a hidden frustration—that she was experiencing but could not share? The reality was that we would not be able to understand her plight until she agreed to work with me to decipher her messages. As I steadily attended to and reflected upon the possible meanings of her perpetual turnings away, she felt challenged to stay engaged, even when I was unclear as to the deeper meanings. Again and again I clarified my essential powerless in our relationship, while pointing out that I could not hope to know, understand, or help her without her willing consent and cooperation. "Each moment is your choice. The power is in your hands."

She said, "But I don't want it to be!" and I responded, "You can accept the reality and pay its cost, or deny the reality, pursue magic, and pay *that* cost—your choice."

Engaging in this manner, we could see that she wanted me with her all the time, just as she had wanted her lost parents. What was it that kept her from holding a sense of herself and me in an internal sustaining relatedness? Was this the seven-year-old confronted with multiple losses? Would holding the relationship with me be disloyal to the treasured memories? Would keeping a sense of relatedness risk a punitive response from her inner controlling voices? I kept wondering about these issues and listening for clues.

Trapped in these longings, Darlene had to grapple with inevitable frustration and anger at the end of each therapy session. And as I described above, her striving for magical control hampered our work during the hour as well, since it left her feeling vacant and not genuinely involved even when we *were* together. Darlene's dilemma was that she could not really be with me *or* herself while we were meeting, unless I actively pursued her.

Occasionally she did have a session that was more genuine than the others. These brief excursions into authentic dialogue provided some relief, even though they were invariably followed by a resurgence of the controlling and rigid "demons" of her ritualized life—the unreal, timeless world where so much of her suffering took place. And as our sessions unfolded, Darlene began to realize that she could not control life and loss. Without risking loss, she could have no gains. Would she end the therapy to avoid facing up to her limitations? What would prevent me from becoming just one more name on the long list of her discarded therapists? Increasingly concerned about her growing pain and exhaustion as she engaged with this recognition and again became more preoccupied with suicide, I suggested a brief hospitalization. I hoped to reduce both the day-to-day distractions and the isolation that were eroding her strength. I also hoped that in an environment where people would react to her from moment-to-moment she might become more engaged, and less involved with her tormenting rituals. Perhaps a period of hospitalization would also offer her, on a minute-to-minute basis, the kind of support and engagement that she felt was helpful during our sessions.

Admission required several calls from me to the hospital. The staff needed my help in building a case for admission with the health insurer, which agreed to only a week's stay. When the admission process was complete, I talked first with the admitting doctor, and then with the doctor assigned to Darlene on the unit.

As I described my prior work with this patient and my hopes for her admission, one doctor asked me to review her medications once again. He wondered if she should be given a higher dosage of a drug that in the past had not proved effective. My focus on the psychology of the patient's dilemma, and on the evolving dynamics of her psychotherapy, was not challenged or disputed, apparently because these aspects of her treatment simply were not significant issues for this physician. The second doctor, who would be working with Darlene during her hospitalization (my God! only a week!) responded to my detailed psychological description by asking dryly, "Do you think this is BPD (borderline personality disorder), BDD (body dysmorphic disorder), or more OCD (obsessive compulsive disorder)?"

I agreed that all of her symptoms could indeed be understood as manifestations of a struggle to avoid grieving her early losses. Her "OCD" behavior consisted of rigid habits involving foods, clothes, bathing rituals, routines of movement, counting, and location of objects in space. I noted that these rigidities allowed her the illusion of "stopping time" by compulsively making each day, activity, and object the same.

But her symptoms could equally be understood as "BDD": an expression of the hatred and rage that she could not tolerate inside herself, focused outwardly on specific aspects of her body surface. Some of this rage was directed inwardly via obsessive berating ruminations and criticisms in which she "proved" to herself that time had not passed. In her body she could see herself as still a little girl who had not physically changed or developed, waiting for the return of her dead mother and grandmother. No breasts, hips, bodily hair, or periods allowed, only smooth girlish skin and a shape without curves.

These psychological mechanisms had already been consciously and meaningfully elaborated by the patient, however, and had diminished through the therapy. As a result, deeper issues were now coming into focus, and a less concrete view of the very same symptomatology could now easily be recognized as "BPD": the rage, splitting, and narcissistic preoccupation. All of these behaviors were connected to her early losses, and so were the developmental delays that had occurred as her perpetual rage screened out the deeper affects.

Whatever descriptive diagnoses we used to categorize aspects of her condition, however, this patient was struggling with a diversity of symptoms by which her underlying psychology tried to deal with emotional pain. It seemed to me essential to understand these complex interwoven issues, along with the course of treatment that had preceded her hospital stay, if we were to provide effective care. But the response to my explanation was swift: "Okay, but do you think she should be on the OCD or Eating Disorders Unit?"

As these kinds of exchanges unfolded, I felt increasingly like an invisible dinosaur. Yes, I knew that hospitals had changed. I also understood that these physicians were forced to provide the best help they could in a very short time, due primarily to the economic exigencies of managed care. Nonetheless, I was shocked. And my concern only deepened when Darlene returned a week later for her first post-hospital session and reviewed her experience on the ward. She described how she had come away from the hospital feeling "processed." She said that the entire focus had been on medications. There had been little or no treatment based on any personal involvement with her. Indeed, the medical staff had only become concerned that she might be suicidal on the last day of her hospitalization, and then only because psychological testing had raised that disturbing possibility, not because someone became concerned after talking with her.

Undoubtedly some of Darlene's observations were colored by her splitting, her rage, and the narcissistic injury of not having been "special enough"; but there was no denying their essential accuracy. Her experience matched what the staff told me. So offended had she been by the exclusive emphasis on medications that she had stopped taking them! In order to maintain some control in the impersonal system of the hospital, she had rendered it powerless by refusing the prescribed medications. After some reflection on this in her sessions with me, she agreed to resume one of them.

It was while I was listening to this patient describe the continuing preoccupation of a hospital staff with medicating patients that I decided to attempt this chapter on psychotherapy and psychopharmacology.

PSYCHOTHERAPY AND PSYCHOPHARMACOLOGY: COUNTERTRANSFERENCE AT THE INTERFACE

Some patients' depressions, anxieties, phobias, etc., disappear in the course of psychotherapy without the use of medication, as a result of significant change and evolution in their characters. In these situations, it is clear that no external additions have been made to their internal biochemistry. If we had measured synaptic neurochemistry in these people, however, would we have found different neurotransmitter levels before, during, and at the end of therapy? The answer is surely yes. There is little reason, after all, to doubt that the impact of emotional turmoil produces measurable changes in the biochemistry of the central nervous system. Similarly, a reduction in these stresses and a return to a less stressed homeostatic state surely introduces changes in one's internal neurochemistry.

Klerman and colleagues (1974) studied a group of 150 moderately depressed outpatients who had responded to a four- to six-week course of amitryptiline. Following the initial treatment course, the patients were put into two groups. One group received once-weekly psychotherapy with an experienced social worker. The second group received a monthly fifteen-minute interview with a psychiatrist to complete rating scales. Each of these two groups was divided into three subgroups. One subgroup received medication; one placebo; one no pill at all. Thus, one could compare the treatment of depressed patients treated with either: medication or psychotherapy alone; psychotherapy combined with medication; or no medication and no therapy (fifteen minutes a month with a psychiatrist doing rating scales would not be considered psychotherapy). The outcome being measured was relapse.

The patients receiving once-weekly psychotherapy and no medication did as well as those receiving medication without psychotherapy. Those receiving medication had a relapse rate of 12.0–12.5%. Those receiving psychotherapy alone had a relapse rate of 16.7%. (This was not statistically significant because the difference between those receiving medication and those receiving psychotherapy without medication was one patient). Thus, medication alone and psychotherapy alone were equally effective by the measures used. However, the effects of medication were discernible much more quickly.

The authors found that the depression measures they used could not discern a difference between the groups receiving medication alone and the groups receiving medication combined with psychotherapy.

Those receiving psychotherapy, although they had a relapse rate similar to those receiving only medication, did better on social adjustment and family interaction scales (work performance, anxious rumination, interpersonal friction, inhibition of communication, submissive dependence, and family attachment). Because of this, the authors recommended that the best treatment would combine psychotherapy and medication, because medications did not address the social and interpersonal issues that can lead to a better adaptation.

Those receiving placebo with psychotherapy had a 28.0% relapse rate, and those receiving placebo without psychotherapy had 30.8% relapse rate, both significantly worse than individuals receiving either medication or psychotherapy alone. Could this result reflect a different attitude towards psychotherapy among patients who, when given a medication, look for a medication effect but find none? Might they, in their initial preoccupation with medication relief, be less attentive to their psychotherapy?

Those receiving neither psychotherapy, medication, nor placebo had a relapse rate of 36.0%.

While it would make sense to repeat this study, prospectively, with a larger number of subjects to test the consistency of these results, it would also make sense to include from the beginning a group receiving intensive psychotherapy alone and placebo alone.

I have seen a number of patients who report that the benefits of their psychotherapy remained, and that their depressions did not recur, even when they faced issues similar to those that had precipitated their initial depression. Some of these patients were initially treated with medication and psychotherapy. Others had responded to psychotherapy alone. Such reports are consistent with the findings reported above. They suggest that in some (or many) individuals the personal learning that occurs in psychotherapy has an enduring effect that may prevent recurrences, or be useful even when a recurrence does arise.

Similarly, as it has become clear that there is a biological component of emotional distress, significant improvements in medications, and therefore function and life, have occurred. Medications produce symptomatic improvement more quickly than psychotherapy does, thus reducing the period of emotional distress. However, the initial hope that our new somatic understanding alone would effect cure has not been realized. The most marked improvement usually tkaes place in situations where both the biological and psychosocial issues are jointly addressed.

Given these considerations, what should we do with individuals whom we cannot effectively reach in psychotherapy? Should we not ask whether the problem might lie in our incomplete knowledge of the process or in the individual practitioner's limitations, even as we also consider the introduction of medication? Depending upon the individual's state, capacity to function, and motivation, when do we introduce or defer medications? We need to ask this question at every juncture in the treatment process, even as we remain keenly aware of the danger that the new emphasis on the biologic will cloud our judgment of the importance of internal and interpersonal psychology. Even when we are using biologic agents effectively, we need to be mindful of the source of change. Medications can relieve symptoms, but they do not affect character.

The advent of effective psychoactive medications has allowed many physician-psychiatrists once again to feel like "real" doctors. Those who had been organically inclined from the beginning now had better biochemical agents to work with. Others who had been trained in psychological approaches that they found to be tedious and less than effective now could take a broader approach. And analytically trained psychiatrists were initially threatened. Would these medications eliminate the need for intensive intrapsychic work? It is possible to see the potential workings of countertransference in these broad outlines.

What of the psychologists and social workers who practice dynamic psychotherapies and psychoanalysis? How are they affected by this change of the last forty years? They often do not have prescription rights, and so may have kept a more consistent focus on intrapsychic work, while asking a colleague to handle medications. These nonmedical practitioners have in many cases been the torch-bearers for psychoanalytic work, and the mainstays of many psychoanalytic institutes. Yet they want prescription rights, and legislative and legal struggles continue around this question. Again, one can see the possibility of significant countertransference issues in their practice.

Given the recent advances in our knowledge of organic functioning, the question of the appropriate integration of the biologic and the psychologic needs continuous attention. How should we approach the weighing of these diverse and overlapping perspectives in a balanced and integrated fashion? Obviously, we can examine, and then agree or disagree with, the points of view of researchers, and the premises and variables of their research, on all of these questions. We must ask ourselves, What is being measured? Who is doing the measuring and from what perspective? What constitutes therapy? What outcome are we examining? Is it symptom reduction, character change, personal growth? What does the patient want and need?

In most cases, we confront not a simple either-or circumstance, but a multivariate situation in which a reasonable understanding requires the balanced integration of many different areas of reality and uncertainty. It is into this nebulous, fast-changing arena that we must venture daily, in order to learn all we can from the mistakes that we are sure to make.

How can we best help those individuals whom the dynamic understandings generated by psychotherapy fail to reach? The first step is to remember that the therapist may be limited by blind spots in his or her own perspective, and that consultation or supervision may be useful in the effort to overcome these and connect better with the patient. And what of those patients so stuck in depression, or whose inner pain so powerfully and clearly neutralizes their ability to achieve reasonable understanding, that they cannot function? In these circumstances, medications can significantly reduce distress and allow patients to use therapy for the deeper understanding of themselves that they need.

There is a vast middle ground of patients; those for whom prescribed medications may or may not serve to hasten and help the work of psychotherapy. How can we know when to prescribe and not to prescribe? And what is the meaning, in clinical terms, of offering or not offering medication? Such questions must be addressed before the clinician decides to reach for the prescription pad.

In an age when television and radio advertisements routinely urge health care consumers to "ask your physician" for medications intended to combat a wide range of conditions, these musings may sound quaintly anachronistic. Insurance companies, HMOs, and public clinics often promote the use of medications as the best way to deal with psychological issues. And why not? A relatively inexpensive "quick fix" makes good business sense, doesn't it? After all, this society simply doesn't have the resources required to provide intensive therapies for all who could use them—even supposing that we as a society really were convinced of the ultimate efficacy of long-term psychotherapy!

Regardless of the contemporary ethos that promotes widespread and *casual* medication use, I believe that there are questions about the meaning of prescribing drugs for patients that are relevant for both patient and practitioner. They are based upon my perspective that the focus of treatment is directed to the search for the core self whenever possible. I find it helpful to ask before prescribing:

Why am I thinking of medications now? Is the patient's distress so intense? Is he or she unable to function or work productively at this time? If so, why? Have we reached some important area of internal distress, and do these symptoms represent the struggle at this interface? Is the patient so blocked that he or she cannot really make use of inner resources to work well at this time? How will medication help? Am I reaching for a short-term gain at the expense of deeper and more enduring work?

Will this medication actually help us get to the heart of the matter? Will it provide a needed respite?

Am I responding to a plea for a magical intervention? Am I colluding in the wish for magic? Am I feeling powerless myself? What does this represent countertransferentially? Am I desperate and joining in the sense of hopelessness? Am I more or less engaged? Is this a way of distancing myself from the patient, or a legitimate response to genuine distress?

Clinical Decisions

These are the kinds of tensions that decision-making about drugs involves. And the therapist cannot hope to evade them by relying on easy generalizations. In spite of my own admitted bias toward psychotherapy and away from drugs, for example, there have been many times when a patient's distress outweighed my concerns about future impact on the treatment progress. And in many other instances, psychotherapy was clearly enhanced by the use of medication.

There have also been treatment situations in which a patient requested medication and I provided it because I sensed that a struggle would have been unproductive. In those cases, I did my best to make it clear that the primary purpose of the medication was to provide us with a "window of improvement," an opportunity to achieve an understanding of deeper issues by reducing the patient's distress with medicine.

Henry

Henry, a 48 year old, unmarried engineer, came to treatment at the recommendation of his priest. He had been troubled since adolescence by numerous compulsions, and these had dramatically increased over the preceding two years. The compulsions included checking door locks, stoves, toasters, and other electrical devices before leaving for work each day. Henry knew, as a professional engineer, that his checking of these devices was unnecessary, but he was compelled to do it, regardless.

Henry presented in the interview as a neat, organized, polite, careful, and controlled person. He was cautious in his inquiries and seemed concerned not to offend me, or anyone else. He lived by rules and described a limited awareness of emotional response in himself. He explained that he lived at home with his elderly father, a retired engineer. Henry's description made the older man sound cold, rigid, authoritarian, and emotionally cruel. Henry painted his mother, who had died many years before, as a meek, self-effacing woman whose job had been to make a home for her husband according to his likes.

Henry told me that he had tried to help her in her tasks and had never overtly resented his father. Since his mother's death, in fact, Henry had seen it as his duty to take care of his father. Was the father grateful, I wondered? Henry paused, then said that he found my question "odd." Smiling, he added, "No, that's not Dad's way. You know how it is." It seemed clear that by asking me to understand his experience as ordinary and acceptable, Henry was revealing that he suppressed any discontent and attempted to gloss over his deeper responses to the terms of this relationship.

Continuing, Henry noted that he had been and remained a dutiful son. He had worked after school as a youth, and had contributed regularly to the upkeep of the household. Rarely socializing, he had attended a local college while living at home. He had dated infrequently while in college. He had felt awkward with women, he said, never having forgotten his father's acerbic comments about "kids these days with short skirts and no morals." Henry pointed out that his father had warned him often of the dangers of getting sidetracked and slipping into "perdition," a state of irretrievable moral failure that could be caused by involvement with sex and drugs. Awkward in his own social involvements, and mindful of his father's anger-laden warnings, Henry had kept to his home and his studies.

In his thirties, he had become friendly at work with a divorced woman, and shared an occasional lunch with her. They had also gone to a movie once or twice, but Henry had felt too anxious to pursue the relationship, although he had once gotten sexually involved with her on a business trip. He had enjoyed the experience, but later felt guilty and had backed away from intimacy with her. Around that time, his compulsive behaviors had became more intense. He went to confession, where he spoke with a comforting and understanding priest (the same person who later referred him for treatment).

Over the two years before we began our work, Henry had struggled with his deepening compulsions. By now he felt compelled to check the furnace, stove, doors, and other devices many times before leaving for work each day. Sometimes he would even leave work and return home to recheck them. He had grown increasingly anxious and had lost several pounds.

During our early sessions as I was inquiring about the circumstances of his life, I asked him if he could account for his anxious concerns. Henry attributed some of his worries to the fact that his now elderly and partially disabled father would face increased difficulties in getting out of the house in the event of a fire. These comments and some others like them made it seem clear that the father was actually more demanding and critical than had so far been portrayed, but Henry never seemed to have any overt complaints. Did he ever find his father annoying? "Oh no," he quickly replied. "That wouldn't be right—he's my father!"

Sensing that Henry would not be able to explore questions of this kind any further at this time, I declined to pursue this remark. Later, however, he noted that his compulsions always seemed to intensify when his father was about to be released from the hospital after another treatment for his heart problems.

I wondered to myself how much of Henry's distress was caused by the increased burden of care he took on with his father's return, and how much actually stemmed from denied anger and the wish to be free of this ungrateful parent[1] whom he was trying so hard to love.

During one session Henry told me that he understood that medication might be helpful, and that he really needed relief. I responded by suggesting that medicines might indeed give him some relief from the distress he felt, and that they might also help him to understand the inner dynamics that were triggering his symptoms. This last comment produced a quizzical look, so I went on to explain that when medications relieved symptoms they also provided some emotional room to make sense of the feelings that were causing the problems. Henry nodded, but he seemed intent on obtaining the medication rather than spending much time thinking about the feelings that made him want it.

Without further discussion I prescribed fluvoxamine, and saw him monthly at his request. During our sessions he pointed out that his symptoms had diminished and that he had resumed his customary activities. We talked at length about his work and his life at home. Although Henry was able to describe his father's harshness indirectly, he never labeled it as such. He did clarify the fact that emotional abandonment, along with actual threats to abandon the family, had been part of his father's behavior during the patient's early life. I wondered aloud, "Might some of these memories and feelings be evoked by your father's decline and the approaching end of his life?" Henry hadn't thought of that, but he found it "an interesting idea."

After a year, Henry decided to taper the medication, and then discontinue it along with his psychotherapy. About a year later, he called to report that his distressing symptoms had returned, and that he wanted to meet.

---

1. I am reminded here of a truism that I first learned in residency training and have later seen to be true in the people I work with, namely, that people can't be free to love until they have recognized and come to terms with their hatred.

Soon after we resumed meeting, Henry noted that he had been thinking about my earlier comments about the "deeper roots" of his anxieties. He said he wanted relief from his symptoms, but he also intended to get to the bottom of them, "This time, I want to figure out what's going on. You were right, there is something inside me."

Associatively, he described a new and growing awareness of feelings about his father, including guilt that seemed to be related to a wish that he could be free of the burden of caring for the old man. He admitted that he was afraid of losing his father's companionship, however, and went on to describe a yearning for other close relationships in his life.

We resumed our work, meeting on a weekly basis. He resumed his medication. Gradually, Henry recognized a feeling that his life was controlled and circumscribed by his father. As he struggled with distress and guilt, he tried to make sense of now conscious and contradictory emotions, as he talked with me and with his confessor. In what seemed to be a kind of conjoint therapy, he worked with both of us to begin confronting the painful feelings he'd kept hidden from himself. For the first time he began to describe flickering feelings of anger, along with some destructive fantasies. Not long after this he discontinued the medication because of its side-effects, but he decided to continue therapy without medication.

During the next year of weekly therapy, memories of childhood privations and denied resentments surfaced with some troubling affects. Meanwhile his father was re-hospitalized for heart surgery. Henry was dutiful in his attention and care, and left work often to care for the older man. Still, he knew that this burden took a heavy toll in stress and fatigue. Once again he described the all-consuming effect on his life of having to provide constant care while holding down a job, and he wondered what purpose his sacrifice really served.

His compulsions returned in full force. He saw in some dreams and associations that his fears of a house fire were related to his own unacceptable fury and his wishes to be free of his father, even as he simultaneously expressed the longing to share "something good" with the old man before the latter died. Gradually, these insights became more keenly focused, more authentic. As he accepted the idea that feelings could be a "blend" (rather than remaining starkly black and white), he also began to see that his negative emotions did not include actions or "real sin." His compulsive actions were in fact a guilt-driven undoing of angry and destructive wishes. With this recognition his symptoms began to diminish, and he could even begin teasing his father about his "crusty" manner.

This mild discharge of accumulated resentment allowed the two of them to engage each other more and to enjoy each other's company. Henry warned his father to watch what he said. Otherwise he might smear grease on the wheels of the old man's wheelchair, "but only to research the effects on the friction characteristics of the wheels!" Gradually, Henry began to assert more of his own needs and wishes at home.

Over the next year, he also sought out the woman he had dated years before. They renewed their relationship, which began to flourish. Henry said that he wanted to marry her, but that he could not take that step while his father still lived. I wondered aloud if that restriction didn't put him in the uneasy position of wanting his father's death so that he could move on with his own life. This query seemed to trouble him. Still, he *had* managed to uncover these powerful feelings without a recurrence of his compulsions. He did wait until after his father's death to marry, and there was a brief recrudescence of the compulsions around the time of the wedding.

Henry's case is an example of a situation in which the initial use of medication not only relieved symptoms, but also allowed for an engagement in deeper therapy. Had I tried to pursue therapy without medication, I don't believe that Henry would have tolerated his discomfort, nor do I believe that he would have begun to examine the underlying issues. He needed some time on his own to mull over the questions that had begun to surface. Had I *only* provided medication, however, Henry's personal life might not have evolved as it did. Our efforts in the initial treatment to raise questions that he had not previously considered, combined with the medications that gave him relief from the disturbing symptoms, allowed Henry to begin examining his life circumstances.

The outcome in Henry's case appears to have been positive. Nonetheless, there have been many situations over the years in which I became convinced that the prescription of medication would impede therapy rather than further it.

Brad

Brad, a 45 year old married man, entered treatment on the behest of his wife. If he didn't change his behavior, she warned, their marriage was over. Brad displayed a smirking disdain and an urbane, put-upon attitude at our first meetings. He boasted of many of brilliant successes in his career. In spite of his accomplishments, however, his behavior often seemed outrageous and provocative. His "jokes" and comments offended everyone, from his boss, wife, and children to his neighbors.

Brad dressed bizarrely at times, and outraged others with his biting sarcasm and his public rudeness. Yet he defended these inconsiderate antics by dismissively resorting to windy harangues about "freedom of speech," his "rights," and his refusal to conform to social conventions and the expectations of others.

When I responded with the word "Bullshit!," Brad laughed and praised the intellectual cleverness of my *riposte*. "Oh, that medical training!" Then he admitted, "I know I'm an odd duck, actually impossible— but that's *your* problem!" I clarified matters by noting that it really wasn't my problem. I suggested that provoking others to respond and react might be a strategy aimed at allowing him to deal with the responses of other people, rather than having to confront what was occurring within him.

We went on in this vein for a number of sessions, and I continually drew the focus back to his internal life and the motivations for his behavior. Gradually Brad became depressed, and began to recall his early life and his sense of having been an outsider in his family and community. As he spoke he saw the repetition in his current life. He had been the talented oldest male in a patriarchal family, and had many genuine accomplishments. Yet he had never really been included in the life around him. Flamboyant alcohol-fueled behavior had been regularly exhibited by both of his parents, and explained as a normal part of the "privileged" high-society life that they were part of. To him it felt "weird," this so-called proof of the special status of his high-flying family. He was lonely and unable to feel a connection with either parent.

Yet the same behavior that had often seemed both provocative and destructive to the young Brad was now firmly entrenched in his own repertoire. Brad's own behavior was a caricature of his parents'. He didn't like my pointing this out, but he saw it. Early in treatment I advised that he stop drinking, and we discussed Alcoholics Anonymous. He did stop the drinking, but disdained the need for support from, or involvement with, others. This was a curious position for a lonely man. Beneath the bravado and the disdain lay a shame that was as yet untouchable. We continued working in his newly abstinent state.

At one juncture I wondered aloud if his current outrageous behaviors weren't related to his early experiences. He seemed to enjoy having the power to make others endure the kind of embarrassment and humiliation he had once experienced. Now he could be the abuser! And could they be serving more than one emotional purpose? His current behavior precluded inclusion, but he now actively caused his own exclusion and thus preempted others. Did that give him the illusion of controlling every situation? Such manipulative behavior also appeared to deny his need for the others, even as it kept him engaged with many different people. Until recently, Brad had regarded other people's tolerance of him as predicated upon their need for *him*. Just as he had once needed his parents, and thus had been required to tolerate their abuse and inconsistency, so others were now forced to overlook his own unacceptable behavior. Brad's "victory" over his early deprivations consisted of the fact that *he* was now in the abusive, controlling position.

Although he saw the logic of my comments, he dismissed them, and in so doing, affirmed them! "That's just the way people are. You need to have power. [Now] it's my turn!"

I pointed out the contradictory denial and affirmation of the words "it's my turn," and went on, " But what about your envy of others?" He looked surprised and taken aback. "Sure," I said. "They seem to get something out of their association with you, and you get so little. You tell me it's meaningless. You tell me that they need you for some purpose, and otherwise would not tolerate you. So they get something and you envy them for that, and make them pay by accepting abuse. But once again, you're alone on the outside—pretending you don't need. Yet you need them to need you! This power of yours seems so sadly empty."

As our examination of his behavior and its origins continued over the next few years, Brad became more subdued. One day he came to therapy and said that he wanted medication. I asked what his thoughts were about it, and what he hoped for. He spoke in his usual disdainful manner about the need being "obvious." Why was I putting him through this? Everyone used medication! Maybe he was my "annuity," and I just wanted to hold onto him in order to collect my fees. Instead of responding, I tried to explore what "holding onto him" and other statements implying exploitation might mean to him. Were we reliving his earlier dynamic with his parents yet again? Was there more to be understood in this particular depression?

This time it was the patient who snapped, "Bullshit!" He wanted medication.

I told him my concern that although medication might relieve some of his distress, it might also help him to avoid confronting more deeply the issues he needed to face. In the past I'd often wondered, for example, how much of Brad's behavior, the source of so much upset and embarrassment to others, might be a way to orchestrate situations in which others would feel something akin to the shame he had experienced. I was convinced that we needed to continue to examine such questions, and I was concerned that the use of drugs might interrupt the process. Could we continue to keep it an open question?

Reluctantly, and with great disparagement, the patient agreed to "indulge" me. He continued the sessions as scheduled, and endured genuine emotional distress from the pain of his depression. Although he engaged in some related acting out outside the office, he managed to continue our line of inquiry during the sessions.

Then one day, Brad turned to me. Regarding me carefully and with a strained expression, he asked if I knew his secret. Puzzled, I replied that I didn't know what he was referring to. He wondered if I had guessed the "secret" which he then named (but which I shall not, to protect Brad's identity and confidence). I reminded him that I had inquired earlier in treatment about this interest, and that he had denied it. In fact I had *not* known his secret, and we now proceeded to examine it: what it meant to him, how it originated and developed, why he believed that I knew it, and why it caused him such shame. Many months later Brad said,

> *"You know, I never would have looked at that or admitted it, if you hadn't said 'no'*
> *when I asked for medications. I wouldn't have faced it! I have been keeping it inside*

all my life." [Italics mine; as noted above, I have not defined Brad's secret in order to protect his privacy.]

I report here what Brad said, and I would like to believe that it is so. Yet, we do not know with certainty that he might not have faced these issues while taking medication.

There were several factors that led me to take different courses with Brad and Henry. Henry presented with an exacerbation of symptoms that had become dystonic in the context of a stable, somewhat repressed, depressive character. He was emotionally closed (defended) against introspection, and was symptom-focused. In contrast, Brad, while hostile and competitive, was seeking engagement in the context of chronic and escalating character issues. He was externalizing his distress and enacting it in the world about him. He was not troubled by symptoms. For him to feel and bear internal discomfort, "the symptoms," was an objective of treatment.

While one could make a similar case that Henry's character was significantly impacting upon his behavior, the difference was that his characterologic issues were ego-syntonic and not bringing him into conflict with others. Brad's need to engage in order to externalize his issues also made him potentially more available for treatment. When Henry had experienced a return of symptoms and considered the questions previously raised in his meetings with me, he returned with an interest in learning about the origins of his issues within his personality. Again medications aid in the reduction of symptoms, they don't alter character. If I sense that we are ready to go deeper, and I feel that medications will help, then I prescribe them. If I feel that the use of medication risks deferring the deepening of necessary characterologic work, I will explore the request, and, as in Brad's case, clarify the potential risk to treatment.

My work with Brad before the symptoms arose led me to believe that with him I was acting as the repository of projected ego capacities, and thus inadvertently signaling him that I believed in his capacity to struggle with his internal conflicts—a kind of positive mirroring absent in his childhood.

In spite of the uncertainties, it seems that patients usually benefit most when the therapeutic emphasis remains focused on the challenge of locating and understanding the origins of the patient's self-created distress, without interposing iatrogenic obstacles. In some instances, as in the case of Henry, my sense of the initial resistance to introspection led me to choose to meet his needs as he experienced them. He wanted symptomatic relief. An attempt to force my view would have become an iatrogenic obstacle to further work. As I see it, medication should be used in psychotherapy with careful consideration of its implications for patient and clinician alike. I need to keep my uncertainties as a constant: how much is what I am doing, or not doing, helping or getting in the way? The dynamic tension of living with this uncertainty is a necessary burden of the work. If nothing else, it helps to keep me humble about what I *really* know, versus what I merely think or believe. Thus, I attempt to elicit interest and curiosity in the personal internal origins of the patient's problems while balancing them with an awareness of the patient's distress and its implications.

Wilson

Not long ago I began working with Wilson, a young man who came for a consultation because of phobias and panic attacks. An accomplished academic, for many years he had lived a circumscribed life, and he was often tense and controlling in his environment. Finding items out of their usual place or similar surprises made him irritable. In the last several years, he had experienced several new symptoms, including panic attacks while driving and sudden surges of anxiety with no apparent precipitant. He reported that his brother, father, and grandfather had all experienced similar symptoms.

The duration and recent escalation of his symptoms, coupled with the family history, had me thinking about the use of medication when he raised the issue himself. He had read about it on the Internet, he said, and knew a bit about research related to pharmacology. He also understood the implications of his familial tendency to develop these anxiety symptoms. Yet he would not consider medication. I commented that it might be useful, given his symptoms, their duration, and his family history, but I pointed out that we would need to understand more about him before it would be reasonable to reach a conclusion. I wanted to know why he was so strongly against the idea. He said he had tried some anxiolytic agents on the advice of his internist, and he "didn't like the sensation." He had also tried behavior therapy with a psychologist. Until recently, this latter intervention had given him some ability to manage the symptoms.

As he spoke, it became clear that he saw the use of medication as evidence of weakness and a compromise of his independence. I saw him as someone with many internal conflicts who was constantly proving his independence to friends and professional colleagues. The external world was the arena in which he was working out internal conflicts.

We began exploring the period during which the previous behavioral techniques had become less useful. During this period of initial history-taking, I mentioned that anxiety was frequently a signal that some emotionally charged memory, wish, experience, feeling, or desire had moved close to awareness, but for some reason remained unacceptable. This notion he considered a bit quaint but interesting. I asked him to note those moments when the anxiety began, and to ask himself what might have preceded it. I was seeking to enlist his conscious cognition as an ally in bearing and examining the anxiety. I hoped to make him "curious" about himself and his symptoms.

At first, the most predictable situation that triggered his anxiety was the fifteen-minute wait before his therapy appointments. I asked him what crossed his mind as he sat feeling his anxiety: What did he imagine, remember, daydream, etc? Where did he feel it? Did it have shape or dimension? If he looked at it or went inside it, what might it tell him?

His first comment was, "You're not like my father; you're kind of quiet."

"Oh?" I said. Quite spontaneously he went on to describe his father's intrusive, overbearing, and controlling manner. In spite of these qualities, however, he felt very close to the older man. I wondered what might have brought his father to mind. He wasn't sure, but he noted that the anxiety had disappeared as he spoke.

As we gathered more history and began exploring, an analytic therapy evolved. Two years into the treatment, Wilson felt that he had suppressed much of his genuine self and had been in a reactive struggle with both of his parents. He had felt obligated to live in opposition to their wishes, and so he could not choose his own path. Anger at himself and guilt about his destructive wishes, along with feelings of separateness and

isolation, underlay his anger at his parents. Three years into the treatment, he was no longer anxious or irritable. Occasional episodes of
inexplicable anxiety were easily resolved as he trained himself to stay with
the feeling and examine his experience. We never needed medication.

What of the many individuals with major or psychotic mood disorders (particularly bipolar disorders), and those individuals struggling with
character disorders who clearly need today's effective medications? Used
appropriately, these drugs unquestionably help people to function in the
world. They can also enhance the work of psychotherapy by helping the
clinician to help patients work through disrupted psychological developmental processes. In most instances, when the affective or psychotic
symptoms are reduced, the character issues and developmental lapses
emerge.

George

George was a thirty-five-year-old man addicted to opiates. I met
him on the ward of a drug treatment unit. Large and muscular with a
deeply intense look, he rumbled down the hallway like a runaway freight
train. Even in his relaxed moments, George's visage and demeanor struck
others as intensely angry. He seemed mystified by this observation and
said that he didn't feel angry at all.

George had a long history of destructive behavior. Beginning in
grammar school, he'd had rampages, most of them directed at property.
His parents had felt compelled to move from several homes because of the
damage George inflicted on doors and walls. In the fifth grade, he had
managed to start several pieces of heavy construction equipment and to
smash them together, resulting in a huge monetary loss. George rarely
assaulted anyone, but if attacked by another, he would respond fiercely.

Prior to George's admission to the drug treatment program, three
men had insulted his girlfriend at a bar and challenged him to fight.
Because George had promised his mother to avoid trouble, he left the bar
with his girlfriend and drove away. Several minutes later, his car was
forced off the road by a truck containing the three men from the bar. One
of them got out of the truck with a chain and began smashing George's
windshield. George jumped out of his car, grabbed the chain, beat his

assailant with it, then picked him up and threw him down an embankment. Next he ran to the truck, smashed the window out with his fist and dragged out the two occupants. After beating both senseless, he flung them down the embankment and drove home.

There was no sadistic glee in George's description of these events. He told the story in matter-of-fact fashion, although his methodical delivery contained a striking intensity of affect and a furious rational logic. George said that he had felt no anger during the incident, and that he felt no anger as he told the story. I found that hard to believe, but I was most struck by his intense but muted and seemingly calm affect. (And, speaking of countertransference, I was also shocked, floored, mystified, and intrigued. It was an extremely powerful experience.)

One day two other patients sought me out to describe another startling incident involving George. On the previous evening, the three had been playing on the grounds surrounding the treatment unit, and had decided to climb a large tree. As they climbed toward a high and precarious point, they discovered that they had unknowingly cornered a large raccoon. The panicked animal turned to attack, and the two men were terrified. George was seemingly unruffled. He stared at the animal for a moment. Then he cocked his fist and with steady deliberation knocked the raccoon out of the tree with a single blow. His silent, intense manner had never changed. There was something so strange—so spooky—about his demeanor that these two patients had sought me out to discuss it, and to recommend that I "talk to George" about his state of mind.

I did so. When I interviewed him, the young man denied any history of racing thoughts, hallucinations, delusions, strange ideas, a revving internal motor, prolonged awakenings, or any other extreme behaviors beyond those already noted. Again, I was impressed with the unrelenting intensity of George's voice, facial expressions, and posture. Although he did not seem fidgety or restless, sitting with him I had the sense that his inner state vibrated with an intense, spring-like tension.

Was this a manic equivalent? Upon reflection I recommended a trial of lithium; it was 1979 and no other agents were yet being used. George agreed, and within two weeks he and the staff noticed a dramatic change. He seemed more at ease and looked less intense. I interviewed him again, and he reported that he "felt different." He could hear music, for example. I wondered what he meant by this, and he explained that he wasn't "busy" in his head. The music made him "feel" something. He felt a new quietness inside—something he had never felt. For example, he'd just spent some time with a female friend, and he'd actually been able to listen to her. He'd been surprised to discover that she was a person, and that he "wasn't just thinking of screwing her." He said that before starting on the medication he would have been constantly scheming to get her into a sexual situation. His head would be "buzzing."

In these many ways, George was telling me that his mind was no longer a jumble of intense preoccupations. When I reminded him of my earlier questions about racing thoughts and struggling with a busy mind (problems he had denied having), he responded, "Doc, how could I know? That's what I'd *always* had, until you gave me that medicine. That was normal for me. I had never felt anything else!"

George then noted that much of his former aggressive and destructive behavior had been a way to temporarily relieve what he now recognized as an inner pressure. This racing, headlong state of near-mania had been with him for as long as he could remember. Like the destructive behavior that had preceded it, the opiates had provided a temporary respite.

Several weeks later, the nurses reported that over several days George had dramatically reverted back to character. I requested a serum lithium level and met with him. He confirmed that he had stopped taking the lithium, mainly because he didn't know how to cope with his new world of feelings and involvements. He explained that he didn't know how to be with or talk to people. They seemed to know "how to be," and he didn't. As we talked, it became apparent that his lifelong struggle to deal with his inner pressures had prevented him from working through many developmental stages and social tasks. As a result, he often felt clumsy and inadequate, like an adolescent who has suddenly lost part of his child-based identity and is not yet sure of his new one.

During the years that followed this exchange, I have worked with a number of people more apparently bipolar than George who, once treated, appeared to have narcissistic character disorders. As one listens to them, it becomes clear that their bipolar disorders have prevented them from growing through specific developmental phases, and that this sense of incompleteness, now revealed, has left them feeling "different," weak, small, inadequate, and foolish. Trapped in this negativity, they often want to stop the medication and return to a more familiar state, a world in which they felt powerful and grandiose. If the therapist can help achieve a pharmacologic stabilization of mood, however, it becomes possible to transferentially live through and work through developmental phases, as these people struggle to resume the growth, however interrupted or sidetracked, that had been denied them earlier.

George's drug program, however, had no provision for an ongoing psychotherapy that would allow him to work through this process. He subsequently left the program, and, I later learned, committed suicide.

Medication and Countertransference: Jeremy

Another category of patients with special needs is the group suffering from borderline personality disorders. These people present with a wide array of symptoms and behaviors. They can have many behavioral manifestations: mood disorders, volatile mood swings that look bipolar, depressions, rages, dissociative experiences, attentional and behavioral disorders, and even brief psychotic episodes. My experience with those who develop behavioral problems and repeatedly demonstrate explosive behavior has been that they often benefit from mood-stabilizing anticonvulsants and low doses of the neuroleptics.[2]

At the same time, however, the characterologic aspects of their disorder predispose them to a yearning for magical interventions that denies their own role in orchestrating their life issues. This tendency confronts the clinician with a significant dilemma. If we believe that medication is useful, how can it be used without encouraging the fantasy

---

2. It has been my frequent experience that the newer anxiolytics and antidepressants are effective for a limited period of time—say one to two years. If during that time the underlying issues are examined worked through, then the discontinuation of the medication or the loss of its effect are not followed by a return of symptoms. With some people, however, I have seen the return of symptoms when there has been inadequate or absent understanding of deeper causes and precipitants.

of a magical external agent that will instantly and effortlessly fill up the patient's emptiness? After all, actions mean more than words to most of these individuals, and prescribing is an action that does put something inside them.

I sometimes wonder: How often is the prescription of medication for such people an expression of the therapist's own sense of futility? ("I need to do something because I feel powerless.") How often is it triggered by anger? ("Take this and leave me alone; I can't stand being with you.") When does the act of prescribing merely embody some aspect of the interaction being enacted, rather than meeting a patient's authentic need for medicine? The answer is not a clear and simple one. Because the dynamics of psychotherapy with individuals who have character problems tend to elicit strong responses in both parties, we can never be entirely certain. In many situations, therapists find themselves caught up in prescribing one medication or combination after another. This may reflect an enactment wherein the patient is showing the therapist through experience his or her own disheartened state, as if saying, "Now you feel my own powerlessness and futility." Not infrequently, this occurs when the therapist has become transferentially removed and desperate, and is substituting a drug for engagement.

The following case history illustrates the crucial importance of working toward a heightened awareness of one's own transferences before prescribing medication. It also shows the clinician's need for frequent consultation, perhaps supervision, and the advisability in many situations of establishing a division of labor between the roles of psychopharmacologist and therapist.

Jeremy, a thirty-two-year-old unmarried man, had worked since his college graduation for a series of social service agencies that worked with homeless veterans. Jeremy was an ardent and articulate advocate for these people. Frequently, he became embroiled in furious controversies with his bosses and with other collaborating agencies because he felt that no one seemed to care about the clients as much as he did. He viewed others as bureaucrats, who were afraid to jeopardize themselves by challenging "the system."

Jeremy also saw himself as the champion of people whom society neglected. He would position himself as the self-righteous opponent of his colleagues, and, as a result, lose his job. Wounded by these dismissals, he viewed himself as a victim of uncaring others, and would wind up in treatment—yet again. I was therapist number eight. Older and younger therapists, male and female, all had failed him. Even those initially perceived as "good" had eventually let him down or else betrayed him in some way.

I had been recommended by his former therapist who said, "He's your kind of patient[3]," and went on to review his history and early development. I agreed to an evaluation.

Jeremy came neatly dressed to his first appointment, and carefully asked where to sit. He seemed exceedingly polite, cautious, and intent on doing his best not to offend. He quickly launched into a story about his last therapy and how it had ended. He said that his previous therapist had hurt him deeply by misunderstanding Jeremy's intentions. The therapist had become angry because Jeremy called his home when Jeremy couldn't reach him at the office. Jeremy explained that he was a patient, after all, and doctors are supposed to help! Again and again, he linked his rights as a patient to his understanding of a doctor's obligation to help those who need care. To myself I wondered if he felt so worthless that only the designation of being a "patient" gave him rights and expectations.

I said that given his past experiences, it might help to define his expectations and to assess realistically what might be achieved in these sessions. He became enraged, screaming that I didn't know how to be a doctor. I was going to reject him as so many other therapists had. He had known it when he saw me open the door! No one liked him! I was just concerned with rules and not people. I was like all of the bureaucrats who didn't care about people. He hated this world and intended to kill himself. He stood up as if to leave, and I responded by saying forcefully that he

---

3. The phrase "your kind of patient" sends chills up my spine. It means trouble. Since I wrote a paper on borderline patients early in my career, and since I had a proclivity for directness before it was fashionable, my friends have referred to me a number of acting out patients. With some of them our work has progressed in an ultimately satisfying way. But although I feel more at ease and less constrained once I have a sense of their painful genetic issues, I still find myself on guard and careful when I meet these people.

needed to sit and talk with me. Then I asked him what he understood about the previous three minutes. What had he understood me to say? He couldn't remember. It was a blur, he said. He just knew that I hated him, and that no one could help him. I asked him if he knew that he had been screaming at me. "Sort of," he said. "But you're a psychiatrist, and that's your job."

No, I said. *Our* job, if we agreed to do it, involved his trying to tell me what he experienced, and also our attempting to understand what went into these experiences. Certainly he might feel furious and disappointed with me, and we could talk about it, but screaming at me and stomping about, threatening suicide, etc., would distract us and interfere with our understanding what was occurring in him. I tried to explain that working together would mean agreeing on what and how we would work together. To this he replied, "You don't like me; you want to control me."

I responded, "No, you'll have to control yourself, but I don't like being screamed at. Do you think you might need to push me away quickly so that you can at least be in charge of, control, the rejection that you seem to believe must occur?" He looked at me blankly.

In spite of his rage, I sensed both desperation and shame. He seemed to consciously love, idealize, and miss his former therapist, pointing out again and again that: "he really knew me." I wondered to myself if the intensity of that relationship had overwhelmed him with yearnings, and if the boundaries of the relationship had come to represent a rejection too painful for him to manage.

In our third session he was screaming again—angry, personal attacks full of vitriol. When I reiterated that such assaults weren't going to help him and that he had to find a way to tell me what disturbed him without being abusive, he became even more enraged. He told me that he paid me "to take this shit." I said that while he might feel full of bile and painful hatred, the so-called "shit" that he wanted to be rid of, it wasn't my job to be dumped on, nor would it help him to do so. If he refused to restrain himself, the hour was over. He began to respond with more abuse. I interrupted him, "Stop, the hour is over. I'll see you on Thursday. If we can discuss this and work on it fine. If not, I won't see you."

We met on Thursday. Jeremy was quieter that day and straining to control himself. He told me frankly that he didn't like me. I was not warm and kind like his previous therapist. I acknowledged that it must be difficult to find me so unlike his former therapist and that he seemed to miss him. I invited him to tell me more of his experience of his former therapist and his initial sense of me. From his comments, it seemed clear that he feared a repetition of his previous therapy, in which he had become too emotionally invested in the clinician, and had then wound up feeling shamed and rejected by the realistic boundaries that separated them.

I felt that clear structure and defined limits, even if these at first seemed cold and clinical, might protect our efforts. Together we worked out a schedule, along with provisions for setting up extra appointments or phone calls, if required. We also defined my role if he should be hospitalized, along with my understanding of what therapy could offer him and what he wished from it.

As Jeremy's treatment began in earnest, struggles with his family and co-workers continued. We seemed to lurch from crisis to crisis. The last session's crisis was forgotten as we attended to *this* session's emergency. Frequent longings for past therapists soon emerged, and these were exacerbated by his resentment of my not having learned, almost overnight, the historical details of his life. Gradually, the repetition of his earliest life scenarios with his parents and brothers became apparent in the living replications in his contemporary life.

While he could recognize the similarities and parallels, they were meaningless to him. "So what?" he would say, or, "I told you, that's how people treat me," or, "Are you trying to say it's my fault?" Then prolonged rages and threats would ensue. His terror of feeling shamed and at fault appeared to be immense. If anything was his responsibility then he was totally flawed.

Slowly, as his feelings and experiences became focused in the treatment, the outside struggles with colleagues diminished. Jeremy then became depressed and suicidal. It seemed clear that issues involving less conscious self-loathing that had previously been played out in his attempts to form attachments outside the office, relationships that he quickly undermined with intrusiveness and paranoid attacks, had been transferred into the treatment. He fantasized continually about a relationship that would make him feel good and whole. If only "X" liked him, he would be fine! It was never consciously me, always another.

We did our best to make sense of this idea, and Jeremy was able to describe the inner sense of emptiness that this "other person's" affection would somehow fill and cure. He also began to see that his self-righteous rages, which made him feel temporarily energized, were followed by an empty and depleted feeling, and a profound, heavy depression. We kept slogging through repeated episodes of fantasies of someone's loving and liking him as a cure for his emptiness and experiences of the rage. But I was increasingly concerned that he was even more isolated, having driven away so many people; I did not recognize my own countertransference wish to escape from being the sole focus of his longings and rage. He looked more depressed, dressed carelessly, and talked more about killing himself.

Then he got into a struggle with his current boss and was fired. He was indignant and threatened legal action for unfair practices. Partially on the basis of this threat he managed to work out a termination package that protected him financially for several months. But his victory, and the capitulation of his boss in the face of his paranoid machinations, only reinforced his paranoia and his despair. Now he was home alone all day. Repeatedly our discussions focused upon the fact that *he* was responsible for keeping himself alive, and I pointed out that this responsibility included getting himself to a hospital if he was unwilling to contain his impulses.

But I was less clear about all the feelings and responses aroused within me. I could sense his shame and exquisite terror at being held accountable for any aspect of his own situation; thus his attempts to hold me and others responsible. The slightest possibility that he was responsible for a problem meant that he was totally worthless, and should die. Some part of me was aware of his desperate and panicky little boy imago left in his room to cry. But only later did I see that, hidden in my sense of his early desperation, lay my masochistic submission to his enraged demands that *I* save him. In part, I had never been with someone who so completely lacked even the rudiments of a soothing internal object. I began thinking of medications to stabilize his mood swings and alleviate his desperation as I began to sense my own parallel feelings.

I was clear that medication, although it might alleviate some symptoms, would not solve his problems or eliminate his issues, but my own feelings got me muddled when it came to working out the details of

prescription and usage. Most significantly, in the face of his rage, desperation, and terror at seeing someone else, I withdrew my suggestion that he
see a pharmacology consultant (I feel incredibly stupid writing this and
remembering my state of mind. This was the masochistic submission.) In
the guise of assuaging his fear by acceding to his wish, I hid from my own
fury and wish to escape from him.

I reviewed Jeremy's past medication experience in an effort to
determine what had been useful and what had not. We decided to try
antidepressants and a mood-stabilizing anticonvulsant. These pharmacologic recommendations seemed reasonable, yet in making them I again
neglected the countertransference aspect of our work; more accurately,
it could be said that I fled from it. Once I began prescribing for Jeremy, he
began to engage me in disputes about medication that increasingly distracted me from the more neutral and observational stance on which our
work had been based. By mixing roles I had clouded our work.

Previously, for example, I had noticed that any shift on my part into
a more responsive mode, smiling at one of his jokes, perhaps, or display-
ing a more relaxed demeanor, would at first please him, but then trigger
an attack based on some sensed criticism or rejection. Eventually I
realized that the attacks served several purposes. First, they punished me
for being different from his idea of me. Second, they were a way to fend
off awakening yearnings for closeness, and the attendant risk of shame and
humiliation. And finally, they emerged from Jeremy's need to continue
seeing me as "only a temporary therapist," a pretense that perhaps
revealed his failure to make peace with earlier losses. He could attend
our sessions only if he regarded me as a stop-gap until he found someone
more suitable. Yet as his world shrank, I was, in fact, of ever increasing
importance to him.

Paradoxically, holding me at a distance had allowed him to stay with
me. He would complain that I was too cognitive, too behavioral, not
empathic, harsh, intellectual, mushy, touchy-feely, too analytic.[4] Medi-

---

4. Unbeknownst to me, he sought out at least eight colleagues during the course of
our time together to find a better therapist, who would not be like me. I learned this
from him many years into our work.

cation, however, meant accepting something from me, thereby bringing us closer. The prescriptions represented my *giving* him something— crossing a boundary—and that step meant a shift away from the distant, unsatisfying, temporary therapist he needed me to be. Medication became a way of taking me inside him, but before he was ready for it.

What was there about my countertransference that contributed to the muddle? There were many facets. Consciously, I worried that he was racing into a downward spiral. His parents were aging, and he still needed to resolve his early issues with them. I liked his determination, but wondered if he would run out of energy. His past therapists had been solid clinicians who had made strenuous efforts. However, his identification with his negative introjects was his link to his parents. These distorted views of him were the only "Jeremy" that his parents recognized. To give up these images and senses of himself meant being invisible in his parents' eyes.

Yet he was compelled to repeat with me, as with his former therapists, the living out of these identities. Clearly I hated his abuse of me, and I quickly engaged it as an issue to be dealt with and contained. Even its lesser manifestations had the power to infuriate me. I'd get caught up in some detail and feel guilty; Had my tone or words really been harsh and sadistic? Was I being too active, too passive, too intellectual? At times I sensed an acquiescence on my part in some small area, and recognized it as masochism. How far away could my retaliatory wishes be? I really wanted to be useful to him. His desperation touched some old pieces of my life. At that time, I had been loath to adopt the attitude that they were beyond help, because that might mean that some aspects within *me* were beyond help. Was something similar taking place here? I wasn't sure.

Our involvement revolved around action and containment, and required the construction of a bounded container within which I hoped we could work on his basic self-hatred and sense of unlovableness. But words were mere window dressing, a kind of background hum for the real arena—action. For example, I might tell him that his screaming and shouting told us that he was distressed, but that it didn't allow us to understand his turmoil. He would regard this idea as meaningless unless I said, "Stop yelling and sit down so that we can talk!" He might comply (submit). However, this latter response was gratifying to him, since my words and tone were the equivalent of actions and kept us in a sadomasochistic relatedness. We were acting-in, as opposed to acting-out. (We later learned that these exchanges soothed him, because they indicated real involvement. He was getting a "real response" from me, "not just words.")

He was a person who literally needed to check the windows or reflective surfaces he passed in order to know that he really existed. Thus he needed proof of my involvement. For some time, I had been startled and saddened by the profound absence of any significant, positive internal objects in his psychological makeup. And yet, even with this awareness of Jeremy's inner turmoil, I failed to consider fully how he might experience receiving something—medication—from me, and then ingesting it.

Although each medication I prescribed for him had some salutary effect, each came with a side-effect or a deficiency that Jeremy experienced as intolerable. As a result, his sessions became more and more taken up with medication issues. His frustration and rage mounted, increasingly laced with *ad hominem* attacks aimed at me. No one and nothing could help. He was self-conscious about his body, and now he was gaining weight. "I'll be a fat pig!" he said. His breasts were larger now, and "You like that, emasculating me!" he announced. "You're such a big man, a doctor, and I'm an experiment! Fuck you!" He hated men whom he saw as more successful than himself. He hated women because they just had to exist and be desirable to be taken care of. "Why is it everyone *else* in the world is helped by medicines, but not me?" Attempts to examine such furious statements were met with dismissal, or accusations that I was trying to shame and blame him.

I noted for later work Jeremy's hopelessness, his sense of being different and apart from all humanity, his palpable self-loathing, and his aversion to physicality. Strikingly, I began to see that anything given to him by others soon became something bad and hurtful. Was his internal experience such that anything taken in from the outside was transformed by his inner being into something bad and painful? Is that why medication ordinarily useful to others hurt him? Somehow, other people's considerations and attempts to aid him always seemed to backfire. (Much later in our work, he did describe his sense that nothing good could survive in him, most importantly the his core-self that emerged periodically in images of a pathetic infant or small child.)

As the months passed, his rage and frustration grew sharper. Often, his reflections and associations about these furious outbursts, were to his abusive and irrational parents, in what appeared to be exact repetitions in his current life of prior experiences. He could not see any relevant connection; in spite of his own description. I had become one of those "others" who failed to understand and help him; who blamed him; etc. Moments after detailing some recent incident of parental excess and outrage, he would wail, "But I know they love me."

From this and many other statements, I began to sense that he needed to be the family scapegoat, which would at least give him a role and a connection to these people. If he were not the hated and hateful scapegoat, he would have no role and no connection at all.[5] What a dilemma. If he gave up his destructive negative introject, he lost them. If he stayed as he was, his life was a painful, futile disaster. And so he built his fantasy hope around the illusion that his parents would be more loving and reasonable if he were not so awful. If *he* was the problem, there was still

---

5. Years after this period of treatment, several incidents graphically played out this scenario. During a visit with a brother and his parents in which there had been no conflict, his mother began telling the family what an awful person the patient had been. He began detailing embarrassing incidents, and saying: "You remember what a terrible person you were?" The patient responded calmly and quietly that it was hard for him to talk about these incidents. They embarrassed him; could they change the subject? His mother took offense and began screaming at him. When the patient said quietly that it was just hard to talk about, his mother flew into a rage, locked herself in the bathroom, and threatened to cut her wrists. His father turned and pleaded with him to apologize and not upset his mother. The patient exploded in rage screaming: "That fucking bitch has been hating me for years". His mother came flying out of the bathroom saying: "You see how horrible he is—It's his fault I get upset. He's the bad one! That's how he talks to his mother." The parents calmed down immediately. The patient left the room in tears and went upstairs, hating himself for screaming at his mother and losing his calmer demeanor. He had once again fulfilled the demand to be the sacrificial "scapegoat," and restablize his parents' state.

hope. If *they* were the problem, the situation was desperate, for he knew that he could not change them. And if others were allowed to like or help him, then he was obviously not "bad," and the contrast with what his parents had taught him would be too painful to endure. With me, he had to be the sick, difficult patient because he would then warrant care. He could not get better because he risked losing the connection with his parents or me.

Tortured by these contradictions, Jeremy strove consciously to do well at a new job and in his relationships. But he unconsciously sabotaged himself at every opportunity, and eventually wound up feeling rejected. For example, even though his previous therapist had liked him, his cloying demands and paranoid hypersensitivity eventually led him to terminate their work. In the end, everything he did had become grounds for sulking rages that would eventually explode in the hour, with no later resolution.

With a sinking heart, I realized that we were on the same track. I felt confused and desperate. I also felt drawn in and resentful. I began to dread our sessions. No matter what I said or did (or *didn't* say or do), he would use it as the basis for another furious rage. Lost and confused in the middle of what Russell called "the Crunch," I went back to firmly clarifying the ground rules and boundaries, and interpreting the rages as strategies aimed at pushing me away. Repeating an earlier refrain, he pointed out that I was "supposed to be able to take it" (echoes of "That's your job!"). I told him once again that I was not there to absorb his abuse nor would I be like him in his earlier role with his parents, even as he became like his parents to me. Once again, I began to dissect every gesture, every shift in voice, and every devaluing and dismissive comment, always asking about the meanings behind them. He was furious with me, but contained his rage enough to stay somewhat engaged.

Gradually, as I persisted in rebuilding the structural integrity of our work, the treatment changed. Jeremy began to see that each rage-filled attack made him feel worse. He could no longer abuse others in a self-righteous rage. We were beginning to find rudiments of the hidden core of genuine self. The treatment was, and is, stormy. But it now progresses within a more reliable frame.

What had led to the earlier deterioration, then? Several things. First, as I reviewed the above scenario I saw that while I consciously felt that our previous work had been progressing and that his most desperate struggles had been moving into the office, his suicidality had scared me. He had no connections but me. And while I had told myself that I didn't want to abandon him, I now recognized that I did. (You cannot "not want" something, after all, without first sensing that you *do* want it.) I felt guilty about having wished to distance myself from him, to abandon him.

These reflections played a large part in my review of the initial decision not to insist on a separate psychopharmacologist after Jeremy had resisted seeing one. My willingness to resort to medication reflected my hope that I might find in it an ally that was stronger than I! It was also related to a yearning for some magical agency that would give me relief from his onslaughts, and protect me from having to be alone with him. Although I had outlined the limitations of medication as I consciously understood them,[6] I had managed to resist and minimize my own unconscious wishes to flee and to continue the enactment.

As I now reengaged with Jeremy, reconstructing the boundary issues around abusiveness and self-containment, the treatment hours became quieter. I was again more fully present. I insisted again that he see a psychopharmacologist. This time, after a significant but engaged struggle, he did. The pharmacologist prescribed the same medications he had been taking. While Jeremy's depression and despair seemed unchanged, his mood became more stable and he was less suicidal. He became embroiled in the same kinds of struggles with the pharmacologist as he had with me. However, I could now examine these episodes in treatment and use them. Most importantly, I could see his rage-filled attacks as a matter of playing out the dynamics of "badness" and rejection. My becoming clearer about the boundaries and his responsibility to not cross them had stabilized my capacity to stay engaged.

The issue was not whether medications "work" or "don't work," or whether they are "good" or "bad." Quite simply, the issue was the manner and meaning of the prescription, when seen in the context of our state of transferential interaction. The

---

6. Here is an example of trying to clarify my purpose consciously and ignoring the deeper resonances in me and the transference. This is the very issue I raised as a criticism of Renik.

medications were extremely useful, as was my reexamining of the countertrans-
ference. Neither tool, used alone, was sufficient.

The real issue for both of us centered on the meaning we gave the medication. Like an attractive woman therapist who dressed in a provocative manner and denied that transference had any part of the work in her drug program (only to find herself in an affair with a patient), I had denied some of the impact the work with Jeremy had upon me, and we had both paid the price for my denial. On too many occasions, I had prescribed the "right" medications in the wrong way as a substitute for my more engaged involvement. It seems to me that errors such as these are widespread. I'm convinced that we all need to understand that medications can never substitute for the engaged transferential work.

I have seen too many instances in the past where unconsciously driven emotional needs overcame the pharmacology of a potentially useful agent—even when that agent was taken as prescribed. This dynamic can be observed in its most visible form when a patient visits a medical doctor and fails to take the prescribed medication because the doctor was "rushed," or "cool," or "didn't explain it," or "I didn't like the way he [she] talked to me."

The bottom line: Medications prescribed in the context of a consciously respectful relationship that considers the transferential interactions do not jeopardize treatment. Medications themselves, whether we use them or not, do not constitute a threat to the deeper emotional resolution of psychological issues. They do, however, constitute yet another potential area for confusion and loss of perspective in the therapeutic struggle for resolution of core conflicts and deficits.

*   *   *

As I said earlier, it was my experience with Darlene's hospitalization that motivated me to approach this very difficult subject. I wrote this chapter out of my conviction that if we ignore the personal nature of our work in response to the economic and social pressures that increasingly affect it, we will lose much of our effectiveness. However valuable medication may be (and it is!), we cannot neglect our own psychology and the issues that attend our own human development, to say nothing of our patients'. If we do, we will be able to provide little more than an impersonal, formulaic involvement—a sterile algorithm based solely on the "magic" of chemistry. And that approach is doomed to failure, because it addresses only one dimension of emotional stability and growth: the biochemical. A failure like that is the reverse of the failure wherein a clinician becomes too wedded to psychological explanations, and so misses out on the benefits that neurochemical agents can provide.

I am convinced that it is possible now for psychotherapists to combine our understanding of psychological development and of the human need for connection with our fast-growing knowledge of the biochemistry of mental processes. We *are* capable of integrating our growing insight into the psychological dynamics of trauma, developmental deficit, distortion, fixation, and impulse with our new expertise in neurobiology and chemistry in a humane and respectful way.

In short, if we can achieve the right synthesis between psychotherapy and psychopharmacology, we can create a broad-based, multidimensional therapy that will continue to advance our understanding of human behavior even as it extends our capacity for helpful intervention. Unfortunately, the human and interactional aspects of psychological work are now being shunted aside in favor of more purely medical tools. Is it any wonder that self-help and alternative approaches to healing are burgeoning? People want to learn through human connection!

Psychology has always been a diverse field, crowded with many different perspectives on human development and the usefulness of psychotherapeutic interventions. I mention this because of the frequency with which people outside the field ask, "What do psychiatrists believe about . . . ?", as if we all shared a single opinion. Similarly, people early in their training often speak with certainty about some particular approach or point of view, as if it represents the only possible way to understand an issue. Of course we all tend to want unambiguous answers that are clear and absolute, and surely the desire for such certainty accounts for the great appeal of medications today, and for the excitement we all feel about the new understandings of brain function that are emerging with our deeper knowledge of neuroanatomy, neurochemistry, and neurophysiology. These new tools seem promising, to say the least. Paradoxically, however, they are raising new questions, and triggering new uncertainties, at an unprecedented rate. Each new discovery seems to provoke more questions about the interrelation of psyche and soma than the one before. As I speak with individuals working in these areas, I am most impressed by those who recognize the enormity and complexity of what they are trying to understand. Have we forgotten that even as our knowledge advances, we must remain respectful about all that we *don't* know in the many fields of knowledge related to psychotherapy?

11

Summary and Guidelines

In many ways, the materials I have presented are elementary; they are part of the fabric of daily practice for psychoanalysts and dynamic psychotherapists. I decided to present them notwithstanding, because the tenor of the times has shifted and the training of therapists has shifted along with it. In most training programs today, the traditional elements of transference and countertransference are no longer emphasized as central to treatment. For that reason I wanted to review these basics, which remain crucial aspects of our practice. Whether one is a psychopharmacologist, a neuropsychiatrist, or a behaviorist, consideration of transference is a fundamental aspect of the treatment experience. To ignore it puts the work at peril.

I hope that I have made clear how pervasive transferences are for both the therapist and the patient, and how inevitable they are in intensive psychotherapy. We live our lives in a sea of transference—at work, at home, at school, in our friendships and elsewhere. Therapy is unlike other relationships in that the dynamics of transference and the way we shape our perceptions and beliefs about others are the focus of the work. The patient in the therapeutic process usually initiates a reenactment scenario, and stressful transferences of this kind are an essential part of the developmental process that is therapy.

Rather than denying or fleeing from his or her own countertransference, the seasoned clinician first metabolizes its content and then finds a way to weave its clinically meaningful content back into unfolding therapies, in such a manner that patients can use it to gain understanding about their own conflicts, drives, character, and interpersonal dynamics.

The clinical examples I have cited depict only a small fraction of the endlessly varied complications and outcomes that take place during psychotherapy. Obviously, they were intended to illustrate only the range of potential responses of patient and therapist, not an exhaustive catalogue of all possible transference scenarios during treatment.

What can we learn from these varied case histories, and from the mistakes that we all make as we struggle to understand our patients and our own involvement in the working process? Although well-intended clinicians may differ over specific transference interpretations and strategies, one general premise seems clear: *In order to deal effectively with transference issues in treatment, the therapist must be willing to shoulder certain new responsibilities occasioned by our rapidly growing understanding of transferential dynamics in the intersubjective environment.* Among those responsibilities are the following:

1. Therapists must work at being able to recognize such transferences when they occur. We need to be vigilant about the possibility that many transferences occur without our awareness during the treatment hour, and that their meanings may only come clear later, after appropriate review and reflection.

2. We need to reflect continuously upon our own involvement and question our own role, which includes our motivations and other treatment-related responses. We must conduct repeated self-analyses of our inner states, with an eye to understanding how these may or may not relate to our patients. The therapist seeking the best understanding of the treatment process and the possible transference meanings within it must:

—break the transference experience down into its component parts;

—differentiate the personal experience from the interpersonal;

—consider the possible relevance of his or her own transference to the treatment (this is the process of *metabolizing*);

—consider the possible reasons that a given issue is arising at this moment with this patient;

—seek possible genetic understandings of the meaning and dynamic of the interaction.

3. If and when this metabolic process begins to yield clues and possible understandings that might be useful for the treatment, it is helpful when the therapist can find a way to introduce these possibilities back into the process for collaborative examination. (The caution here is that the clinician needs to remember that these are possibilities and only possibilities.)

4. In many instances the therapist will say nothing about these responses and possible insights. Time may be allowed for further data to emerge, and for patients to recognize and discover their own meaning. These mini-re-creations, the transference reenactments, contain multiple meanings that can only become clear over time as the process unfolds. No single explanation can hope to lay bare the multiple meanings generated by the psychotherapeutic process.

5. While enactments are an inevitable part of the process, they must be carefully examined, and should never be dismissed as merely predictable byproducts of intensive psychotherapy or psychoanalysis. Nor should the recognition of their inevitability be employed as a screen for acting out by the therapist. My own experience has taught me that those of us who hope to work within the transference/countertransference framework require ongoing supervision, continuing personal treatment, and regular peer assessment.

Aspects of Enactment

Resonance

While in an enactment situation, defined by part-object projective dynamics, the therapist may feel that he or she is the recipient of some foreign affect, projected by the patient. However, the actual source of such resonances is located in the therapist's own life. The patient's reenactment has stirred up some personal issue within the clinician, and this inner turmoil has an affective kinship with the patient's own experience. Thus the sense of harmonic resonance.

Inclusion and Disclosure

Having metabolized the enactment interaction, the therapist looks for the most useful way to reintroduce various aspects of his or her own experience and understanding. Sometimes one responds spontaneously. At other times, one may notice a sense of distance, or a sense of involvement, and that becomes the point of departure for discussion. Or one may wonder if the circumstance isn't related to some particular and defined circumstance that has been called to one's own mind.

Disclosures seem most helpful when they include a cogent description of the connection between the transference materials and their possible genetic origin in the patient. This step, the reintroduction of the material, is crucial. It should be stressed that the self-disclosure by the therapist is not of personal material from his or her own life. Much more important, it is the disclosure of a response to the patient that has occurred during the course of treatment *and that seems to contain possible meanings for the patient's treatment.*

The recommendation that countertransference disclosures be accompanied by a possible genetic interpretation of their meaning and origin comes from the need to convey to the patient that what the therapist is saying about him— or herself is an attempt to understand *the patient* through the therapist's experience of the patient. The disclosure does not stem from the therapist's preoccupation with his or her own feeling state. Nor does it represent a mere reaction to the patient. Disclosing this kind of material is a way to try to make sense of the patient's own experience. Without such explicit guidelines, therapists run the risk in their disclosures of burdening patients with their own emotional content, or "blaming" the patient for their own feelings. In this regard, Hoffman's (1983) warning about the dangers of overvaluing one's own experience and making grandiose assumptions about how quickly one can understand complex patient issues bears careful scrutiny.

So, do we disclose transference details, or not? What information should be disclosed, and what held back? Under what conditions is disclosure advisable, and to what purpose? How do we integrate disclosure materials back into treatment? And how do we work with undisclosed but palpably present affective materials? Once we recognize that our work must draw us actively into the turbulence of the patient's transferences while also reactivating our own, the need for effective guidelines to help us negotiate this more engaged form of therapy becomes apparent.

A Rule of Sense

While guidelines often take the form of rules or recipes or lists of do's and don'ts, they can also be assembled as a loose framework that remains flexible even while it provides a guiding paradigm. The countertransference guidelines that I have begun to clarify are all implied by a single practice principle that might be called "A Rule of Sense." Framed as a question, it simply asks: *How does what I'm experiencing and considering make sense in light of the patient's genuine treatment needs as I understand them?*

While such a broad generalization as this could be taken as an open avenue to rationalize anything, I assume that the reader hears it as I mean it: as an invitation to the kind of considered examination that I have presented throughout this book. Sometimes I can do it myself; in the many instances where I cannot be clear about what makes sense, I keep quiet, think, get supervision, or talk to a peer group.

Personal Analysis

Freud's early assertion that practicing psychotherapists should return to analysis every five years takes on increased urgency when we begin to grapple more directly with the intersubjective aspects of our work.

My own experience, and that of the colleagues with whom I've discussed this, has convinced me that second and third analyses may result in dramatic improvements in one's emotional and work capacity. The good news for therapists is that as our own narcissistic strivings become less intense with the passing of the years, we become more able to see ourselves in perspective, and better able to make use of the analytic process. In addition, our journey through various life stages brings forward old and new issues that must be reworked in their newer incarnations if healthy growth is to continue. For all of these reasons, periodically renewed analytic scrutiny is essential.

Supervision and Consultation

There is little doubt that regular supervision by senior consultants, along with regular peer group meetings, can help us to focus on the dynamics of transference and countertransference and give us fresh insights into other events that unfold within the treatment dyad.

Over twenty-five years of regular weekly meetings, a colleague and I have gained an understanding of each other's work that is still deepening. Many times, our discussions have helped us to avoid the traps of our own characters and to minimize our shortcomings, even as they provide us with ever new perspectives that refresh and enliven our work.

I've also attended a monthly peer group meeting for the past eighteen years. These sessions allow me to hear different viewpoints, and sensitize me to aspects of practice that I tend to overlook or under-emphasize. Like the weekly meetings, I return to the office after these exchanges with a renewed sense of curiosity and humility.

I've also found it useful periodically to consult with, or be supervised by, practitioners who know me less intimately. Discussions of this kind shed new light on issues and problems that are less readily apparent in more familiar surroundings. The underlying theme in all of this seems compellingly clear:

As practitioners, we cannot work alone without running the risk of falling prey to our limited and biased views. Nor can we hope to avoid the countertransference pitfalls that constantly surround us without plenty of outside advice and supervision.

SPECIFIC CONSIDERATIONS

Active and Dramatic Interventions: A Summary

In earlier chapters I outlined a series of forceful treatment interventions in which I disclosed my reactions to patients' transferences and reenactments. Before making those disclosures, I carefully reviewed my decision to introduce these materials in light of the following considerations:

1. It is essential that disclosure be used only to further the goals of treatment. Because reactions to events or comments that take place during a therapy session come from multiple sources in both individuals, our responses must be filtered from a number of different perspectives: the patient's and our own transferences, the sense of where we are in the treatment process, the possible meanings that we can discern in the material, and so on, as we decide whether to disclose or not, what to disclose, and how best to introduce the material.

2. Any disclosing of verbal responses must be related to the ongoing interaction between therapist and patient. Although that interaction may trigger personal issues within the practitioner, such issues should not be the focus of the dialogue in the treatment hour.

3. The therapist should be careful to avoid generalizations about the patient. Disclosures work best when they are restricted to a description of the therapist's reaction to a *specific* interaction. That principle was at work when I told a patient that *in certain specifically defined circumstances*, I did not like being subjected to her behavior. Eventually this patient was able to come to the conclusion that she was struggling with a general sense of being hateful and unlovable, and that she was seeking to confirm this

premise through her behavior. A less circumscribed response from me about her behavior might have felt like a devastating confirmation of her deep fear that she was unlovable.

4. For most patients, there is a need to know directly from the therapist that the latter feels something in response to the patient's comments or actions during the treatment hour. For many people, it is enough to sense it in the therapist's voice, expression, and demeanor. Other people require more overt and direct acknowledgement, because they do not believe that they really exist, either for themselves or for the clinician. These are the people who frequently provoke the most immediate and dramatic responses, as these best confirm to them their ability to reach the clinician affectively. The therapist should examine the meaning to, and impact upon the patient of such responses, as well as the patient's need for them.

   While therapists must recognize privately that their responses are related to their own psychological states, it is rarely appropriate to define this to the patient, beyond the general acknowledgement that the response included personal dimensions. The therapist's neurotic and characterologic substrate is not relevant to the patient's struggle for insight, but it is the responsibility of the clinician to remain aware of this aspect of his or her personality, and to manage it effectively.

5. Disclosure materials should not be presented until the therapist has a clear sense of the possible genetic origin of the transference dynamic within the patient. Disclosure under other circumstances can make the patient feel responsible for the therapist's feelings, which could injure the patient through an unprocessed reaction. In the context of the search for deeper meaning, however, the focus remains upon the patient's intent to communicate and the therapist's interest in this goal. The therapist's reaction is data that may be useful in this pursuit. This mitigates the likelihood of holding the patient responsible for the therapist's feelings.

6. The potential meanings of patient enactments should be presented as "possibilities" that can be jointly examined and consid-

ered by both members of the treatment dyad. It is disrespectful to assume that the therapist can grasp what is occurring within a patient through a pure leap of intuition.

7. The timing of interventions is significant. The therapist must work first to understand the meaning of his or her response in terms of the ongoing treatment, and in terms of the question: What is the meaning of this enactment? One helpful approach is to raise questions to the patient about how the phenomenon under scrutiny manifests itself: You've felt this way before; "This seems like"; "If this is like—, I wonder what occurs to you." If attempts at understanding prove fruitless and the situation recurs, it is probably time for an introduction of the clinician's response during the session: "I find myself feeling—, and I'm not sure what it might mean about what you're saying?" Sometimes delaying too long the overt recognition of a clear and definable experience in the treatment can deteriorate into a protracted, destructive stalemate, as both parties avoid and circumvent the experience.

Subtle Enactments and Active Interventions

By their very nature, subtle enactments are complex experiences and difficult to define. Some are very brief. Some occur acutely, others recur chronically. As defined earlier, these subtle enactments are the basis for the most common form of mutual transference, the times in treatment when patient and therapist are comfortable together and assuming a congruency in their understandings and perspectives, and they should be regarded as prime areas of potential analytic work.

In previous chapters, I described my sense of mutual outrage with my patient Frank regarding healthcare changes and practices. I also noted a colleague's concern for her patient Richard's alarming potential for masochistic overextension. Those feelings seemed perfectly natural at the time they occurred, but later reflection showed that they were greatly intensified by the dynamics unfolding during the treatment hour. Many such experiences have taught me to expect this phenomenon, and to remember that the treatment process often intensifies affects, even familiar and comfortable ones. In an effort to maintain my therapeutic awareness during these periods of benign and non-distressing affective response, I have worked out some guidelines that have been consistently helpful:

1. Whenever I note one of these comfortable, ego-syntonic responses to a patient, but lack a clear understanding of why I am experiencing it, I first register the feeling and any accompanying fantasy or impulse, then search my experience for similar moments with this patient. I also scrutinize the reaction to see if it has any historical relevance for either of us.

2. The more comfortable I feel with such an issue or feeling, especially when some heightened affect is linked to it during the treatment hour, the more I begin looking for a subtle transferential enactment in which I may have become enmeshed. Such feelings are, for the most part, consonant with my positive sense of myself in my professional capacity. It's important to remember that even comfortable recurrent states must be noted and then examined.

3. Because such "innocent" feelings do not draw attention to themselves with dysphoric affect, I remind myself that I must be especially vigilant in reviewing my own psychological state. When I do come upon personal referents, I search within myself for their possible relevance to both this particular patient's dynamics and to the current transference. I also look to see if my affective response is a clue pointing toward some other subtle way in which I may be joining the patient.

4. Over time I may note the recurrence of a general theme or a vague but identifiable constellation of feelings, as happened in the case of Frank, where "shared mutual outrage" became an issue. Careful attention in these instances will sometimes culminate in a spontaneous recognition or unexpected clarification of the phenomenon. During a particularly challenging moment a few years ago, for example, a patient asked me to describe what I felt in more depth and detail. This was a unique treatment experience for me, and, as it turned out, my willingness to

catalogue my own responses to the situation we had just experienced and begun to examine encouraged the patient to examine her own associations.

5. As I noted earlier, not all subtle enactments require overt confirmation. Sometimes patient and therapist alike can leave enactment issues in the realm of the merely sensed. These affects are apparent to both parties, but do not have to be directly acknowledged across the transitional space. Instead I may explore these feelings simply by wondering aloud about "what it would be like" to experience the inner states the patient has described. At other times, I may choose to confirm the patient's affective experience by saying something like, "And when you sensed that, what else was occurring?"

(Guidelines 2 and 4 especially are key helpers that I rely on to alert me to the presence of subtler, less dramatic mutual transferences.)

Spontaneity

Much of what I have written emphasizes thoughtful care and restraint. Yet when the kind of considerations and safeguards I have been describing are built into one's moment-to-moment experience, there is plenty of room for spontaneous responses and engagements.

Erotic Countertransferences

Erotic countertransferences have been part of intensive psychotherapy from the beginning, but they were denied in our scientific forums until quite recently. Their emergence over the past two decades into the field of psychoanalytic discourse has enhanced our understanding of our clinical work, and encouraged increased scrutiny of and honesty about our own involvement in the process.

The growing acceptance of open examination and discussion of erotic transferences in the therapist strikes me as hopeful, allowing us as it does, to explore the dynamics of patient–therapist interaction far more effectively. This new openmindedness should help to eliminate the destructive secret enactments that have burdened our work in the past.

1. The therapist can enhance his or her understanding of the treatment by noting the presence or absence of erotic responses. The next step is to ask how such responses are related to one's own life and experience separate from the patient. After this initial reflection, the thoughtful clinician will probably want to ask: What is the relevance of my response to the patient's therapeutic work? If it is not seemingly relevant, why is it present within me? On the other hand, if such erotic/sensual energy seems to be absent, why is that the case?

2. The clinician who seeks to understand his or her own erotic feelings and fantasies in the treatment setting should chart their arrivals and departures. When do they occur, and how frequently? Do they erupt within the hour, or at its start or finish? Afterward, in dreams, etc? Are there any fluctuations in the intensity of the feeling? Any variations that provide information about corresponding shifts in the transference?

3. The next question has to do with the nature of the fantasy itself. In many cases, the therapist who examines the details of the fantasy within him— or herself may discover clues about the patient's issue.

4. Further assessment of the targeted erotic fantasies should focus on whether or not they are syntonic, dystonic, aversive/distasteful, anxiety-provoking, pleasing, or something else. Once again, a careful examination will help us to understand our responses and their possible relationship to treatment.

5. As I have noted in the foregoing discussion, I'm convinced that any explicit confirmation or acknowledgement of erotic responses by the clinician is disruptive to treatment. Such disclosures too often address the therapist's needs, rather than the patient's.

    The relevance of this last guideline can be seen in the following treatment incident. I noted sexual feelings during the first few minutes of each treatment session with a woman suffering from an acting-out character disorder. After a few minutes the feeling would disappear.

Try as I might, I could not define any specific behavior or communication that triggered this response. After lengthy reflection, I told the patient that she seemed "somehow different" during the first minutes of each session. The patient responded that she knew exactly what I meant; she always sought to "bring men to attention" during the opening moments of a conversation. She laughed openly about the all-too-predictable sexual responsiveness of men.

Without confirming her supposition, I asked her to reflect upon what it might mean, to be able to so predictably elicit a sexual response from men. The patient began to describe her need for power, and her feeling that she had no psychological resource except her sexual allure. She said that she had always relied on sexual provocation to feel confident that men were truly present and paying attention to her. That discussion led, understandably enough, to her grief over the disconnectedness and abandonment in her own life, and her sense of worthlessness and fury.

6. It should be noted that both hetero– and homoerotic transferences require careful scrutiny of the sort suggested in these guidelines. I have not separately examined the homoerotic dimension in the present work. Transference can unfold along any gender direction, whatever the conscious and concrete sexual preferences of the people involved may be.

Obviously, too, the same guidelines for self-examination and transference scrutiny are applicable whatever the vector of the transference. It should also be remembered that some individuals may be frightened of, and resistant to, the emerging awareness of erotic transferences that do not correspond to their own conscious sexual preferences. And as I noted earlier, eros is not always eros. Erotic feelings may conceal fears of loss and feelings of emptiness, powerlessness, or other nonsexual dimensions of experience.

As I mentioned in the introduction, my hope in writing this text was to alert beginning practitioners to this aspect of the work of psycho-therapy. Other authors, Gabbard, Tansey and Burke, and Maroda, Epstein, and Feiner for example, have written thoughtfully and in greater depth about the countertransference and related issues. I commend their works to you and hope that this book has served as an introduction.

On a final personal note: I have been surprised at how challenging and distressing it has been to review my own errors. Yet each review has shown me new perspectives and understandings that I missed in previous examinations. Our work never ends.

Bibliography

Adler, G. (1985). *Borderline Psychopathology and Its Treatment*. New York: Jason Aronson Inc.

Balint, M. (1968). *The Basic Fault*. London: Tavistock.

Beebe, B. and Lachman, F. (1988). The contribution of the mother–infant mutual influence to the origins of self- and object representations. *Psychoanalytic Psychology* 5(4) 305–337.

Bollas, C. (1983). Expressive uses of the countertransference. *Contemporary Psychoanalysis* 19;1–34.

———— (1987). *The Shadow of the Object*. New York: Columbia University Press.

Bowlby, J., Ainsworth, M., Boston, M., and Rosenbluth, D. (1956). The effects of mother–child separation: a follow-up study. *British Journal of Medical Psychology*, 29, 211–256.

———— (1958). The nature of a child's tie to his mother. *International Journal of Psychoanalysis*, vol XXXIX, part V, 1–23.

Buie, D. H. (1981). Empathy: Its nature and limitations. *Journal of the American Psychoanalytic Association* 29:281–307.

Davies, J. M. (1994). Love in the afternoon: a relational reconsideration of desire and dread in the countertransference. *Psychoanalytic Dialogues* vol. 4(2):153–170.

Demos, V. (1984). Empathy and affect: Reflections on infant experience. J. Lichtenberg and M. Bornstein, and D. Silver (eds.), *Empathy*, 2: 9–34, Hillsdale, NJ: Analytic Press.

Deutsch, H. (1926). Occult processes occurring during psychoanalysis. *Psychoanalysis and the Occult*, ed. G. Deveraux, pp. 133–146. New York: International Universities Press, 1953.

Ehrenberg, D. B. (1982). Psychoanalytic engagement. *Contemporary Psychoanalysis* 18:535–555.

———— (1984). Psychoanalytic engagement, II: affective considerations. *Contemporary Psychoanalysis* 20:560–599.

Epstein L. and Feiner, A. (1979, 1993). *Countertransference* 10:213–234. New York: Aronson.

Escalona, S. K. (1968). *The Roots of Individuality, Normal Patterns of Development in Infancy*. Chicago: Aldine Publishing Company.

Ferenczi, S. (1926, 1980). The further development of an active therapy in psychoanalysis. *Further Contributions to the Theory and Technique of Psycho-Analysis XVI*. New York: Brunner/Mazel.

Freud, S. (1893). Studies on hysteria, *Standard Edition*. 2:21–47.

———— (1920). Beyond the pleasure principle, *Standard Edition*. 18:7–64.

———— (1923). The ego and the id, *Standard Edition*. 19:19–28.

———— (1937). Analysis: Terminable and interminable, *Standard Edition*. 23:216–253.

Gabbard, G. (1994). Commentaries on papers by Tansey, Davies, and Hirsch. *Psychoanalytic Dialogues* vol. 4(2): 203–213.

———— (1996). *Love and Hate in the Analytic Setting*. Northvale, New Jersey: Aronson.

Gill, M. (1982). *Analysis of Transference, Vol. I Theory and Technique*. New York.

———— (1993). One-person and two-person perspectives: Freud's "Observations on transference-love." In: *On Freud's "Observations on transference-love,"* Ed. E. S. Person, A. Hagelin, and P. Fonagy. New Haven, CT: Yale University Press.

Gorkin, M. (1987). *The Uses of Countertransference*. Northvale, NJ: Aronson.

Guntrip, H. (1971). *Psychoanalytic Theory, Therapy, and the Self.* New York: Basic Books.

Havens, L. L. (1973). *Approaches to the Mind.* Boston: Little, Brown.

——— (1976). *Participant Observation.* New York: Aronson.

Heimann, P. (1950). On countertransference. *International Journal of Psycho-Analysis*, 31:81–84.

——— (1960). Counter transference. *British Journal of Medical Psychology*, 33:9–15.

Hoffman, I. Z. (1983). The patient as interpreter of the analyst's experience. *Contemporary Psychoanalysis* 19:389–422.

Hogarty, G., and Anderson, C. (1986). Family psychoeducation, social skills training, and maintenance chemotherapy in the aftercare treatment of schizophrenia. *Archives of General Psychiatry* 43:633–642.

Jacobs, T. (1986). On countertransference enactments. *Journal of the American Psychoanalytic Association* 34:289–307.

Kernberg, O. (1975). *Borderline States and Pathological Narcissism.* New York: Aronson.

——— (1984, 1986). *Severe Personality Disorders, Psychotherapeutic Strategies.* New Haven: Yale.

Khan, M. (1964). The function of intimacy and acting out in the perversions. *Sexual Behavior and the Law*, ed. Slovenko, 397–412, Springfield: Thomas.

Klein, M. (1946). Notes on some schizoid mechanisms. *International Journal of Psychoanalysis* 27:433–438.

Klerman, G., DiMascio, A., Weissman, M., Prusoff, B., Paykel, E. (1974). Treatment of depression by drugs and psychotherapy. *American Journal of Psychiatry* 131:186–191.

Kohut, H. (1959). Introspection, empathy, and psychoanalysis. An examination of the relationship between mode of observation and theory. *Journal of the American Psychoanalytic Association* 7:459–483.

——— (1968). The psychoanalytic treatment of narcissistic personality disorders. *The Psychoanalytic Study of the Child* 28: 86–113. New York: International Universities Press.

——— (1971). *The Analysis of the Self.* New York: International Universities Press.

———— (1977). *The Restoration of the Self*. New York: International Universities Press.

Kopelowicz, A., Corrigan, P., et al. (1996). Biopsychosocial rehabilitation. In: Tasman, A., Kay, J., Liberman, J. A., eds. *Psychiatry*, Philadelphia: W. B. Saunders Co. 1513–1534.

Kopelowicz, A., Liberman, R. P., et al. (1997). Efficacy of social skills training for deficit versus non-deficit negative symptoms in schizophrenia. *American Journal of Psychiatry* 154:424–425.

———— (2001). Recovery from schizophrenia. Direction in Psychiatry, Vol. 21:287–306.

Kumin, I. (1985). Erotic horror: desire and resistance in the psychoanalytic situation. *International Journal of Psychoanalytic Psychotherapy* 11:3–20.

Levenson, E. A. (1996). Aspects of self-revelation and self-disclosure. *Contemporary Psychoanalysis* 32:237–248.

Little, M. (1951). Countertransference and the patient's response to it. *International Journal of Psycho-Analyisis*, 32:32–40.

———— (1981). *Transference Neurosis and Transference Psychosis*. New York: Aronson.

Loewald, H. (1980). On the therapeutic action of psychoanalysis (1960) in *Papers on Psychoanalysis* 221–256, New Haven: Yale University Press.

———— ibid. (1978). Instinct theory, object relations, and psychic structure formation. *Journal of the Psychoanalytic Association* 26:493–506.

Mahler, M. S., and LaPierre, K. (1965). Mother–child interaction during separation individuation, *Psychoanalytic Quarterly*, 34:483–498.

————, Pine, F., and Bergman, A. (1975). *The Psychological Birth of the Infant*. New York: Basic Books.

Maltsberger, J. T., and Buie, D. H. (1974). Countertransference hate in the treatment of suicidal patients. *Archives of General Psychiatry* 30:625–633.

Maroda, K. (1991). *The Power of Countertransference*. New York: Wiley.

———— (1999). *Seduction, Surrender, and Transformation*. Hillsdale, New Jersey: The Analytic Press.

McLaughlin, J. T. (1981). Transference, psychic reality, and counter-transference. *Psychoanalytic Quarterly* 639–664.

———— (1986). The play of transference: some reflections on enactment in the psychoanalytic situation. *Journal of the American Psychoanalytic Association* 35:557–582.

———— (1991). Clinical and theoretical aspects of enactment. *Journal of the American Psychoanalytic Association* 39:595–614.

———— (1993). Work with patients: the impetus for self analysis. *Psychoanalytic Inquiry* vol. 13:365–389.

Ogden, T. (1979). On projective identification. *International Journal of Psycho-Analysis* 60:357–373.

Racker, H. (1968). *Transference and Countertransference*. New York: International Universities Press.

Rako, S. and Mazer, H. eds. (1980). *Semrad: The Heart of a Therapist*. New York: Aronson.

Renik, O. (1993). Analytic interaction: conceptualizing technique in light of the analyst's irreducible subjectivity. *Psychoanalytic Quarterly* LXII:553–571.

———— (1995). The ideal of the anonymous analyst and the problem of self-disclosure. *Psychoanalytic Quarterly* LXIV 466–495.

———— (1996). The perils of neutrality. *Psychoanalytic Quarterly* LXV 495–517.

Reynolds, C. F., Frank, E., et al. (1999). Nortriptyline and interpersonal psychotherapy as maintenance therapies for recurrent major depression. A randomized controlled trial in patients older than 59 years. *JAMA*. Vol. 281, 1:39–45.

Russell, P. (1976). *The Crunch*. Widely distributed by hand in the Boston community.

Sandler, J. (1976). Countertransference and role responsiveness. *International Review of Psycho-Analysis* 3:43–47.

———— (1990). On internal object relations. *Journal of the American Psychoanalytic Association* 859–880.

Schwaber, E. (1992). Psychoanalytic theory and its relation to clinical work. *Journal of the American Psychoanalytic Association* 40:1039–1057.

Scott, J. (2000). Treatment of chronic depression. *New England Journal of Medicine* 342:1518–1520.

Searles, H. (1959). *Countertransference and Related Subjects*. New York: International Universities Press.

————— (1959). Oedipal love in the countertransference. *International Journal of Psychoanalysis* 40:180–190.

————— (1961). Sexual processes in schizophrenia. *Psychiatry* 24:87–95.

Segal, H. (1964, 1973). *Introduction to the Work of Melanie Klein*. New York: Basic Books.

Sokolsky, L. (1993). *The Therapist's Experience of Direct Disclosure of Problematic Countertransference To Higher Functioning Patients*. (Doctoral Thesis) Massachusetts School of Professional Psychology.

Sullivan, H. S. (1953). *The Interpersonal Theory of Psychiatry*, H. S. Perry and M. L. Gawel eds. NewYork: Norton.

Stern, D. (1985). *The Interpersonal World of the Infant, A View From Psychoanalysis and Developmental Psychology*. New York: Basic Books.

Stolorow, R. and Lachman, F. (1984). Transference: The future of an illusion. *The Annual of Psychoanalysis* 12/13:19–37.

Stolorow, R., Brandshaft, B., and Atwood, G. (1987). Principles of Psychoanalytic Exploration. *Psychoanalytic Treatment: An Intersubjective Approach* 1–14. Hillsdale, NJ: Analytic Press.

Tansey, M. (1994). Sexual attraction and phobic dread in the countertransference. *Psychoanalytic Dialogues* vol 4(2): 139–152.

Thase, M., Greenhouse, J., et al. (1997). Treatment of major depression with psychotherapy or psychotherapy—pharmacotherapy combinations. *Archives of General Psychiatry* 54:1009–1015.

Tansey, M. and Burke, W. (1989). *Understanding Countertransference*. Hillsdale, NJ: Analytic Press.

Tronick, E. (1989). Emotions and emotional communication. *American Psychologist* 44: 112–119.

Winnicott, D. W. (1947). Hate in the countertransference. *Collected papers: Through paediatrics to psycho-analysis*, 1958, London, Tavistock publications; New York, Basic Books.

————— (1958). The capacity to be alone. *The maturational process and the facilitating environment*, 1965, NewYork: International Universities Press.

———— (1960). Counter-transference. *The Maturational Process and the Facilitating Environment*, 1965, New York: International Universities Press.

———— (1971). Playing: Creative activity and the search for the self. *Playing and Reality*, London: Tavistock Publications Ltd.

Wrye, H. K. (1993). Erotic terror: male patients' horror of the early maternal erotic transference. *Psychoanalytic Inquiry* 13:240–257.

Zukav, G. (1980). *The Dancing Wu Li Masters, An Overview of the New Physics.* New York: Bantam Books.

Index

Dr. Wishnie is a 1966 graduate of the Albert Einstein College of Medicine. He completed his psychiatry residency at the Mass. Mental Health Center and a concomitant research fellowship at the Mass. General Hospital in 1970 where he studied psychological aspects of coronary artery disease. From 1970 to 1972, he served in the NIMH Clinical Research Center in Lexington, KY where he adapted psychodynamic techniques for work with drug addicts with significant criminal histories. Out of his work came his book, *The Impulsive Personality*. In 1972, he returned to Boston to work and teach at the Cambridge Hospital Department of Psychiatry, Harvard Medical School. During these years he continued to consult at the Veterans Administration clinics and hospitals working with drug addicts and had an appointment at the Boston University School of Medicine. Dr. Wishnie taught and consulted on the intensive treatment of individuals with severe personality disorders. In 1999, he graduated from the Massachusetts Institute for Psychoanalysis.